To: _____

From: _____

With heartfelt gratitude, thank you for purchasing this book. Thank you for inviting me into your home, vehicle, church, workplace, hotel room, or wherever you are reading this book. Thanks for listening.

Jasmine Gordon

38 Reasons for Unanswered Prayers

> *Catch the foxes for us,*
> *the little foxes that*
> *spoil the vineyards,*
> *for our vineyards*
> *are in blossom.*
> Song of Solomon 2:15 (ESV)

Jasmine Gordon
Servant

Copyright © 2020 Nichole "Jasmine" Gordon
ISBN 978-1-7353091-2-5

All Rights Reserved

All Rights Reserved. No part of this book may be reproduced or transmitted in any form or by any means, electronically or mechanically, including photocopying, recording, or by an information storage and retrieval system without permission in writing from the author of this book.

Scriptures marked (KJV) are taken from the KING JAMES VERSION (KJV): KING JAMES VERSION, public domain.

Scripture quotations marked (NIV) are taken from THE HOLY BIBLE, NEW INTERNATIONAL VERSION®, NIV® Copyright © 1973, 1978, 1984, 2011 by Biblica, Inc.™ Used by permission. All rights reserved worldwide.

Scripture quotations marked (NLT) are taken from the Holy Bible, New Living Translation, copyright © 1996, 2004, 2007 by Tyndale House Foundation. Used by permission of Tyndale House Publishers, Inc., Carol Stream, IL 60188. All rights reserved.

Scripture quotations marked (ESV) are taken from The Holy Bible, English Standard Version® (ESV®), copyright © 2001 by Crossway, a publishing ministry of Good News Publishers. Used by permission. All rights reserved.

Scripture quotations marked (AMP) are taken from Copyright (c) 1954, 1958, 1962, 1964, 1965, 1987 by The Lockman Foundation, La Habra, CA 90631All rights reserved. https://www.lockman.org.

Scripture quotations marked (GWT) are taken from GOD'S WORD is a copyrighted work of God's Word to the Nations. Quotations are used by permission. Copyright 1995 by God's Word to the Nations. All rights reserved.

Editor:
Darlene Oakley

Proofreader:
Ruby Porter

Published by:

DOMINIONHOUSE
Publishing & Design, LLC
P.O. Box 681938 | Orlando, Florida 32868 | 407.703.4800
www.mydominionhouse.com

*****

Author Contact:

www.mwbint.org
Email: mwb8870@gmail.com
718.781.0571 | 804.720.6080

Epigraph

If you have SALVATION on a layaway plan, it's time to pick it up. It's paid for, in full.

-Jasmine Gordon

"Beloved, the Christian journey is like a relay. There will be setbacks, delays, obstacles, and distractions. Along the way, you may get a pebble in your shoe. Don't ignore it because it's a tiny one. Stop! Take it out of your shoe so you can walk more comfortably."

Preface

Author's Reflection

✽✽✽

From My Heart to Yours

May I remind you of the exceptional love that Jesus has for you. He willingly gave Himself to be tortured and humiliated in the presence of thousands of on-lookers. He did it so you can experience life everlasting with Him. He promised you the splendor of heaven. *"The Lord is not slack concerning His promise, as some men count slackness; but is longsuffering toward us, not willing that any should perish, but that all should come to repentance."* (2 Peter 3:8-10, NKJV)

My friend, if any of the content in this book should offend, hurt or cause you to feel uncomfortable, it is not my deliberate intention to do so. However, it may be just what is needed to get you back in line with God's Word. My greatest desire is to encourage and empower you to foster a relationship with your Creator. As a messenger of God, I have first-hand knowledge that some messages are not always soothing or comforting to the flesh.

Nevertheless, the correction and reprimand of God is much like pruning, the cutting away of dead things. Yes, it will be painful in the beginning, but the result will be stunning growth and fruitfulness. *"My child, don't reject the LORD's discipline, and don't be upset when he corrects you. For the LORD corrects those he loves, just as a father corrects a child in whom he delights."* (Proverbs 3:11-12, NLT)

Think of the track and field events in sports. You were chosen to run the last leg of the relay because your teammates have confidence in you and already see you as a winner. As you approach the finish line, don't look to the left or the right. Keep going! Pick up the pace! I know it feels like you are running out of breath. But, NO! You are running out of time!

Focus on your teammate who is about to pass the baton to you. Strategically, position yourself to receive it so that there will be no delay in the relay. Now, you have successfully received it. It's in your hand. The finish line is in view. Don't get weary; and, don't allow the baton to fall. Don't get distracted by those running alongside you. You must endure whatever pain and push through to the end.

Beloved, the Christian journey is like a relay. There will be setbacks, delays, obstacles, and distractions. Along the way, you may get a pebble in your shoe. Don't ignore it because it's a tiny one. Stop! Take it out of your shoe so you can walk more comfortably. If the pebble is left undisturbed until it's convenient for you to remove it, it may be too late. Even a tiny pebble can cause a significant amount of damage to your foot that may require medical attention.

That being said, perhaps over the years, you have been engaged in some things that were detrimental to your salvation and relationship with God; but, because they were not enormous things that jolted your attention, you ignored them. Double-check to see what pebble you may have picked up. Is it a pebble of unforgiveness? Is it a pebble of resentment or hate? Could it be a pebble of lying or gossiping? What about a pebble of jealousy or disobedience?

How is your walk with God? Have you identified any pebble that is preventing you from walking holy? If God should call you home now or return to earth, would that pebble prevent you from being prepared? Whatever the pebble may be, get rid of it before it transforms into a mountain. It will be much harder to move then.

Remember, the finish line is in view. The Holy Spirit is your coach, the angels are your cheerleaders, and I am your motivator. I am encouraging you not to allow time to run out before you reestablish a better and stronger relationship with God. Receive Him by faith. *God having provided some better thing for us, that they without us should not be made perfect. (Hebrews 11:40, KJV)*

With Love,
Servant of Jesus Christ,
Jasmine Gordon

Dedication Page

I seize the opportunity to dedicate this book, another reader's guide, to all my friends, my family, my followers, as well as myself, who desire to live a pure, honest, and holy life in the sight of God and man. I dedicate it to the spiritually blind individuals who are ignorant of Satan's devices and trapped by his lies.

I would also like to dedicate it to the millions of people who are living dangerously carefree and hopeless. They are misinformed, uninformed, and misguided by many would-be leaders who are teaching that demons are not real, and that there is no sin, devil, or Hell. It is dedicated to the presumptuous individual, who knows what sin is and the consequences of it. Yet, he still chooses to disregard God's commands and continues to live in and practice sin without any remorse.

"Render therefore to all their dues: tribute to whom tribute is due; custom to whom custom; fear to whom fear; honor to whom honor."

Romans 13:7

Acknowledgments

I must first acknowledge the Holy Spirit, who is my primary source for learning. I express an attitude of gratitude to Him for teaching and downloading the revelation that has inspired me to seek more information that will assist us in our transformation unto salvation.

I am humbled and honored for the privilege to pen another inspirational reader's guide. No matter where I am or what I achieve in life, it is the result of someone aiding me along my journey, which propels me into my destiny. I am mindful of the fact that I did not achieve, arrive at, or gain the knowledge to write by myself but through the contribution of my astute editor, family and friends, mentors, teachers, and my pastor, Marsha Minott.

I would be remiss if I failed to say thanks to Millicent Alexander-Spencer for enlightening us about pride in "Reason 28." To you, the beloved supporters, known and unknown, thanks for your assistance in aiding the circulation of my books. Each time you purchase a book or tell someone about it, you are helping me encourage, enlighten, equip, educate, and empower our fellow sisters and brothers.

Thank you. May God continue to bless you and your family.

"Acknowledging authority and positioning is the key to physical and spiritual success. One can only follow the principle of what he or she knows and understands. To know God is to seek and fear God. To fear God is to understand His ways and character. He rewards those who seek Him diligently."

Table of Content

38 Reasons For Unanswered Prayers

Reason 1
Anger 21

Reason 2
Backbiting. 29

Reason 3
Bestiality/Zoophile. 37

Reason 4
Bitterness/Resentment. 43

Reason 5
Corrupt Communication/Idle Jesting 47

Reason 6
Covetousness 53

Reason 7
Disobedience 59

Reason 8
Doubt/ Unbelief 65

Reason 9
Envy 71

Reason 10
Fear 75

Reason 11
Gluttony. 81

Table of Content

38 Reasons For Unanswered Prayers

Reason 12
Going Against God's Word 87

Reason 13
Hate 91

Reason 14
Home Life. 97

Reason 15
Homosexuality 103

Reason 16
Hypocrisy 111

Reason 17
Idolatry 115

Reason 18
Immaturity 121

Reason 19
Incest 133

Reason 20
Jealousy 141

Reason 21
Lust 151

Reason 22
Lying/Deception 165

Table of Content

38 Reasons For Unanswered Prayers

Reason 23
Malice 171

Reason 24
Mammon 177

Reason 25
Masturbation 189

Reason 26
Murmuring 197

Reason 27
Not God's Will .203

Reason 28
Pride 209

Reason 29
Rebellion 215

Reason 30
Rejection 221

Reason 31
Selfishness 227

Reason 32
Sorcery 237

Reason 33
Stealing 245

Table of Content

38 Reasons For Unanswered Prayers

Reason 34
Unforgiveness 251

Reason 35
Ungratefulness 259

Reason 36
Wavering 267

Reason 37
Witchcraft 273

Reason 38
Wrong motive 295

Final Words: From My Heart to Yours 301

Words of Encouragement 303

Call To Salvation 308

Repentance Prayer .310

Note of Thanks 311

References 312

About the Author 313

Contact the Author .314

Introduction

If I regard iniquity (sin) in my heart, the Lord will not hear me.
(Psalm 66:18, KJV)

Now we know that God heareth not sinners: but if any man be a worshipper of God, and doeth his will, him he heareth.
(John 9:31, KJV)

First and foremost, this book is not written to condemn or belittle anyone, but, instead, to encourage, enlighten, empower, and uplift you and me. It is a roadmap which will show us how to be prepared and stay ready to inherit eternal life with Jesus Christ. I am not the Holy Ghost police, neither am I trying to be one. According to Romans 3:23, "...for all have sinned, and come short of the glory of God...." *(KJV)*, my sin may differ from yours, but we do sin. We all have struggles, shortcomings, and weaknesses. The Lord has allowed me to pen this, another reader's guide, to alert us and draw our attention to the various obstacles that caused us to live, continuously, with unconfessed sin, daily. Bear in mind that I am not an expert on any of the topics I write about, but as the Holy Spirit led and inspired, I wrote. Most of the content is biblically based.

This book will reveal the most ignored sins that we commit, daily. It will bring awareness to the things we participate or have participated in but never considered dangerous enough to, negatively, affect our relationship with Christ and our destination, and so, repentance never crossed our mind. The Bible refers to these things as the little fox that spoils the vines. *"Take us the foxes, the little foxes, that spoil the vines: for our vines have tender grapes."* (Song of Solomon 2:15, KJV)

God loves us so much. It pains His heart to see us choose the wrong path, out of ignorance. Through this book, He wants to reemphasize that He is returning sooner than we think, for a church without blemish. He reminds us that He will not compromise His words for anyone. His desire is for us to pay close attention to the little things that we may have taken for granted, not knowing that they can deprive us of our salvation. Instead of blaming our pain and suffering on others, witchcraft, society, culture, generation, or bloodline, God wants us to know that our actions may include one of these 38 reasons.

There are multiple reasons for blocked blessings and unanswered prayers to which we are ignorant. Even though sin is **not the only reason** our prayers may go unanswered, Psalms 66:18 clearly states that it is a significant factor. Whether we are a prayer warrior, an intercessor, or just someone who loves to pray, there will be a moment when we will experience no result and no answer to our prayers. Put simply, prayer is a mere conversation between God and us, and is the principal means of communicating about our situations to Him. Prayer has the power to open doors and close doors, to elevate and dismantle, and to make things move or standstill. One may conclude that a BIG sin may be lingering in our lives; hence, our situation remains the same, and our prayers unanswered. Again, **sin may not be the reason.**

During a telephone conversation, a friend asked me what the title of my book was. "*38 Reasons for Unanswered Prayers*," I answered. After a long pause, "Really!" she exclaimed. "Is there a reason why my prayers are not being answered? Should I be kneeling for 24 hours? Or it depends on the type of prayer being prayed?" she asked. "Hmm, now I am curious to read that book. I did not know there could be reasons why my prayers are unanswered." Of Course, I left her in suspense eagerly awaiting its completion.

Surprisingly, one of my sisters gasped at the mention of the title as well. "38! I did not realize there were so many." In awe, she continued, "Wow! On a serious note, you gave me something to think about. We need to examine ourselves thoroughly. That means we have been blaming God for things of which we are guilty. Wow! What a revelation."

Here are a few reasons our prayers may have gone unanswered: **Wrong timing, wrong motive, religion, lack of faith, and our refusal to ask, seek and knock.**

Perhaps, you may be wondering why I chose the number 38? The number 38 means slavery and bondage, which is, precisely, one of the disadvantages attached to sin. The number 3 represents the "Trinity" (Father, Son, & Holy Spirit), and the number 8 represents "New Beginning." The Trinity has come to redeem us from slavery and bondage so we can experience a new beginning with Him. Reader, I admonish you. Please don't take the contents of this book lightly.

Journey with me, through the pages of this reader's guide, to discover the reason or reasons that you may hear "no," "wait," or silence when you pray.

Unless otherwise indicated, all scripture verses are taken from the King James Version.

Behold, the Lord's hand is not shortened, that it cannot save; neither his ear heavy, that it cannot hear: ²But your iniquities have separated between you and your God, and your sins have hid his face from you, that he will not hear. ³For your hands are defiled with blood, and your fingers with iniquity; your lips have spoken lies, your tongue hath muttered perverseness. (Isaiah 59:2-3)

²⁴Because I have called, and ye refused; I have stretched out my hand, and no man regarded ... ²⁸Then shall they call upon me, but I will not answer; they shall seek me early, but they shall not find me.... (Proverbs 1:24 & 28)

Please read these scriptures from the version of your choice:

- *Ezekiel 3:18-21*
- *1 Thessalonians 5:14*
- *Galatians 6:1*
- *James 5:19-20*
- *Matthew 25:1-13*
- *Micah 3:2-4*
- *Job 35:12*

"Anger is a choice. You choose when and where to express it. Therefore, you can decide to keep it on life support, or you can pull the plug and let it die. Getting rid of anger is a challenge, but it is doable."

Reason 1

***

Anger

He that is slow to anger is better than the mighty; and he that ruleth his spirit than he that taketh a city. (Proverbs 16:32)

Anger. She could not disguise it anymore. From a distance, a booming sound echoed, across the neighboring properties, night after night. Tension, from neighbors, blanketed the atmosphere. With a big sigh, one neighbor uttered, "The neighborhood nuisance is awake."

A strong feeling of displeasure and agonizing pain was felt as the child fiercely defied her. "Mother, why do you mistreat me? he asked. "God is watching, and He will get you for mistreating me." Even though she tried putting her best on the outside, she found it hard to control her anger towards him. As it relates to the child, Tony, her rage was deafening through her silence. The daggers from her eyes pierced, intensely, into his soul. Every breath she took, anger screamed. The language of her body spoke anger!

Have you ever found yourself in a situation, when anger got the better of you–when someone rubbed you the wrong way, and your heart began to race and sweat trickled down your face–when you shook like a leaf and lashed out with a sudden outburst? Where did that come from? Sorry, beloved. That is the spirit of anger that you refused to acknowledge and let go.

Anger is a possessive spirit, but only with your permission. It will intensify its stronghold, but only with your assistance. I compare anger to a disease that is deeply embedded within your emotions but is curable. This disease (anger) is inflicted by something or someone else. Sadly, it is medicated, incubated, and entertained by you. This tormenting spirit that, secretly, harasses you, continuously, can be restrained, if you so desire. Failure to let the anger go will propel you into saying and doing regrettable things and later encountering embarrassment. Its sole intention is to rob you of your joy and tarnish your character. Surprisingly, you continually defend its action; thus, you entertain and incubate anger.

Over the years, I encountered individuals who defended their anger. Whenever asked about the anger that they exhibited, they would make excuses to justify their actions. Some individuals might say, "I got it from my father," or "it runs in my family," or "I was born that way." Others may say, "Leave me alone. That's just me. I can't help it." Yes, you can help it if you so desire. Each time you justify the reasons for your continual outbursts, you give power and permission to the spirit of anger to indefinitely reside in your space. It has been said, that what you don't know won't hurt you. I beg to differ. Actually, what you don't know can KILL you.

Once you are born again, you are given a spiritual blood transfusion. You no longer have the right to claim your parents' or foreparents' demons. Your DNA has changed. You are, now, a part of the family of God–washed in his fountain, and cleansed by his blood. You have become heirs of God and joint-heir with Jesus Christ. The generational and bloodline curse of anger that runs in your family will no longer be your inheritance. The power to break, uproot, and destroy that bondage has been placed in your mouth. Activate it.

I discovered that whatever anyone seriously wants to do, they will do without hesitation. Ponder this. If you are a smoker in a "No Smoking" environment–whether in flight for eleven hours or being admitted to the hospital for weeks, would you smoke? If you answer "No", to the above, it merely means that you have made a choice to stand your ground; and you have the will power to say, 'No" to anything or anyone.

Reason 1 - Anger

Anger is a choice. You choose when and where to express it. Therefore, you can decide to keep it on life support, or you can pull the plug and let it die. Getting rid of anger is a challenge, but it is doable. Ephesians 4:26 reminds us to, "Be ye angry and sin not: Let not the sun go down upon your wrath." This means that it's okay to be upset or to be disappointed with someone or something; but seek to resolve the issue at hand before it takes root. Don't allow it to reach the point of ill feelings or resentment. Many refer to their anger as righteous indignation, but you know that there is nothing righteous about the anger you feel.

Deliverance from this or any other spirits depends on you. However, you must, first, acknowledge that you have a problem and then seek to identify the root cause of that problem. Many times when a negative situation occurs in your life, you plunge straight into denial-pretending as if nothing has transpired- as if you are not hurt. There are some pressing, pertinent questions that you need to ask yourself such as: What is the root cause for the anger I exhibit? What triggers my anger? When you find the answer, you also need to know what you used to numb the pain and where the memories are hidden. Don't keep secrets for satan anymore. Exposing the spirit of anger will break its stronghold on your life. No longer will it have your permission to hold you hostage. You must muster the strength to deal with the findings.

Anger, like any other spirit, can disguise itself very well. Invading spirits will leave their host, when the host decides to renounce, reject, and rebuke them. You must, also, be aware of the open doors that are allowing this spirit or any other to come and go as they please. Lack of knowledge of spiritual warfare can cause human beings to be vulnerable to the possession and torment of demonic spirits. People of God, you need to know the spirits that are at work. Identify them and serve them notice.

"My people are destroyed because of lack of knowledge...." (Hosea 4:6) We can be destroyed not only by what we don't know, but, also, by what we refuse to learn). Let's take a close look at this tree. Can you identify with any of the fruit below?

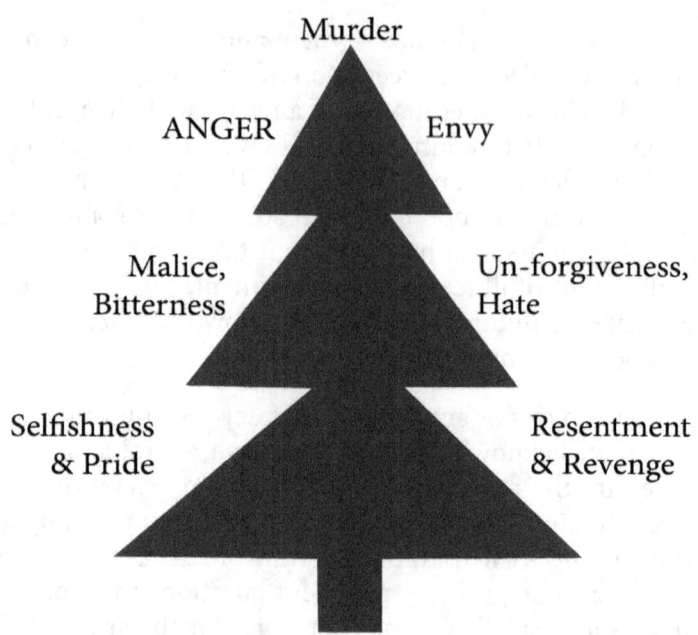

It's obvious that without a seed, there will be no root. Without a root, there will be no tree; and, without a tree, there will be no branch to produce fruits. Therefore, if you don't like the fruit, get rid of the tree from the root.

If whatever makes you angry is not dealt with promptly, it will turn into resentment. Resentment turns into revenge; revenge springs up into hate; and hate blossoms into bitterness. Bitterness branches off into unforgiveness. Unforgiveness escalates into anger; and anger overflows into malice, which can gives birth to murder. Did you notice the long process it takes before anger actually surfaces? You have a choice.

Possible root causes for your anger

- Being lied to or about to others
- Being ignored

Reason 1 - Anger

- Feeling guilty
- Feeling fear
- Feeling of inadequacy
- Feeling of insecurity
- Victim of rape, incest, or molestation
- Feeling of rejection
- Feeling of abandonment by parents, spouse, friends, society
- You were given up for adoption
- Feelings of betrayal
- Loss of income
- Domestic abuse or Divorce
- Being cheated out of your inheritance
- Being cheated out of your grades in school
- No love, affection or attention from your spouse or parents
- Being cheated on by spouse or girlfriend/boyfriend
- You were bullied in school or are being bullied at work or elsewhere
- Discouragement because you have not accomplished your goals
- Unexpected sickness or death
- Feelings of oppression, possession, depression

If the reason for your anger is not listed, feel free to add it or them. Yes, you may be feeling trapped and consumed with anger. Nonetheless, freedom and deliverance are possible. You have the power to destroy the spirit of anger from your life.

Your body, emotions, mind, and spirit have suffered the physical and emotional pain and feelings of hurt. Yes, you wear the scars and have paid a dear price. Nonetheless, it is not in vain. Your painful experiences were the prerequisites for you to be able to effectively help someone else who has gone, or will be going, through something similar or less than what you have gone through and want to commit suicide. With confidence, you will be able to encourage those who are sharing your experiences or worst.

Gaining control of one's emotional state of mind increases enjoyment of one's life and allows one to live it to the fullest. If you exercise self-control, you are an overcomer and more than a conqueror. Remember, being ANGRY is different from ANGER. And, continuously, reliving the pain, nursing the wounds, and displaying the scars, will only hurt you. Again, anger is a choice. Let it go.

Jesus is coming sooner than we think. Let's get ourselves aligned with the Word of God so we won't be left behind.

Prayer

Almighty God, King of Kings and Lord of Lords, I worship and adore you. Lord, you are the horn of my salvation and I will hold on to you for life. You are my deliverer in the time of trouble. How majestic is your name, O God!

Holy Spirit, I need you to intervene in my chronic situation right now. You know the intent of my heart. Nothing is hidden from you. As an X-ray and CAT scan machine would, you read my innermost parts. While I can hide my faults and struggles from others, I cannot hide them from you. Father, I acknowledge that I have become a host for the spirit of anger. Rescue me from myself and the deadly grip of anger. Lord, I have been struggling and entertaining this rage since _____ until now. Lord, I am asking you to uproot the hostility within me. God, this unexplainable agitation that I feel

Reason 1 - Anger

is tormenting. Father God, I know it is not your will for me to live this way. At times, I don't even want to be around myself because my attitude stinks. Lord, there are so many things about me that I dislike. Help me to fix them. Teach me your ways, O God, and show me your path of righteousness.

Father, I know my behavior has displeased you numerous times, but thank you for not giving me the punishment I deserve. Thank you for not giving up on me. Oh Lord, my God, in you, I put my trust. Save me from this spirit of anger lest it destroy me. I permit you to uproot everything that is causing rage, irritation, and hostility to have such a stronghold in my life. Deliver me, O God, let me not be consumed by the spirit of anger, in Jesus' name.

Foul spirit of anger, through the power of the blood of Jesus Christ, I bind you, and I strip you of your assignment. I command you to leave my body now in Jesus' mighty name. Spirit of Anger, with every power vested in me, I denounce, I renounce, I reject, and I rebuke you in Jesus' mighty name. I cast you out into outer darkness and dry places, never to return, in Jesus' name.

Lord Jesus, replace anger with love. Replace the spirit of bondage with freedom. Replace the spirit of heaviness with praise and worship. Replace sadness with joy so I can smile again.

"Did you know that while you are talking about who is wearing this, who is living in sin, who is not Godly, and who is going to hell, you are committing sin? You are gossiping, judging, criticizing, and being malicious. How do you think God feels about such behavior?"

Reason 2

***

Backbiting

Lord, who shall abide in thy tabernacle? Who shall dwell in thy holy hill? He that walketh uprightly, and worketh righteousness, and speaketh the truth in his heart. **He that backbiteth not with his tongue, nor doeth evil to his neighbor, nor taketh up a reproach against his neighbor.** *(Psalm 15:1-3)*

I am guilty of backbiting, tale-bearing, slandering, and gossiping. I am not exempt from this chapter. I concur that juicy details about people's business sound good to the flesh. It can be challenging, at times, to restrain oneself from interjecting one's opinion in such conversations. Depending on who or what it's about, the temptation to share the tale with a friend or a family member is an even greater challenge. However, there will come a time when the Holy Spirit convicts us, saying, "Enough is enough." When we speak ill of each other, we are not only hurting them, we are also hurting God. It's worse, if we confess to being born-again Christians and are in a leadership position. From us, He expects better.

Many are looking to the Church for a place of refuge and safety. Unfortunately, many have experienced discomfort and pain. According to Hebrews 10:25, *we should not forsake the assembling of ourselves together... but exhort each other because the return of Christ is fast approaching.* In other words, when we come together in one accord, we will be able to strengthen and encourage each other. Hence, the verse "Iron sharpeneth iron; so a man sharpeneth the countenance of his friend." (Proverbs 27:17) Do we really encourage and sharpen each other's countenance?

Backbiting is defined as, "Malicious words regarding someone who is not present." Backbiting, gossiping, tale-bearing, criticism, and slander are all an abominable disease of the tongue, for which God expresses a strong dislike. A backbiter talks negatively, sometimes with evil intentions about another person behind his or her back to tarnish the individual's reputation. Then, to stay true to our deceptive form, we smile and pretend to be innocent when we are face-to-face with the individual we have just maligned. When the conscience chimes in and conviction takes place, we may try to justify our action by saying, "But it's the truth." Yes, it may be the truth, but what if the person whom we speak about finds out that we are sharing his or her business with someone else? Was it ours to share?

Believe it or not, backbiting, along with the other diseases of the tongue, so to speak, are driven by a spirit that respects no one–whether we preach like Paul, cast out demons as Jesus did, baptize in Jesus' name, or the Father, Son, and Holy Ghost. This spirit of backbiting makes individuals go out of their way to assassinate the character of their fellow sisters and brothers, without remorse.

Beloved, this behavior happens so frequently that it seems like the practiced norm. Going forward, let us allow our spirit man to be in control of our tongue. It will be a devastating thing if our conscience is seared. We will be less sensitive to the feelings of others, while at the same time, we will continue to cause each other harm.

Criticism

"To avoid criticism say nothing, do nothing, and be nothing." & "The final proof of greatness lies in being able to endure criticism without resentment." (Elbert Hubbard)

It is so sad that a church member will be excommunicated for committing fornication, adultery, or murder, but gets a pass although they are known for gossiping, holding grudges, resentment, and unforgiveness. They are also given a pass, despite their regular sowing

Reason 2 - Backbiting

of discord among brethren, carrying news to the pastor, lying to each other, exhibiting jealousy, and criticizing others. Criticism is just as deadly as backbiting and these other diseases of the tongue, yet, it is so rampant among believers. Whether we are known or unknown, we can almost guarantee or expect to be criticized by someone. For example, if you fail at something, you will likely be called worthless and no good. If you appear not to try hard enough or achieve enough, people classify you as mediocre and as one with no ambition. If you are exceptionally gifted or hold a high position in society, some may call you a show-off or a brown-noser or that you're only ordinary, just like everyone else.

One of the most crucial and unconscionable one is being criticized for using your God-given gift or talent to educate, win souls, and build the kingdom of God. Sometimes, you may hear believers mumble among themselves, "She thinks she can pray more than anyone else" or "He is not the only one who can discern, I can see too," or "I am not intimidated by anyone's gift. God gave me gifts and talents too." Wouldn't it be surprising if those whom we criticize and condemn make it into the kingdom of God, and our reward for all our effort and ethical behavior is everlasting damnation? Will it be worth it? Judge not!

Did you know that while you are talking about who is wearing this, who is living in sin, who is not Godly, and who is going to hell, you are committing sin? You are gossiping, judging, criticizing, and being malicious. How do you think God feels about such behavior? If you should die after the last word comes out of your mouth, where do you think you would spend eternity? Do you think God would compromise with you and give you a break because you go to church on a particular day?-or because you were baptized in one specific name?-or because you refused to adorn yourself in a specific way? Do you believe you would be given a pass to heaven because you speak in tongues, heal the sick, and cast out demons? Again, unless there is authentic repentance, not only from your lips but your heart, all the good deeds you have done won't matter. What was the condition of your heart at the time of your expiration? It will not matter what you have done in the past or who you have built yourself up to be in the eyes of others. God cannot compromise or overlook any sin.

Dear Reader,

May I remind you about the story of Miriam, Moses' sister in Numbers 12:

Now **Miriam and Aaron spoke against Moses** because of the Cushite woman whom he had married (for he had married a Cushite woman); ²and they said, "Has the Lord really spoken only through Moses? Has He not spoken also through us?" **AND THE LORD HEARD IT.** ⁵The Lord came down in a pillar of cloud and stood at the doorway of the tabernacle, and He called Aaron and Miriam, and they came forward. ⁶And He said, "Hear now My words: If there is a prophet among you, I the Lord will make Myself known to him in a vision And I will speak to him in a dream.

⁷"But it is not so with My servant Moses; He is entrusted and faithful in all My house. ⁸"With him, I speak mouth to mouth [directly], clearly and openly and not in riddles; And he beholds the form of the lord. Why then were you not afraid to speak against my servant Moses?" ⁹and the anger of the Lord was kindled against Miriam and Aaron, and He departed. ¹⁰But when the cloud had withdrawn from over the tent, behold, Miriam was leprous, as white as snow. And Aaron turned and looked at Miriam, and, beheld, she was leprous. (Amplified Bible)

God is the same yesterday, today, and forever. He does not change. If we continue to be critical of each other, we will pay dearly, whether with our bodies or with our lives. I encourage you to dig deep into your own life and see what needs fixing and adjustment. Criticism can leave a lasting and devastating effect on an individual's feelings. It can cause someone to have low self-esteem or harbor resentment and anger, or even walk away from God. Be reminded of Luke 17:1: "Jesus said to his disciples: 'Things that cause people to stumble are bound to come, but woe to anyone through whom they come." (NIV)

Reason 2 - Backbiting

My friend, when we have decided to walk with Christ, we have shed the old sinful nature and adopted the spirit of love. The Bible tells us that love speaks and thinks no evil. Criticism is the opposite of love. If you are one who says, "Let's pray for Sue," but then proceed to disclose all of Sue's business or personal matters, you can be in trouble with God and it can prevent your prayers from being answered. Some individuals only pretend to care about those whom they are getting ready to talk about. Sadly, their intent can be easily discerned by not what comes out of their mouth, but what is embedded in their heart. You should not allow anyone to turn you into a gossiper or an outlet for negative news. Protect your mouth and ear gate and use your tongue as an instrument for blessing and restoration.

Tale-bearing: *He that covereth a transgression seeketh love; but he that repeateth a matter separateth very friends. (Proverbs 17:9)*

A tale-bearer is a person who, maliciously, gossips or reveals secrets and usually sows seeds of discord. Where there is no tale-bearer, there is no strife. Psalm 50:16-21 references the tale-bearer's judgment. The tongue is an unruly evil full of deadly poison. It cannot be tamed. A tale-bearer continually uses his or her mouth to build strife. As of today, when someone confides a secret in your trust, you must keep it to yourself. Resist the temptation to pick up the phone and start calling all your friends to say, "Guess who got a divorce?" or "Guess who was caught in adultery" or "Did you hear what happened to Tony?" Even though it may be the truth, it is a betrayal of trust. Besides, it is not your story to tell. And it may keep your prayers from being answered.

[16]But to the wicked, God says: what right do you have to recite my laws or take my covenant on your lips? [17]You hate my instruction and cast my words behind you. [18]When you see a thief, you join with him; you throw in your lot with adulterers. [19]You use your mouth for evil and harness your tongue to deceit. [20]You sit and testify against your brother and slander your own mother's son. [21]When you did these things, and I kept silent, you thought I was exactly like you. But I now arraign you and set my accusations before you. (Psalms 50:16-21, NIV)

When you are about to judge or criticize someone for some insignificant reason, ask yourself what your faults, bad habits and imperfections are. Would you want someone talking about those to everyone else behind your back? Could this be the sin that's preventing your prayers from being answered?

Control your tongue. Jesus is coming sooner than we think. Let's get ourselves aligned with the Word of God so we won't be left behind.

Prayer

Almighty God, you are my peace. You are my strong tower. Thank you for being my shield and buckler. The heavens declare your glory, and the world shows the excellent work of your hands. You are awesome in my life, Almighty God.

Lord, I am guilty of backbiting, tale-bearing, gossiping, slandering, and criticism. I have sinned. I have sown seeds of discord. I have disappointed you with my mouth, and I broke your heart. Lord, as your Word said, whatever is stored in my heart, flows through my mouth. Therefore, I surrender my heart to you so you can detox me.

Father, I beseech you, let the words of my mouth and the meditation of my heart be acceptable in your sight, O Lord, my strength, and my redeemer. Anything that I speak, let it be uplifting to the listener. Anything that I think about or harbor in my heart, let it be pleasing to you, O God. Lord, You are the One who repurchased me with Your life from the brink of death and destruction. I acknowledge You as my source of strength. Keep me from presumptuous sins, O God. Lord, I pray that backbiting, tale-bearing, slandering, and gossiping will have no more power or dominion over me. Help me to exercise self-discipline and consider other peoples' feelings.

Lord, thank you for delivering me from these diseases of the tongue. Put a watch over my mouth that I may talk right, walk right, and think right. Harness my tongue with words of encouragement. I ask, in Jesus' mighty name. Amen.

Reason 2 - Backbiting

[12]Now we ask you, brothers and sisters, to acknowledge those who work hard among you, who care for you in the Lord and who admonish you. [13]Hold them in the highest regard in love because of their work. Live in peace with each other. [14]And we urge you, brothers and sisters, warn those who are idle and disruptive, encourage the disheartened, help the weak, be patient with everyone. [15]Make sure that nobody pays back wrong for wrong, but always strive to do what is good for each other and for everyone else. (1 Thessalonians 5:12-15, NIV)

"Bestiality is on the rise. It's trending as if it's this best thing on earth. Throughout multiple reports on various news channels about individuals caught in the act of bestiality, all reporters classify bestiality as either a criminal act, crime, animal abuse, animal cruelty, brutality, horrible action, demented corruption, or disturbing sexual assault. The list continues."

Reason 3

***

Bestiality/Zoophile

A man must not defile himself by having sex with an animal. And a woman must not offer herself to a male animal to have intercourse with it. This is a perverse act. (Leviticus 18:22-23, NLT)

*B*estiality? What does this mean? It is the act of a human having sexual intercourse with animals incapable of giving consent. A zoophile is a person who has an extremely strong sexual attraction for animals, but they may or may not engage in the practice of bestiality.

There are some topics or subjects we would prefer to sweep under the rug or pretend as if they don't exist. Thinking about them makes you want to puke, let alone talking about them. Nonetheless, being silent about subjects like these can suggest agreement to those who crave and indulge in such behavior. One may argue that if no one speaks out or is fighting against it, then no one cares; therefore, it is legal to pursue.

During my teenage years, I heard of instances where men were accused of having sexual encounters with donkeys, dogs, goats, cows, monkeys, pigs, and horses, but the stories seemed far fetched. In my little mind, such an act was impossible to imagine, so I never gave much thought to the accusations. However, since I became an adult, I have seen and read about the tug-of-war between authorities and citizens wanting to legalize bestiality in various countries and states.

You may have heard about Malcolm Brenner, an author, a journalist, and a zoophile who told his story in a documentary of being in love with Dolly the dolphin in the early 1970s. Anyone who researches

Malcolm Brenner will find the word "zoophile", proudly, displayed next to his name. Malcolm stated that he doesn't think anyone was born zoophile, but he has a vivid memory of being molested at the tender age of five by his psychiatrist, and having a mother who was a cold, distant character which may have contributed to him turning to animals.

"I think I found animals to be a safe and secure repository for my sexual desires," Malcolm said. "I knew that there was something different about my sexuality; that wasn't normal like other guys.... I wanted desperately for it to be normal; to have a relationship with a woman.... I first realized that I was attracted to animals when my father took me to see a movie called the shaggy dog; strangely enough, I found myself getting an erection at five years old. After that, I was aware that something was different about my sexuality." Malcolm mentioned that his first physical encounter with an animal was at age 11, with the family dog.

This next statement by Malcolm blew me out of the water. He said, "One hundred and fifty years ago, black people were considered degenerate subspecies of human beings, and at the time, miscegenation (the mixing of racial groups through marriage, sexual relationship and more) was a crime in many states as bestiality is a crime in many states. **I am hoping in a more enlightened future; zoophile will be no more regarded as controversial or harmful than interracial sex is today.**" Hmmm. He is implying that bestiality should not be considered an offense; and if the ban could be lifted off the crime of interracial marriage, there should be freedom for those who want to have sex with animals, as well.

I have seen individuals, ranting and raving–expressing their disagreement with many countries and states, where same-sex marriage is explicitly forbidden. Yet, these countries have refused to ban or pass the law against humans having sex with animals and making animal pornography. In other words, in their eyes, it is not right for someone to be involved in such despicable behavior such as bestiality, but two human beings of the same sex, who love each other are deprived of expressing their love through marriage.

Reason 3 - Bestiality/Zoophile

Bestiality is on the rise. It's trending as if it's this best thing on earth. Throughout multiple reports on various news channels about individuals caught in the act of bestiality, all reporters classify bestiality as either a criminal act, crime, animal abuse, animal cruelty, brutality, horrible action, demented corruption, or disturbing sexual assault. The list continues. Like a child or an adult who was raped, no consent was given to the rapist. Hence, the victim is violated and taken advantage of. It is abuse. The same goes for the animals.

My friends, take a second look at the Scripture portion below. Because of Jesus' crucifixion and His amazing grace, it is no longer mandatory for anyone to be put to death for their sins, today. *"Rather, he is patient for your sake. He doesn't want to destroy anyone but wants all people to have an opportunity to turn to him and change the way they think and act."* (2 Peter 3:9, GW) However, the fact remains that these practices are wrong, sinful, and offensive in the eyes of God. Genesis 2:20-22 clearly shows that God, deliberately, sought and, specifically, handpicked a companion (woman) for man. Never forget that our body is the dwelling place for the Holy Spirit. Don't pollute or contaminate it with ungodly practices.

Perhaps, you are thinking that this doesn't go for you, and I am glad it doesn't, but you would be surprised by how many individuals struggle with either the feelings or the practice. A girlfriend of mine once told me that, while she was on the internet researching information to complete her class assignment, shockingly, an image of a woman and her dog in a compromising position popped up in front of her face. She said, as quickly as she glanced at it, it seemed as if it got into her spirit; she had no peace. She explained angrily, "The memory of this disgusting image kept flashing in my mind. Each time it does, I felt a funny sexual feeling. Oh, no! This is impossible; I will not accept this in Jesus' name! I prayed nonstop. I had to take the bull by its horn and quickly cast it down and out of my spirit!" No, she has never acted upon the feelings, and yes, she overcame that demonic attack through the power of prayer and the blood of Jesus Christ.

Beloved, guard the gate of your eyes and ears; be careful of what you look at or to what you listen. Be extra cautious of who you allow to touch you or be intimate with you because spirits are transferable. Overall, guard your mind and protect your spirit. This kind of behavior is abnormal. A demonic spirit is definitely behind this perversion. We have to pray for deliverance for the individuals who are being molested by the spirit of bestiality and zoophile. According to Malcolm, at age five, he encountered two horrific things. Do you remember what they were? Were they coincidences? Who was this psychiatrist? What else was he involved in, in addition to pedophilia? Could it be that the spirit of zoophile was transferred to the child Malcolm at that time? I firmly believe that something spiritual happened to Malcolm as a child, or perhaps, even as a toddler. Parents, protect your children. Avoid sending your children to unsupervised sleepovers, camping, picnics, and other such adventures.

If we confess our sins, he is faithful and just to forgive us our sins, and to cleanse us from all unrighteousness. (1 John 1:9)

The man gave names to all livestock and to the birds of the heavens and to every beast of the field. But for Adam, there was not found a helper fit for him. 21So the Lord God caused a deep sleep to fall upon the man, and while he slept, took one of his ribs and closed up its place with flesh. 22And the rib that the Lord God had taken from the man he made into a woman and brought her to the man. (Genesis 2:20-22, ESV)

A man must not defile himself by having sex with an animal. And a woman must not offer herself to a male animal to have intercourse with it. This is a perverse act. (Leviticus 18:22-23, NLT)

Prayer

God, all honor belongs to you. I give you the glory, I give you the praise, and I worship you. Gracious Father, thank you for your

Reason 3 - Bestiality/Zoophile

amazing grace and unlimited mercy. Thanks for not disowning me in my folly. Lord, you are truly amazing. Hallelujah!

My God, I am in deep trouble. Lord, I have allowed the spirit of bestiality to invade my mind and spirit. Lord, as embarrassing as it may sound, I have found myself lusting after animals uncontrollably. Lord, I have tried so hard to shake and ignore this feeling. Still, it seems to overpower my mind. O God, I come boldly before your throne to confess my disgusting behavior and to seek your deliverance.

Lord, I acknowledge you as my savior, my deliverer, my lifeguard, and my redeemer. Father, thanks for giving me multiple chances at life. Lord Jesus, you told me in Joel 2:32 that you will deliver me if I call on your name. Jesus, son of David, have mercy on me. Help! Lord, I have failed you; despite your warning against human sexual interaction with animals, I have turned away from your ordinances. I have become filthy in your eyes and the eyes of men. O God, deliver me from this demonic invasion. Deliver me from this spiritual bondage, and set me free from this spiritual attack. Lord, I know I have caused great embarrassment and shame to your name. Please forgive me for the terrible choices that I have made. Cleanse and heal me completely. In Jesus' mighty name.

You foul spirit of bestiality, I rebuke you in the name of Jesus. I command the power of God to paralyze you. I renounce and reject you from my life. May the blood of Jesus destroy you. I serve you notice written with the blood of Jesus. I cast you into outer darkness and dry places, never to return again. You are not welcome in my space anymore. Amen.

"If a man has sex with an animal, he must be put to death, and the animal must be killed. If a woman presents herself to a male animal to have intercourse with it, she and the animal must both be put to death. You must kill both, for they are guilty of a capital offense." (Leviticus 20:15-16, NLT)

"Bitterness not only affects you but many people who are connected to you through bloodline or by association. I heard a preacher once say that bitterness is like acid that destroys the container in which it is placed."

Reason 4

***

Bitterness/Resentment

Let all bitterness and wrath and anger and clamor [perpetual animosity, resentment, strife, fault-finding] and slander be put away from you, along with every kind of malice [all spitefulness, verbal abuse, malevolence]. (Ephesians 4:31, AMP)

It is possible to be angry and sin not. However, it is impossible to resent or have bitterness within you against someone and be sinless. Bitterness lingers because you are in pain from having been hurt by someone or disappointed about specific circumstances, which was not forgiven. Refusing to address the issue that's causing the pain will lead to the seed of bitterness. A person is not born exhibiting bitterness and anger. There is always an underlying factor that contributes to and feeds the spirit of anger and resentment.

There are nine fruits of the spirit, and bitterness is not one of them. *Make sure that everyone has kindness from God so that bitterness doesn't take root and grow up to cause trouble that corrupts many of you. (Hebrews 12:15, GW)*

Beloved, make every effort to live in peace with everyone and be holy. Without holiness, no one will see the Lord. Make every effort to fix the situation before it becomes uncontrollable. No one is worth losing your salvation over. I implore you to get to the place in God, where you can look beyond the individual who may have caused your uneasiness and quickly identify who is behind the attacks on you. Bitterness will ruin your relationship with God and man and triggers other sins, such as unforgiveness, anger, hatred, murder, and much more.

If you want to know if you are a carrier of bitterness or resentment, walk into a room where the individual who hurt you is. There will be an awkward feeling. Your tone of voice changes to a grumble or mumble if you are compelled to exchange a word to him or her. Another way to identify if you are harboring bitterness and resentment is you may be judgmental of others; or, you may exhibit paranoia thinking someone is always talking about you. You may be harsh or snappy with your answers. You may criticize and complain about everything and everyone. There are times when you may experience sudden outbursts of anger, especially when things are not going your way. And here is the big one. You are easily offended and very sensitive. Some may refer to it as "thin skin."

Sometimes bitterness lends itself to severe dislike, which eventually turns to hatred. For example, you might find yourself being very disagreeable or cynical about the suggestions or ideas that come from the individual whom you dislike. Finally, if you would move mountains to seek revenge or cause sorrow and pain to the individual who hurt you, then you are, indeed, consumed with bitterness.

Perhaps, you are saying none of the above describes you. Bitterness can be expressed in various ways. Individuals who are holding on to bitterness usually refuse to forgive his or her offender and sometimes categorize the individual with others as a result. The offended one talks himself into believing that everyone sets out to hurt them. They think they are an island and can stand alone. They appear to be self-sufficient and don't need anyone. They may even verbalize, "I am a loner. I don't have, and neither do I need any friends." A person who has bitterness within may cry for no apparent reason. They tend to express a spirit of sadness and brokenness as they, continuously, host their pity parties. You can probably identify with a few of the above mentioned characteristics but play it cool, disguising the existence of bitterness.

Bitterness not only affects you but many people who are connected to you through bloodline or by association. I heard a preacher once say that bitterness is like acid that destroys the container in which it is placed. It is time to disperse that acid so you can be whole

Reason 4 - Bitterness/Resentment

again. Scripture clearly states that without holiness, no man will see God. There is nothing holy about bitterness and it's fruit. You are the container that is holding the so-called acid of bitterness. Don't allow it to destroy you. Dig up the root of bitterness and get rid of the poisonous fruit of grudges, hostility, resentment, anger, unforgiveness, fault finding, and wrath.

Jesus is coming sooner than you think. Get yourself aligned with the Word of God. Don't get left behind.

Prayer

Lord Jesus, I must have you with me. I dare not tread this journey alone. Without you, Lord, I am a complete failure. Without you, I am a mess. Without you, I am like sounding brass and noisy cymbal. Lord, you have been so merciful to me. You are superb. You are magnificent. Lord, thank you for your goodness and your mercy that brought me through. Thank you for looking beyond my faults and seeing my needs. Thank you for prolonging my life. Thank you for not allowing the enemy to destroy me in my transgression.

Father, I approach your mercy seat with bitterness in my soul. Answer my prayer speedily, O God. Forgive me for allowing the roots of bitterness to spring up in my heart and trouble me. Search my heart, O God. Uproot every evil seed that caused bitterness to overpower me. Father God, empty me from all bitterness and fill me with unconditional love. Give me the strength to let go of this evil. Lord Jesus, enable me to destroy the roots of bitterness and demolish every tentacle. Deliver me from the gall of bitterness and empower me to forgive those who have inflicted me with pain and harm. Father, I have decided to renounce, denounce, and reject the spirit of bitterness. Spirit of bitterness, I cast you into outer darkness and dry places, never to return again. Give me your grace to continue to walk in my deliverance as an overcomer. In Jesus' name. Amen.

"Whoever conceals their sins does not prosper, but the one who confesses and renounces them finds mercy." (Proverbs 28:13, NIV)

"We don't have to participate in every event or conversation. Instead, we ought to be the light in the darkness. I guarantee you, the individuals who are sharing the ungodly jokes or leading the discussion are carefully observing our reaction."

Reason 5

***

Corrupt Communication/Idle Jesting

But I say unto you, that every idle word that men shall speak, they shall give account thereof in the day of judgment. ³⁷For by thy words thou shalt be justified, and by thy words thou shalt be condemned. (Matthew 12:36-37. NIV)

Communication can be verbal as well as nonverbal, and the way we communicate gives us the power to uplift, tear down, persuade, manipulate, convert, and influence.

When we speak, can we honestly tell if the person, to whom we speak, is being educated or encouraged? Is God pleased with our daily conversations? Many times, we are carried away, during our conversations with friends or family, and, eventually, say the wrong things. Conversations or arguments, in which persons are engaged and where the spirit of anger shows up and the frightening words that proceed out of their mouths, are unimaginable.

Do not forget that the conception of good and evil begins in our minds. After the mind entertains specific ideas for a while, it gives way for the mouth to voice it, thus giving birth to the idea. For example, an innocent telephone conversation with an old friend might begin very simple, but 30 or 60 minutes later, after reminiscing on the past, we might find ourselves using profanity or swearing. If there is a feeling of uneasiness or guilt after the conversation has ended, then we know our conversation was not pure or seasoned with grace. The uncomfortable feelings we experienced is a sign that the Holy Ghost was not in agreement.

Another trap that plagues most Christians is our willingness to accept sexual compliments, not realizing that it segues into many unwanted temptations, whether in the form of emotional or physical adultery or fornication. We believers must be mindful of our speech or what we allow our spirit to receive because it can often take us down a pathway that was never intended.

Idle Jesting

The New Living Translation version of Proverbs 10:19 says, "Too much talk leads to sin. Be sensible and keep your mouth shut." The interpretation: Unnecessary spoken words may cause one to talk out of context, blurt out loose words, and exaggerate stories (lying). James calls the tongue an "evil poison." David said he would guard his ways and restrain his mouth with a muzzle that he might not sin with his tongue while in the presence of the wicked (ungodly). Sadly, when we are in the company of unbelievers who tell profane jokes and stories, we laugh and give our input, not realizing that we are entertaining their corrupt conversation. We are an accessory to what they are doing or saying. Even if we do not voice it ourselves, our mere participation in it makes us just as guilty. It is effortless to pick up and repeat bad habits if we're not careful. As such, believers must be wary at all times and sharply alert.

You may have heard someone say, "Oh come on. There's nothing wrong with that. It's just a little joke." How many times have you heard, "You are too heavenly minded that you are no earthly good" or, "God has a sense of humor, too, lighten up." May I repeat this Scripture so it can be rooted in our spirit of how God views idle talk and filthy, ungodly communication. "But I say unto you, that every idle word that men shall speak, they shall give account thereof in the day of judgment. For by thy words thou shalt be justified, and by thy words, thou shalt be condemned." (Matthew 12:36-37, KJV)

Beloved, "[t]here is a way that appears to be right, but in the end, it leads to death." (Proverbs 14:12, NIV) Death means spiritual or physical destruction. "But as he which hath called you is holy, so be

Reason 5 - Corrupt Communication/Idle Jesting

ye holy in all manner of conversation; Be ye holy for I am holy." (1 Peter 1:15-16, KJV) "Nor should there be any obscenity, foolish talk or coarse joking, which are out of place, but rather thanksgiving." (Ephesians 5:4, NIV)

We don't have to participate in every event or conversation. Instead, we ought to be the light in the darkness. I guarantee you, the individuals who are sharing the ungodly jokes or leading the discussion, are carefully observing our reaction. Even though they crave the laughs and participation, they are expecting us to be an example. Those individuals will be the first to call us out if we should speak contrary to our faith. If our action and character lines up with God's Word, believe it or not, we will be the first one they run to for advice. You may have had that experience. Be sure that, after engaging in a conversation, you are not feeling guilty but, instead, God was glorified; the listener was edified; and, the devil was terrified.

Jesus is coming sooner than we think. Let us get ourselves aligned with the Word of God. I don't want to be left behind, do you?

Prayer

Dear God, your name is excellent above the earth. Lord, I praise you with all of my heart and I give myself to you. Lord, I honor and adore you. Thank you, Lord, for keeping me in my right mind. Thank you for the mobility of my limbs. Thank you for watching over me continuously. Father, you are magnificent, you are superb, you are gracious.

Father God, I humbly bow before you. Flush out every ungodly, filthy word that is deeply embedded within my spirit. Lord, I am asking you to forgive me for entertaining and participating in corrupt conversations and idle jesting. Lord, I am a man/woman with unsanctified lips. Cleanse me, O Lord. Burn every filthy, sinful word out of my mind, right now, in the name of Jesus. Cleanse my soul, cleanse my heart, and renew the right spirit within me. Father

God, as I renew my mind daily, help me to say and listen to the right thing. Help me to engage in the right conversations and not laugh at unclean jokes. I command my mind to stay upon you as you keep me in perfect peace. May my words be seasoned with your amazing grace so that they may bring blessings and encouragement to the hearer. Lord, I surrender my tongue to you. Restrain me from entertaining or speaking anything that will be displeasing to you. Anoint my words, O God, so that whenever I speak, the devil will be terrified; the listener is edified; and, you are glorified. In Jesus' name. Amen.

Let no corrupt communication proceed out of your mouth, but that which is good to the use of edifying, that it may minister grace unto the hearers. (Ephesians 4:29)

Reason 5 - Corrupt Communication/Idle Jesting

"May your words be filled with the anointing so that when you speak, God will be glorified; the listeners are edified; and, the devil is terrified."

"The sin of covetousness is one of the most subtle and dangerous sins that is rarely spoken or preached about these days. But, it is a sin that competes with God for our hearts, which makes Him angry."

Reason 6

***

Covetousness

¹What causes fights and quarrels among you? Don't they come from your desires that battle within you? ²You desire but do not have, so you kill. You covet but you cannot get what you want, so you quarrel and fight. You do not have because you do not ask God.
(James 4:1-2, NIV)

To covet means you strongly desire and will do anything to obtain someone else's property or possession, without guilt or regard for their feelings or their loss.

Born in a poverty-stricken family, Molly's mom, Sarah, sold bottles and cans to take care of the family. Sarah became the sole breadwinner after her husband fell ill with cancer. There were days when Sarah and 8-year-old Molly walked miles away from home to sell bottles and cans. Disappointingly, not even one bottle or a can was sold. As they strolled back home with the load, little Molly's friends and neighbors mocked and jeered her. Molly refused to buckle under pressure from her peers. Instead, Molly comforted her mom, saying, "Mom, don't worry; God will provide our food." "Mom, when I grow up, I will not allow you to do this anymore. I will have my own business, a lot of money, a nice car, and a big house so you, dad, and I can all live stress-free with plenty of food."

Twenty years later, as she had envisioned, Molly owned one of the most elegant five-star restaurants in the city. As Molly's silver Benz pulled out of her gated community for work each morning, she could be seen cruising down the boulevard, followed by her mom in her pearl-white Lexus. Then, Molly's dad's health took a turn for the worse. Sarah stayed home with her husband that week. With dad not doing well, Molly decided to close the restaurant early so she could spend some time with her dad. On her way home one night, Molly was in an accident. As she crawled out of the destroyed Benz without a scratch, she realized that the car was totaled. Unknown to Molly, she was being watched and had been followed for weeks. The perpetrators did not hide their faces or their agenda.

Not only was Molly forcefully cheated out of her car, but she was also robbed of every cent she had with her. And, as if that weren't enough, they insisted that Molly take them to her bank to make a withdrawal. On their way to the bank, one of the robbers told Molly that she was a show-off who forgot where she came from and didn't deserve all she had.

Who were the individuals that exhibited such cruelty toward Molly? They were her childhood friends who mocked and jeered her and her mom for picking up and selling bottles. How did they know where she was? One of the mockers happened to be the security guard at the entrance of her gated community and another was the maintenance man. Can you see the spirit of covetousness at work here? Reread the definition. Covetousness can be exhibited in various ways; for instance, there are those presumptuous individuals who are determined to have another woman's husband or another man's wife regardless of who gets hurt. Some will go to any length to close down a person's business and will stop at nothing to make someone suffer financial instability. Some will go to great lengths to make a person lose their job, knowing that it will affect their income and cause them to be unable to meet their financial obligations for their car payment, rent, or mortgage.

The sin of covetousness is one of the most subtle and dangerous sins that is rarely spoken or preached about these days. But, it is a sin that competes with God for our hearts, which makes Him angry. It is the foundation for envy, jealousy, uncontrollable greed, and a strong lustful desire for money and material gain. Covetousness can motivate one to commit adultery, steal, kill, work witchcraft, and get involved with sexual immorality (pornography and prostitution), which eventually assassinates his or her character. Covetousness stems from lust. Your eyes have seen it and now you must have it, no matter the cost or the consequence.

Beloved, sin never satisfies. The sin of covetousness cost satan his position in heaven. Now, he is busy planting the seeds of greed in our hearts, which can prevent our prayers from being answered and block us from entering our promise land. According to Ravi Zacharias, "Sin will take you farther than you want to go, keep you longer than you want to stay, and cost you more than you want to pay."

Do not allow the constant need for material things to cloud your judgment, harden your heart to the warning in God's Word against the sin of covetousness, and consume your loyalty to the Holy Spirit. Be careful how you compare yourself to your friends or family members who appear to be thriving while it seems as if you are stagnant. The circumstances or stories surrounding one person's progress and the other person's downfall or stagnancy can be different. When you compare, perhaps you are saying, you don't mind her or them having it; but, you should have it or more, as well.

As a human, living in this competitive world, jealousy, envy, and covetousness will always try to raise their ugly heads. I am sure it's not your desire to associate with these spirits. However, if you allow Christ to take center stage in your life, they will have no power or dominion over you. It doesn't mean that you won't be tempted. It doesn't mean that you will suddenly have everything you want. And, it doesn't mean that you will be perfect overnight. It means that you are submitting your desires to your Creator, permitting him to let His ideal will manifest in your life. And, in turn, you will be more Kingdom-minded than materially driven.

Finally, covetousness and its relatives are rooted in the heart; so, use the Word of God to uproot and displace them. Remind yourself of God's promises daily. He promised to supply all your needs. He promised that you would be like a tree planted by the rivers of water. He promised that your leaves will not wither. He guaranteed that anything you put your hands to will be successful. Stand on those promises and apply His words to combat the spirit of covetousness.

Jesus is coming sooner than we think. Let us get ourselves aligned with the Word of God. I don't want to be left behind, do you?

Prayer

Hallelujah! Lord, I glorify your name in all the earth. Master, I worship you; I exalt you; I revere you, my Lord and my King. I love you, Lord, and I lift my voice to worship you. You have been my glory and the lifter of my head. You have been my defender, my judge, and my jury. Thank you for giving me life. Jesus Christ, I confess with my mouth and my heart that you are Lord.

Lord, I have been discontented and unsatisfied with my blessings. I have proven myself to be ungrateful to you. Lord, I kept breaking your tenth commandment, allowing my spirit to be consumed by covetousness. Lord, I have allowed greed to get the better of me; deliver me, O God. Wash me thoroughly. Cleanse me, purge me, and purify me from this iniquity and transgression, O God. Search my heart and remove every residue of covetousness from my spirit.

Father God, I promise to be satisfied with who I am and who you have called me to be. I will be contented with the blessings that I already have, be it small or significant.

Spirit of covetousness, the Lord rebukes you. I command you, in the name of Jesus, to be stripped from your assignment. I renounce you, reject you, and denounce you in Jesus' name. I cast you into outer darkness, never to return again. May the fire of God consume and destroy your works. Lord, as of today, I express sincere gratitude for everything that you have entrusted to my care. Lord, refresh my vision to see all that you have desired from me. Lord, I accept your

Reason 6 - Covetousness

decision for my life. I will utilize the opportunities you've sent and will send my way. Thank you, Jesus, for your unconditional love.

Thou shalt not covet thy neighbor's house, thou shalt not covet thy neighbor's wife, nor his manservant, nor his maid servant, nor his ox, nor his ass, nor anything that is thy neighbor's. (Exodus 20:17)

"As born-again Christians, when we desire to be used by God, we don't get to choose when we disobey or obey. We don't get to toss a coin and say heads, disobey and tails, obey. God demands respect, fear, and complete obedience."

Reason 7

***

Disobedience

Know ye not, that to whom ye yield yourselves servants to obey, his servants ye are to whom ye obey; whether of sin unto death, or of obedience unto righteousness. (Romans 6:16)

Regrettably, I struggle with the spirit of disobedience, of which I am so embarrassed. There are times when I've clearly heard the Lord instructing me not to go to a particular place or not to do a specific thing, but I turned a deaf ear and did it anyway. The sad part is, I tend to turn a deaf ear when it doesn't accommodate my fleshly desire. Father, please forgive me.

I've observed that if God's instructions cause our flesh to be deprived in any way, we make excuses and plunge into denial about whose voice we are hearing. To justify our disobedience, we'll often say, "I think it's my mind." However, deep within, we know it is the Holy Spirit nudging us not to do that, or not to go there.

As born-again Christians, when we desire to be used by God, we don't get to choose when we disobey or obey. We don't get to toss a coin and say heads, disobey and tails, obey. God demands respect, fear, and complete *obedience*. He will not be satisfied with leftovers, mediocrity, or presumptuousness. Disobedience can kill. It can cause us to miss our destiny and prevent us from receiving all that God has for us. Obedience is not something we can turn on or off as we have the mind. Disobedience opens the door for other spirits to invade our environment, afflict our health, frustrate our intellect, steal our finances, and cause misery in our family life. When God gives us a command to do or not do something, it is for our safety, protection, and spiritual growth.

I've heard of individuals who were told not to marry the person they were dating, but disregarded the warning and suffered the consequences. A few months down the road, hearts were broken because of infidelity, and divorce papers were served. In one instance, one spouse was hospitalized because of physical abuse, and the other was incarcerated. In other cases, some lost their lives at the hand of their spouse, because of disobedience.

What were you told not to do, but you did anyway, in spite of the warning? Were you warned not to buy that car or that house or start that business or join that pyramid (or partner/susu), as some may call it? Countless times, we sin against God by disobeying His words. We, then, justify our behavior by declaring that we are living under grace, thus taking advantage of its benefit.

"Thou shalt not tempt the Lord thy God." Disobedience is the first and last sin. It will prevent our prayers from being answered. According to the Word of God, we are the servant of whomever we choose to obey. A great example is when God tells us to hold our peace and not confront or say a word to the person who verbally or physically hurt us, but we do anyway. In that instant, we've obeyed satan's whisper to confront him or her, and in essence we made satan our master.

Beloved, here are a few individuals who paid the consequence for disobedience:

> Adam and Eve lost dominion over the earth. They lost eternal life in paradise. They lost freedom because they ate from the tree that God asked them not to. *Genesis 3:24*
>
> Moses missed the Promised Land because he struck the rock instead of speaking to the rock. *Numbers 20:11*
>
> The young prophet lost his life because he allowed the old prophet to manipulate him to visit his house, eat, and drink

when the Lord instructed the young prophet not to stop or eat anything on his journey back home. *1 Kings 13:26*

Saul lost his throne to David, and his relationship with God because he refused to listen to God's command. Saul thought he knew what God wanted and kept the excellent looking animals to make a sacrifice unto God despite the instruction to kill everything. *1 Samuel 15: 28*

Samson disobeyed God in many ways. He knew not to touch carcasses of the dead, yet, he ate honey from the body of the lion he'd killed. Samson took vengeance into his hands and lit the tails of 300 foxes with fire and unleashed them in the cornfield of the Philistines, destroying all their shacks, corn, and olives. Samson knew he shouldn't have been with Delilah or shave his head, yet he revealed the secret of his strength, which eventually led to his eyes being plucked out by the Philistines and, ultimately, the loss of his life. *Judges 15:4-5 & 16:17-30*

My friend, may the above lesson appeal to your spirit man to walk in total obedience. Disobedience is a destructive legacy to leave behind and a deadly inheritance to receive. He that has an ear let him hear what the Word of God says: *"To be obedient is better than sacrifice."* There is an excellent reward for those who obey the words of God. Your spiritual eyes will be opened. You will have a closer connection with God. Your knowledge will increase. You will be able to express Godly wisdom and be free to enjoy God's salvation plan for your life. [31]*So Jesus was saying to the Jews who had believed Him, "If you abide in My word [continually obeying My teachings and living in accordance with them, then] you are truly My disciples.* [32]*And you will know the truth [regarding salvation], and the truth will set you free [from the penalty of sin]." (John 8:31-32, AMP)*

Let us make up our minds to do what is right in the eyes of God and obey His teachings instead of what feels satisfying to our flesh. God could call you home at any moment. Will you be spiritually ready to spend eternity with Him? Or will you hear, "Depart from me I never knew you."

Jesus is coming sooner than we think. Let us get ourselves aligned with the Word of God. I don't want to be left behind, do you?

Prayer

Spirit of the living God, fall afresh on me. Melt me and mold me into a character like yours. Empty me, O God. Empty me from all impurities. Empty me from inward sins and carnal weakness. You are my refuge and my strength. You are my present help in the time of trouble. O God, thank you for being my rock of Gibraltar, thank you for being my soap. Wash away the sin of rebellion from me, Father God.

Father God, for far too long I have ignored your instruction and advice and, blatantly, refused to accept your rebuke. Forgive me, O Lord. Father, I am guilty of allowing the spirit of rebellion to control my ways. Father God, I ask for your forgiveness for entertaining and embracing the spirit of rebellion and disobedience. Forgive me for disobeying you, your words, and the Holy Spirit.

Father, let not disaster or destruction come upon me. Have mercy on me, O God. Don't allow any trouble or desolation to overwhelm me.

Spirit of disobedience, I rebuke you in the name of Jesus. I will no longer yield my mind, my thoughts, my tongue, or any member of my body to you. In the mighty name of Jesus, I command you to loose your stronghold from my life. I cast down every high thing that exalts itself against the power and anointing of God on my life. May the supernatural fire of God destroy you. You foul spirit of disobedience and rebellion, I renounce, denounce, and reject you, in Jesus' name. I bind you and render you powerless, in the mighty name of Jesus. I cast you into outer darkness and into dry places, in Jesus' mighty name.

Reason 7 - Disobedience

Help me, oh God, not to continue in the spirit of disobedience or rebellion. Deliver me from these spirits that I may not suffer the anguish and disaster attached to them, in the mighty name of Jesus.

As of today, I replace the spirit of disobedience with the spirit of obedience. I will follow the commandments of God and continue to walk in compliance with God's Word for the rest of my life. Amen.

"Why do you call me 'Lord, Lord,' and not do what I tell you?" (Luke 6:46, ESV)

Then Peter and the other apostles answered and said, 'We ought to obey God rather than men.' (Acts 5:29)

"Most importantly, you must believe and understand His instruction manual, the Bible. It is designed to keep you from making fatal mistakes while He leads you along the path of righteousness."

Reason 8

***

Doubt/Unbelief

But let him ask in faith, with no doubting, for the one who doubts is like a wave of the sea that is driven and tossed by the wind.
James 1:6 (ESV)

After scrutinizing human behavior, I've learned that we are quick to believe most things. We will not hesitate to do or try the things in which we believe, even when we do not know all that those things entail or the possible outcome. We are willing to invest our last dime and make extreme sacrifices so we can be financially independent and have a better life.

You may have heard and seen individuals who have made huge investments in various organizations or companies without thinking twice. Why? Because it is being advertised that these companies have excellent benefits. Moreover, the investors strongly believe there will be a high return on their investment. Over time, everything seemed well. Yet, eventually, the companies or organizations crumbled, leaving clients homeless, jobless, and penniless.

Sadly, the one who gave His life suffered humiliation and shame on our behalf. Yet, we refuse to believe that He will perform as promised. Our action or reaction to certain situations tell us that we do not think the Words of God are real. Have you ever noticed that we only ponder long and hard when God gives us a command or instruction? We, distinctly, hear His voice directing us, but instead of being still and listening, attentively, we run to our friends, asking their opinion. Only after that do we then say, "Let me pray about it. I want to make sure it's God telling me to do that."

Have you ever prayed, asking God for a fixed amount of money, but by the end of your prayer, you had asked God for about five different amounts? The prayer might have sounded like this: "Lord, the rent is due. The children have to go back to school. The car needs repair; and, I don't know where to turn or to whom I should go for help. Lord, I am asking you to provide for us $10,000. Father, if you can't give me that amount, $5000 will go a long way. Father, even $3000 would be helpful..." and so on.

Without a doubt, you are unstable in your decision. Don't try to be modest or feel sorry for God. He is the one who says come boldly before His throne of grace so you can obtain mercy and find help in the time of need. The moment you start giving Him options is a sign of doubt that He will come through for you. Perhaps, you are thinking that He has done it for others but it may not happen for you. Even though, deep within, you know that God can honor your request, you doubt His ability to or whether He would give you $10,000. In this case, you are struggling with double-mindedness, uncertainty, and unbelief. God cannot answer your request or meet all your needs if you are not sure of what you want. When you doubt God's power or will, you are saying He can't get things done, and you do not trust Him enough to leave your situations in His hands.

Doubt is the manifestation of mistrust and lack of faith in God. If you walked into a restaurant at 10:30 AM asking for lunch but were given a breakfast menu instead, does that mean there would be no lunch? No. In fact, from where you were standing, you couldn't see what was going on in the kitchen. Furthermore, your timing was off since the items on the lunch menu wouldn't be available before noon.

Beloved, even though it seems as if God is not moving on your schedule, He is always working behind the scenes on your behalf. Don't allow doubt to cause you to miss out on God's best for your life.

The absence of faith and the lack of belief is the plight of an unbeliever. What I am about to say may sound harsh, but it is the written words of God. When you disbelieve the Word or the voice of God, you are

Reason 8 - Doubt/Unbelief

already doomed. If you ponder on that saying, you will see that it is the truth. If you don't believe in something, you won't participate, and as a result, you will not get the benefits attached.

"He that believeth on him is not condemned: but he that believeth not is condemned already because he hath not believed in the name of the only begotten Son of God." (John 3:18) To receive from God, you must believe and accept His divinity: His death, burial, and resurrection.

Most importantly, you must believe and understand His instruction manual, the Bible. It is designed to keep you from making fatal mistakes while He leads you along the path of righteousness. Unbelief and doubt open the door for other sins to come in, take dominion, and plant strongholds. If you refuse to believe that fornication is a sin, for example, then you will continue to defile your temple, which can, eventually, lead to diseases that will destroy your life. To sin is not unbelief, but unbelief is a sin. Unbelief and doubt can result in the inability to receive from God. Take for instance, a Rubik's cube. Just because you might not understand how it was created and you are unable to align and match all the colors evenly doesn't mean it is unsolvable. Neither God nor His ways are as complicated as many make them appear to be. You will never understand everything He does, is doing or will do. All you need to do is believe Him and have faith in the process. Trust the maker and designer of all the colored blocks that make up your life. Trust that He knows how to solve the puzzle and make them all line up. Don't waste precious time trying to figure out God's agenda. Just trust Him whether you see or understand what is being asked of you or not.

Jesus said unto him, "Thomas, because thou hast seen me, thou hast believed: blessed are they that have not seen, and yet have believed." (John 20:29)

Prayer

Sweet Holy Spirit, sweet heavenly love, thank you for being here with me. Thank you for being my guide; thank you for being my lawyer, my jury, and my judge. Lord, I praise your Holy name. I honor and adore you. Almighty God, you reign supreme over my life.

Father God, please, forgive me for putting more faith and belief in others and material things than I've placed in you. Father, double-mindedness has kept me tossing back and forth like the waves-unsure in which direction to turn. Forgive me for allowing doubt and double-mindedness to strangle my faith. Forgive me, O God for doubting your ability to see me through my dark and lonesome days. I realize that I continuously speak faith but walk in doubt. Help me, Jesus.

Lord, I have allowed the spirit of doubt to destroy my mind and my judgment. I am sorry for doubting your words. Lord, I let doubt and unbelief prevent me from enjoying my relationship with you. Unbelief robbed me of your perfect will for my life. Lord, when I looked back, I saw that John the Baptist doubted that you were the one and wondered if he should look for another. Thomas wanted to feel the scar in your side because he doubted that you rose from the grave. The women, who were praying for Peter's deliverance from jail, questioned Peter's appearance on their front porch. Abraham and Sarah committed infidelity because Sarah doubted your ability to make her conceive at her age. Lord, it is evident that the spirit of doubt and unbelief have perplexed your people for a long time. Break that spirit off me, O God, let it not be rooted in my children or grandchildren.

Almighty God, as I activate my faith, I release myself from the spirit of doubt and unbelief. Through the power of the Holy Ghost, I command my mind, heart, and soul to line up and believe your written and spoken words. I claim victory over every negative whisper that has caused me to doubt your sovereignty and ability to do exceeding, abundantly, above anything that I may think or ask. As

Reason 8 - Doubt/Unbelief

of today, I believe that I am healed, delivered, and set free through the power in the name of Jesus Christ. I will no longer lean on my own understanding. I acknowledge you, Lord, as my all-powerful source, provider, and protector. Take full control of my life and my affairs. Let me not be a hindrance to myself anymore.

Father God, thank you for healing my unbelief. Uproot and destroy any lingering spirits of doubt and unbelief within me, lest I be condemned, according to your Word. Thank you, Lord, that my relationship with doubt and unbelief has come to an end. Thank you, Jesus, that my struggle with the spirit of uncertainty is over. In Jesus' name. Amen.

Trust in the Lord with all your heart; and lean not unto thine own understanding. (Proverbs 3:5)

"Envy is not a new kid on the block. It has been in existence since creation. Isaiah 14:12-14 reveals how satan, presumptuously, verbalized his intentions towards God's position and possession."

Reason 9

✳✳✳

Envy

A heart at peace gives life to the body, but envy rots the bones.
(Proverbs 14:30, NIV)

*I*s envy one of your weaknesses? Are you envious of anyone? I imagine your instant response is No; but, would that be the truth, or would you be in denial?

Envy is dissatisfaction with your accomplishments because of other people's success. It is resentment of someone because of his or her qualities, status, popularity, etc. Envy has the potential to hurdle bitterness towards someone's lifetime achievement, gift, or talent, and cause one to develop hatred. Envy, being similar to covetousness and jealousy, can cause you to be resentful and hateful of your friends, your family members, and even individuals whom you don't know. One can be envious of another person's physique, children, spiritual growth, or even his or her ability to articulate well.

Even though there is a similarity in behavior between envy, covetousness, and jealousy, there is a difference between them. One can be covetous and jealous and internalize it for a long period without acting on it. However, envy, on the other hand, is tormenting. It produces feelings of discomfort and uneasiness that can force its victim to react in a negative manner towards the individual who is envied. It is not a sin to be tempted with envy, but it is when you act upon that which you are feeling. I don't think anyone wakes up in the morning saying, "I am going to envy someone today." Like any other sin, envy is either driven by your fleshly desire or an evil spirit. Therefore, it is always seeking to invade someone's territory, inveigling him or her to walk out of the perfect will of God. Many may have struggled or may still be struggling with envy.

Envy is not a new kid on the block. It has been in existence since creation. Isaiah 14:12-14 reveals how satan, presumptuously verbalized his intentions towards God's position and possession. *"For thou hast said in thine heart, I will ascend into heaven, I will exalt my throne above the stars of God: I will sit also upon the mount of the congregation, in the sides of the north: 14I will ascend above the heights of the clouds; I will be like the most-High."*

Clearly, you see and hear the spirit of envy spewing out of satan's heart because he was dissatisfied with his position and possessions in heaven and became extremely envious of God. Hence, he schemed with the angels to usurp authority over God to take God's place. Thank God, he did not succeed.

My sisters and brothers, if you are feeling a sense of discontent with your position and possessions and strongly desire another person's property, you are exhibiting the spirit of envy. Where envy and strife are, there are confusion and every evil work. As born-again Christians, it should be our priority to check ourselves regularly, keeping our hearts pure from envy, covetousness, and jealousy. With these works of darkness holding space in our hearts, our prayers will be hindered, leaving no space within us for the Holy Spirit to dwell. The Holy Spirit is our oxygen. We cannot live without him.

Jesus is coming sooner than we think. Let us get ourselves aligned with the Word of God. I don't want to be left behind, do you?

Prayer

Dear God, I acknowledge that Jesus Christ is Lord. I believe that he died, was buried, and resurrected to deliver me from the traps of the enemy. Forgive me for partaking in the sin of envy.

Reason 9 - Envy

Foul spirit of envy, I rebuke you in the mighty name of Jesus Christ of Nazareth. I close every portal that I have opened, permitting you to invade my life. May the fire of God destroy you. Father, teach me to be happy for someone else's blessings and breakthroughs. Let me not sabotage or hate anyone for their possessions, but sincerely rejoice and celebrate their accomplishments.

Deliver me, O Mighty God, from this wicked spirit of envy. May every evil seed, root, and spirit that is attached to envy be paralyzed and neutralized by consuming fire in Jesus' name.

Envy, the Lord rebukes you. I bind you in the name of Jesus and I cast you into outer darkness and dry places. You shall have no more power or authority over me.

Father God, thank you for removing my heart of stone and replacing it with a brand new heart of flesh. I decree and declare that I am cleansed. I am redeemed, and I am being made whole through the power of the Holy Ghost. According to your words, O God, thank you for allowing my heart to be at peace so my body can have life. Thank you for NOT allowing my bones to be eaten up by the spirit of envy.

Father, I thank you for deliverance in Jesus' name. Amen

Let not thine heart envy sinners: but be thou in the fear of the Lord all the day long. (Proverbs 23:17)

"Fear is always found in the company of doubt and unbelief and can be very destructive when entertained. Fear steals your joy, peace, dreams, and potential."

Reason 10

***

Fear

Fear not, for I am with you; be not dismayed, for I am your God. I will strengthen you, Yes, I will help you; I will uphold you with my righteous right hand. (Isaiah 41:10, NKJV)

Fear is like faith in that you have the ability to exhibit both. Faith tells you that you can and fear interjects, telling you that you cannot. Fear is always competing with faith. When you believe you can and take action, faith is activated. When you sit back in your La-z-boy, in the pity party park, telling yourself that it's not going to work, you activate the spirit of fear–not simultaneously, because fear and faith cannot coexist. But, you have the potential to activate either fear or faith, depending on your belief system. *For God hath not given us the spirit of fear, but of power, and of love, and of a sound mind. (2 Timothy 1:7)* Therefore, if you continue to walk around exhibiting worry and fear, it means you're disregarding the comforting Words of God and yielding your ears and mind to satan and have become a walking billboard for him, advertising fear and worry.

If you allow fear to become a stronghold, it will be crippling, tormenting, and tortuous to your daily life; and, it will sabotage your destiny. Hence, "fear not" and "do not be afraid" together is written 365 times in the Bible. Fear is a feeling of agitation and worry caused by the presence or perceived imminence of danger. This kind of fear is instrumental to your survival mechanism because it alerts you of impending danger so you can protect yourself. However, there is a kind of fear which causes people to withdraw, be inactive, or keep from making progress. This fear means you are not depending on God or believing in His promises. Jesus told His disciples to "fear not" and "do not be afraid" 21 times during His time with them.

Fear is always found in the company of doubt and unbelief and can be very destructive when entertained. Fear steals your joy, peace, dreams, and potential. Fear is the opposite of faith. When a believer exhibits confidence with determination, he or she can move mountains and every challenging situation must be subjected to the power within. Many are fearful of this pandemic and other diseases and viruses, but fear has negatively affected individual lives over the years more than any pandemic, epidemic, or endemic.

What are your fears? Why do you fear?

Fear is a crippling agent that may be preventing you from moving towards your spiritual assignment. It will arrest your attention, distracting you from your purpose as it sabotages your destiny. Fear is the culprit that prevents most people from receiving God's best. Fear can contribute to stagnancy, laziness, and unproductivity. Do you recall the parable about the men who received the talents in Matthew 25:14-30? The one, who got one talent, hid his. The passage tells us that the one who received one talent was afraid, so he hid his talent. The passage doesn't say of what he was afraid. Could it be that he feared he would not be as productive as the other men? Is it possible that he felt inferior when he saw how the other men were working their talent and multiplying their ability and getting things done? The bottom line is, because he hid his talent and refused to use it, he missed the opportunity to see how great and successful he could have been.

Beloved, God wants us to use our gifts and talents to empower our brothers and sisters, bring joy and happiness to the broken-hearted, encourage those who are without salvation to seek and develop a relationship with Him, enlighten the unlearned, populate Heaven, and plunder Hell. Never think your gift is useless or too small or not as special as someone else's. Each of us has a significant purpose in the kingdom of God. Your blessings, breakthrough, and deliverance may be connected to your gifts and talents. Unfortunately, you may never find out if you insist on entertaining fear and disobey God's direction.

Being a glory carrier, you are uniquely anointed to destroy yokes and every foul spirit that comes against marriages, health, singleness, families, churches, and finances. Today, I encourage you to obey the Word of God over the whispering spirits that come to deceive you. Fear has no fear; it doesn't matter who you are. Its sole mission is to harass, intimidate, and paralyze God's chosen people. Fear has the power to rob you of what is rightfully yours. Do not be its victim.

When you keep your eyes on Jesus fear cannot distract you. Give fear back to its owner. It's not from God

Prayer

Heavenly Father, I thank you for hiding me under your wings of love and for taking care of me in my moments of despair. Thank you for your mercy, which is brand new every morning. Thank you for your faithfulness towards my family and me.

My Father and my fighter, I place my heart in your hands. Deliver me from the spirit of fear. Father, even though you, repeatedly, told me not to fear 365 times, I disobeyed and gave place to the spirit of fear in my life to stunt my spiritual growth, weaken my anointing, and hinder me from receiving all you intended for me to have.

O God, let my love be perfected in you, as your Word says that perfect love casts out all fear. Lord, I know you did not give me a spirit of fear. Instead you gave me power, love, and a sound mind. With the power, I bind up the spirit of fear and render it powerless in my mind, body, and soul. With that love, I embrace you as my Lord and savior. With my sound mind, I cover every area of my life with the blood of Jesus Christ.

Fear, I serve you notice written in the blood of Jesus Christ. I strip you of your assignment. I command you to leave my life and environment right now. I cast you out into outer darkness and into dry places. I close every open door through which you came, in the mighty name of Jesus. Fear, I will not allow you to intimidate me anymore; I renounce, denounce and reject you, in the name of Jesus. You can no longer prevent me from walking in my purpose or answering the clarion call.

Thank you, Holy Spirit, for delivering me from the spirit of fear in Jesus' name. Amen

For God hath not given us the spirit of fear; but of power, and of love, and of a sound mind. (2 Timothy 1:7)

Reason 10 - Fear

"It takes obedience to fear God. Whenever we desire to be used by God, we don't get to choose when we disobey or obey. We don't get to toss a coin and say heads, disobey and tails, obey. God demands respect, fear, and complete obedience."

"Gluttony is named one of the seven most deadly sins. Solomon says if you are a man given over to your appetite, might as well you put a knife to your throat."

Reason 11

***

Gluttony

He that is slow to anger is better than the mighty; and he that ruleth his spirit than he that taketh a city. (Proverbs 16:32)

Like an out-of-control, loaded freight train so was her appetite. Food had become her best friend and confidant to the point that she ate around the clock. As her weight hastened towards 300 lbs, she was often heard saying, "I have to lose some weight. I need to lose at least one hundred pounds", while still eating–her eyes brimming with sadness, pain, and discomfort.

Excitedly, she started juicing–making green shakes and salads. She did, tremendously, well, until the third day. She made her green shake, as always; but, alongside the shake was a massive plate of fried rice, macaroni and cheese, buttered rolls, and pigs' feet. My heart rent for her as I watched her slowly dig her grave with her teeth, so to speak.

With every passing moment, she became a slave to her appetite–held hostage by food. The more she struggled to free herself from its deadly grip, the tighter its stronghold became around her throat. Her will power and resistance to breaking the addiction to food was in the far distance. When the cravings intensified, she tried filling her stomach at home so she wouldn't be tempted to visit the restaurants. Unfortunately, like a magnet, her eyes and her nose would pull her towards the restaurants or the fast-food joints. Not being able to resist, she ate again.

As soon as she finished eating, a canvas of guilt veiled her face. Like raindrops, her tears fell and feelings of disgust and disappointment encapsulated her. "Why do I keep doing this to myself? I want to stop, but, I can't, and most of the time, when I eat, I am not even hungry. So, why? Why? Look at me! I can't tie my shoelaces. I can't walk a short distance without being out of breath. Bending forward is torture. Creaming my feet is impossible; and, lying down is uncomfortable. I have lost control. I don't want to be like this!"

To gain discipline and self-control of her cravings, she attempted fasting–to no avail. In the midst of the fast, the memories and the taste of Johnny's Café's succulent jerk pork, and Golden Corral's all-you-can-eat buffet flooded through her mind. Unable to withstand the temptation, she drove eleven miles in the night to get some food, depending on which one was open at that time.

As she began to gulp down the meal, a look of disappointment blanketed her face. Insipid, I suppose; but she continued eating. Immediately, after she completed her meal, her facial expression changed. She clutched her chest while rubbing her stomach. The physical torment was visible.

In anguish and grief, the woman sobbed and screamed for help. With her friends, she shared her struggles and relationship with food. Embarrassingly, she explained that, once she is awake, there is always an urge to nibble on something. Sometimes, she would awaken between the hours of 2 and 4 a.m., and feel as though she was being forced out of bed to raid the refrigerator or the pantry. She further shared that after eating, the heartburn, the heart palpitations, the loud burping, and flatulence began, and with such discomfort, going back to sleep seemed impossible.

"I felt disgusting and terrible about myself. Yes, I have been praying for deliverance from this spirit of gluttony."

Dear beloved, the dictionary defines a glutton as a person who eats or drinks excessively. The Bible calls gluttony a sin. And if it's a sin, like any other sin, it is driven by a spirit. In my opinion, a demonic

Reason 11 - Gluttony

spirit of suicide influences gluttony. Ponder it for a moment. If an oppressive spirit is causing you to overeat, it can cause you to consume more than your body needs to function. As a result, doors are open to self-debilitating diseases such as diabetes, high blood pressure, heart attack, or stroke, caused by blocked arteries, due to a build-up of cholesterol. If you find yourself eating, even when you are not hungry or spending your last dime on food that you don't need or getting up at various times in the night to raid the refrigerator, you are oppressed by the spirit of gluttony.

Gluttony is named one of the seven most deadly sins. Solomon says if you are a man given over to your appetite, might as well you put a knife to your throat. Wanting to get rid of gluttony should be one of the perfect reasons to fast. Starve that demon to death and gain self-control. With God, all things are possible.

Here are 13 ways you can defeat gluttony:

1. Remind yourself of the physical consequence that your body will pay.
2. Be accountable to your heart, liver, kidneys, and arteries.
3. Check with your doctor to see what nutrients and vitamins your body may be lacking.
4. Be sure to eat on time at least five small balanced meals per day.
5. Make drinking water a critical part of your life.
6. Speak to the food, and let it know that you are in control.
7. Eat a balanced diet with extra protein and vegetables.
8. Drink a glass of water and/or eat a bowl of salad before the main meal.
9. Make a list and prep your meals for the week.

10. Don't wait until you are hungry before you eat, because it will cause you to over-eat.

11. Juicing and shakes are great ways to curb appetite and get necessary nutrients.

12. Reward and encourage yourself for every effort you make and goals accomplished.

13. **FIGHT DEPRESSION, OPPRESSION, AND POSSESSION WITH PRAYER AND FASTING.**

Prayer

Glory to God in the highest. Lord, my soul, magnifies you, my spirit praises your name. Lord, I revere you. Thank you for strengthening me. Thank you for holding me with your right hand of righteousness. Thank you, Lord, for being the lifter of my head. Lord, you are fantastic. You are superb. You are lovely. Thank you, Jesus.

Dear God, as I get ready to enjoy this meal that you provided, I ask that you bless and sanctify it, in Jesus' name. Lord, as I sprinkle your blood over it, please remove any contamination, bacteria, or germs that may be attached to it, in Jesus' name. Help me not to abuse or waste this food by over-eating. Help me to curb my appetite. Give me the will-power to say I have had enough. Give me the courage to walk away from the table, even if the plate is not empty.

Father, unless you provide my daily meals, I have no means or ways to acquire food, and I am tired of using the same food to dishonor your temple through binge eating. May the Holy Ghost alert me when I have had enough. Spirit of gluttony, I take authority over my entire body. I rebuke you and render you powerless, in Jesus' name. You will not force me to overeat or eat unnecessarily anymore.

Heavenly Father, I desire to satisfy my spirit man instead of the cravings and growling of my stomach. Help me, O God, to have a

Reason 11 - Gluttony

balance where I will feed my spirit man as much or even more than my flesh. In Jesus' name. Amen.

When thou sittest to eat with a ruler, consider diligently what is before thee: [2]And put a knife to thy throat, if thou be a man given to appetite. [3]Be not desirous of his dainties: for they are deceitful meat. (Proverbs 23:1-3)

"It is impossible to disobey God and still be victorious. Partaking of the things, which the Bible forbids, is outrightly going against the Word of God. When we do not listen, believe, or follow His direction, we are deliberately disobeying His advice."

Reason 12

***

Going Against God's Word

He that turneth away his ears from hearing the law (commandment), even his prayer shall be abomination. (Proverbs 28:9)

It is impossible to receive knowledge, wisdom, or understanding from a teacher, if we do not believe what he or she teaches. It is, also, a strong possibility that we may not receive anything from the teacher because we refuse to exercise respect for his or her authority, consistently disregard instructions, contradict his or her guidelines, and go against his or her jurisdiction. Remember, we are talking about the reasons why our prayers are unanswered.

Answer these questions honestly. If you are continuously being disrespected and rejected by your spouse, would you bend over backward to grant him/her favors? How would you feel if your spouse never listened or did anything you asked of him or her but still insisted that you jump to his or her beck and call without hesitation?

Many times, we try to contradict the Word of God with our intellect, seeking to change or twist His words to justify our action. Yet, we expect Him to move on our behalf, promptly. We tend to insert our feelings, opinions, and ideas when interpreting Scripture. That's fine if our interpretation is not misleading or changing God's original intention towards His people. Let's not forget, Jesus is the Word who became flesh. We should not expect our prayers or requests to be granted if we continuously wrestle with and against the word of the Word (Jesus) with a rebellious contradicting attitude.

It is impossible to disobey God and still be victorious. Partaking of the things, which the Bible forbids, is outrightly going against the Word of God. When we do not listen, believe, or follow His direction, we are deliberately disobeying His advice. Let's not think for a moment that we are doing God a favor when we decide to believe and accept His terms. We are preserving our spiritual retirement package and long-term benefit for the future. Revelation 22:18-19 reminds us that if we add to His words, plagues shall be added to us, and if we take away from His words, our life shall be taken out of the Book of Life. Most individuals purposely misinterpret Scriptures, notably the Ten Commandments, for convenience.

My friend, unless the Holy Spirit reveals the interpretation of His Words to us, it is impossible for us to understand and interpret, effectively. Therefore, after reading a verse or chapter, if we are not clear on the interpretation of it, continue to seek God for the revelation. He has promised not to hide anything from His friends. Let us not persuade others to see or believe our version or our point of view until we've received that revelation so we don't lead others astray.

There are many verses in the Bible to which we refuse to adhere, but not because they are outdated, abolished, or invalid. The Ten Commandments seem to pose a challenge to many; hence, it has been distorted by men who believe and preach that it is no longer valid and, moreover, we are under grace. Yes, indeed, we are living by grace but it doesn't change God's commandments or His mind. His words stand forever. Matthew 24:35 states: *Heaven and earth shall pass away but my words will not pass away.*

...[F]or I assure you and most solemnly say to you, until heaven and earth pass away, not the smallest letter or stroke [of the pen] will pass from the Law until all things [which it foreshadows] are accomplished. Matthew 5:18 (AMP)

Reason 12 - Going Against God's Word

Prayer

Lord, I give you my all. I give you my soul. Have your way in me. Lord, every breath that I take and every moment that I am awake, have your way with me. Lord, I will always place you before. Thank you for being on my side. Thank you for not allowing the hand of the wicked to remove me nor the foot of pride to overtake me.

Father, please forgive me for going against your words, your laws, and your commandments. Forgive me for rejecting and neglecting your teaching and direction. Lord, I have been sitting in darkness, bound by affliction because I've refused to yield to your words. I sincerely ask you to regulate my mind, rearrange my thoughts, and turn my heart back to you so that my prayers will not remain an abomination to you.

Father God, I realize that my self-centeredness and my intellect have gotten in the way of my salvation. I submit and surrender myself to you right now, in Jesus' name. Lord, I thank you for your never-ending mercy, your unconditional love, and your amazing grace towards me, O God. Father, as of today, I will take the time to seek your wisdom through your words. Grant me knowledge and understanding of your words, O God, and keep me in perfect peace, as my mind continues to rest upon you. In Jesus' name. Amen

Such as sit in darkness and in the shadow of death, being bound in affliction and iron; Because they rebelled against the words of God, and contemned the counsel of the most High. (Psalm 107:10-11)

"Hating each other can be destructive to us mentally, physically, emotionally, and spiritually. Hate will trap us unto death."

Reason 13

***

Hate

But he that hateth his brother is in darkness, and walketh in darkness, and knoweth not whither he goeth, because that darkness hath blinded his eyes. (1 John 2:11)

Martin Luther King Jr. said, *"Darkness cannot drive out darkness, only light can do that; Hate cannot drive out hate, only love can do that."*

Hate can be instrumental to our salvation, and it can also be destructive to our lives, depending on what's causing us to hate. Hating evil would be a natural thing to do if we are in love with God. (Psalm 97:10) We should hate the assembly of evildoers. (Psalms 26:5) Being born-again and proclaiming salvation and the name of Christ, we should hate all sin and ungodliness.

However, the Word of God repeatedly warns us not to harbor hatred and bitterness towards our sisters and brothers. Hating each other can be destructive to us mentally, physically, emotionally, and spiritually. Hate will trap us unto death. Murder, as we know it, is taking the life of another; yet God compares hating your brothers and sisters to a murder. As we already know, without repentance, murderers cannot inherit eternal life. (1 John 3:15)

Not too long ago, I was engaged in a lengthy conversation with a church sister. Our main topic was about the unconditional love, greatness, and favor of God. We were basking in His presence-expressing how much we love God and don't want to miss heaven.

If you were listening to us, you would have thought that we were having a revival.

Then arose the topic about her grandson and his mother that really struck a nerve. Uninterruptedly, I listened to her bare her soul, verbalizing her dismay and disappointment with the child's mother. Shortly after that, the disgruntled sister blurted out, "I hate her, I can't stand a bone in her. If I had the power to kill her, I would. I will never forgive her!" She exclaimed. My mouth flew open, my lips hanging until they were parched.

After catching my breath, I was not sure how to proceed with our conversation. However, I was lead to share with her the story of the crucifixion. I began by saying that a group of wicked, heartless, callous men forced Jesus to carry on His back two pieces of extremely heavy wood attached, and formed a cross. Along His journey, with this load on His back, He fell multiple times. Without sympathy, they kept on beating Him. His back was ripped open, exposing muscle and, quite possibly, bones. They spat upon Him. He was humiliated, mistreated, and embarrassed in the presence of thousands. "Nevertheless, He took it all and kept on going just for you and me," I explained.

After Jesus got to the intended destination, the unsatisfied, vindictive, self-centered men took the cross that Jesus struggled with on His back. They erected it and began nailing Him onto it, while He was still alive. "What was the first of the seven sayings of Jesus, while He was, painfully, hanging on the cross?", I asked her. "Father, forgive them, they not what they do," she replied. I continued to share with her what the Lord revealed to me about the crucifixion and those words.

When I asked God why He allowed the men whom He created to humiliate Him in such a despicable way? He answered, "Yes, I could have erased them with the breath of my nostrils, but it was a part of salvation's plan. I wanted to show humankind that despite the persecution, heartache, betrayal, and hurt they will experience, there is room for forgiveness. I wanted them to understand that

Reason 13 - Hate

no matter what atrocities and turmoil they may face, they can still love unconditionally without resentment or make excuses for their harmful actions. I also wanted to teach them how to see each other through my eyes and not their physical eyes."

When I got through reminding her of the price Jesus paid so that hate would have no place in our mind and soul, she got quiet and broke down into tears.

Beloved, have you ever found yourself hating anyone? Have you ever verbalized the words, "I hate him," or "I can't stand her?" Have you ever felt as if the word hate is too strong, so you resort to saying, "I don't know, but there is just something about him or her that doesn't sit well with my spirit?" Hmm? Have you ever been there? My sisters and brothers, the return of Jesus Christ is rapidly approaching. We can't afford the spirit of hate to prevent us from entering the kingdom of God. Remember, *"Know ye not, that to whom ye yield yourselves servants to obey, his servants ye are to whom ye obey; whether of sin unto death, or of obedience unto righteousness?"* Therefore, when we harbor hatred in our heart, we are obeying satan. Evidently, we have become his servant.

Even though Jesus was in excruciating pain, He did not use it as an excuse or allow it to stop Him from demonstrating genuine forgiveness and compassion. His selflessness is an excellent example for us to adopt and apply to our lives each time we are betrayed and hurt by someone. If we allow our feelings or emotions to dictate to us, we will be at odds with many of our sisters and brothers. Jesus took His feelings out of the way and was able to extend forgiveness from a place of emptiness.

My friend, let go of the memories of the pain and the past. Empty yourself so you can live a fulfilled life without cancer, diabetes, high blood pressure, or any other sickness that may be destroying your body due to hate and unforgiveness. Begin to see the individual/s who hurt you through the eyes of Jesus Christ. Remember, there is nothing that you will ever go through that can compare with what

Jesus went through and, yet, without hesitation, He forgave His abusers.

Just close your eyes for a moment, and visualize yourself being at the scene of Jesus' crucifixion. All of His sufferings were to ensure that we have a secured place in heaven. Do you think He is pleased with us when we hate each other and exhibit ungodly behaviors? Don't allow His death to be in vain. Get rid of hate and replace it with Godly love. Of course, I know it won't be easy to get over the hurt, but if you surrender it all to God, you will overcome and walk in victory. It is time to take your Christian walk and relationship with Jesus Christ seriously.

Jesus is coming sooner than we think. Let us get ourselves aligned with the Word of God. I don't want to be left behind, do you?

Prayer

O God Almighty, I repent for embracing the spirit of hatred in my heart. Wash my heart from all iniquity. Purge me from unrighteousness, and remove from me all my trespasses. Lord, my heart is heavy with hatred for_____. Please, release me from this darkness. Lord, I am imprisoned by my hateful heart. Deliver me, O God, from the spirit of hate that has come to prevent me from receiving eternal life. Search every crevice and corner of my heart, O God and uproot every speck of hatred that is hidden inside.

Father God, hatred has veiled me with darkness, and I don't want to live like this anymore. I don't want to be blinded by the grim darkness. Father God, because of hatred, I can't think right. I can't live right. I can't behave right, and I am not enjoying my Christian life in You. Cleanse my heart with the blood of Jesus Christ. Sanctify my heart, O God, and make it think holiness instead of hatred. I bind up the strongman that is influencing the spirit of hate. Spirit of enmity, through the power of the Holy Ghost, I bind you in the name

Reason 13 - Hate

of Jesus. I command you to leave my life and go cast yourself into outer darkness and into dry places, in Jesus' mighty name.

Thank you, Lord Jesus, for restoring a brand new heart and delivering me from the spirit of hate. Amen.

"Have you ever noticed or stopped to wonder why we treat non-family members and friends better than we do our own spouse and family? Yes, we should love and care for others as well. Nonetheless, I would like to draw our attention to that which we often overlook because we think we are doing nothing wrong."

Reason 14

***

Home Life

For this is the way the holy women of the past who put their hope in God used to adorn themselves. They submitted themselves to their own husbands. ⁷Husbands, in the same way be considerate as you live with your wives, and treat them with respect as the weaker partner and as heirs with you of the gracious gift of life, so that nothing will hinder your prayers. (1 Peter 3:5&7, NIV)

Hmm, why would your homelife prevent your prayers from being answered?

At times, we take our spouse and family members for granted–ignoring their needs and cries for help. We fail to see that it is God's intention and will for us to esteem our family in a high position, showing unconditional love and care for each other. It is His desire for us to foster that love, share His values, and practice them at home. My mom's favorite saying was, "Learn to dance at home before you can dance abroad." In other words, we should first practice how to treat and respect or family members who are at home.

Husbands, wives, parents, children, sisters and brothers, be kind with your words and gentle in your actions. Exhibit love at the moment when the other person is not lovable. Be patient with each other. Learn to control your temper and your words. Whenever these fruits are seen in each other, without a doubt, there will be peace, joy, goodness, and faithfulness dancing around your home. These are the fruit of the spirit.

38 Reasons For Unanswered Prayers

Have you ever noticed or stopped to wonder why we treat non-family members and friends better than we do our own spouse and family? Yes, we should love and care for others as well. Nonetheless, I would like to draw our attention to that which we often overlook because we think we are doing nothing wrong.

Answer the following questions honestly. Get some paper or a notebook and a pen and write your answers down. Your answers could be a part of your prayer list–something else to pray about. Get out of denial.

> How do you treat your spouse?
>
> How do you speak to each other compared to the way you speak to your friends?
>
> Do you compliment each other?
>
> What happens during and after an intense argument?
>
> Was there an apology or does resentment linger day after day?
>
> Do you respect each other?
>
> How about intimacy? Is that the only time you show affection and give your undivided attention?
>
> Do you desire your spouse or someone else?
>
> Do you make and spend time with the children?
>
> Do you honor your children's request?

Reader, if you are not married or in a relationship, answer the following questions.

> How is the relationship between you and your children?

How do you treat your parents?

What is your relationship like with your siblings?

How is your relationship with your grandparents, aunts, uncles, cousins?

If there is a negative answer to any of the above questions, there is a need for repentance. One cannot effectively love, praise, and represent God or preach to others while the relationship at home is in turmoil. Regrettably, our priorities are shifted. We are weaved into the web of busyness and the cares of the world, which takes a toll on our daily lives. Consequently, some family foundation is weakened, while some have been completely uprooted and appears beyond repair. I do agree that some relationships can be toxic and would be futile to rebuild. Nonetheless, there are relationships that hit rock-bottom, to the point of no return in our eyes, but how do we know for sure that God can't turn things around? He is omnipotent, all knowing and can do just about anything. He being the master architect, He can fortify any relationship and put it back together as long as it is His perfect will. With God, all things are possible if we believe.

Listed below are some Bible verses that remind us how to treat each other.

[12] *Now we ask you, brothers and sisters, to acknowledge those who work hard among you, who care for you in the Lord and who admonish you.* [13]*Hold them in the highest regard in love because of their work. Live in peace with each other. (1 Thessalonians 5:12-13, NIV)*

[4]*Love is patient, love is kind. It does not envy, it does not boast, it is not proud.* [5]*It does not dishonor others, it is not self-seeking, it is not easily angered, it keeps no record of wrongs.* [6]*Love does not delight in evil but rejoices with the truth.* [7] *It always protects, always trusts, always hopes, always perseveres. (1 Corinthians 13:4-7, NIV)*

Show proper respect to everyone, love the family of believers, fear God, honor the emperor. (1 Peter 2:17)

Do nothing out of selfish ambition or vain conceit. Rather, in humility value others above yourselves. (Philippians 2:3)

So in everything, do to others what you would have them do to you, for this sums up the Law and the Prophets. (Matthew 7:12)

Bearing graciously with one another, and willingly forgiving each other if one has a cause for complaint against another; just as the Lord has forgiven you, so should you forgive. (Colossians 3:13, AMP)

Prayer

Hallelujah. Glory to God.

Father, here I am again repenting for neglecting my household and other family members. Father God, please forgive me for not treating them the way I would like to be treated. Father, according to your word in Colossians 3:16, *Let the spoken word of Christ have its home within my heart and mind—permeating every aspect of my being as you teach me spiritual things and admonish and train me with all wisdom, with thankfulness in my heart to God.*

Lord, I thank you for not giving up on me. Thank you for not neglecting me as I have done to my spouse and family members. Thank you for not allowing me to feel inferior or less important as I have done to my household. Lord, as of today, help me to treat and esteem my spouse and family members better. I awaken my conscience to be sensitive to the needs of my husband/wife, my child/children, my parents, and my siblings.

Father, I thank you for opening my eyes to see these obstacles that are preventing my prayers from being answered. Praise God.

Holy Spirit, I invite you to reside in my home continuously. Liberate us from darkness. Remove the scales from our eyes so we can see each other through your eyes. In the mighty name of Jesus, I bind every interfering, sabotaging spirit that has come to drive a wedge

Reason 14 - Home life

between my family and me. Through the power in the blood of Jesus Christ of Nazareth, I strip you from your assignment against my home. I cast you into outer darkness and dry places.

Thank you, Lord, for resurrecting our loving and Godly feeling towards each other. For this reason, we can embrace each other without resentment and unforgiveness.

Thank you, Lord. Amen

Anyone who does not provide for their relatives, and especially for their own household, has denied the faith and is worse than an unbeliever. (1 Timothy 5:8, NIV)

"Many practice this behavior out of curiosity, while some are confused and are struggling to identify with their identity. Still, some have encountered tragic sexual experiences such as rape or even betrayal from their heterosexual relationship and, as a result, choose to enter into this lifestyle."

Reason 15

✱✱✱

Homosexuality

Or do you not know that wrongdoers will not inherit the kingdom of God? Do not be deceived: Neither the sexually immoral nor idolaters nor adulterers nor men who have sex with men nor thieves nor the greedy nor drunkards nor slanderers nor swindlers will inherit the kingdom of God. (1 Corinthians 6:9-10, NIV)

*H*ow did I get here? I ask myself repeatedly. I am a successful businessman, married to a stunningly beautiful woman. Our union produced adorable, grown children. I couldn't have asked for more. I have it all, yet I feel empty. My wife and children are always there and would have given their lives for me, but I am still lonely. We are debt-free but I am so miserable. Why?

Like lightening, various thoughts flash across my mind. Thoughts of suicide, feelings of leaving my wife, thoughts of unveiling my secrets to my family, and the list goes on. Unable to win the war that rages daily in my mind, I veil myself with anger and selfishness. Numerous times, I've felt as if I were in a boxing ring being knocked down in every round, anticipating the ringing of the bell so the fight could stop. As the battle intensified, I became more battered, bruised, and broken just knowing I was hurting the person whom I vowed to love, honor, and protect.

With every passing day, it's gotten harder to live with myself and more challenging for my wife to tolerate me. With whom can I share my struggles? How do I break this news to my wife? How will she handle it? Will my children abandon me? If they have questions, can I be honest with them knowing I am not honest with myself? Drowning in my sorrows, I gasp for air slowly submerged in my pain.

The most painful part? Over the years, my body showed up for intimacy with my wife, but my mind was elsewhere making love with someone else. The more I tried to break this extramarital affair, the more I feel the urge to continue. My emotions were entangled in a web of lies, trapped in mental bondage, as my physical body struggled to emerge from beneath the rubble of falling debris. I feel like I am being eaten alive.

Refusing to continue living this lie, I decide to move out of the marital home and move in with my partner. Soon after, the longing and passion we felt for each other over the years suddenly diminished. We argue and fight constantly. It's as if I jumped from the refrigerator into the freezer. I take an unplanned vacation by myself and delve into some deep soul searching. Deep within, I know my actions are not right because I have no inner peace, I feel torn and unfulfilled. I need to get to the root cause of the manifested bizarre behavior I portrayed in adulthood. Hence, I make an appointment to meet with the little boy within me. I need answers.

As a strict and thorough journalist would, I dig way beneath the surface for clues and answers. All that were hidden in the closet, shoved under the rug, buried in concrete vaults were finally exposed. Honesty showed up. Tears trickle down my face as the bitter memories start to emerge. As I journey along the dark memory lane, fear consumes me; fear of the unknown. I am afraid of what I might have seen and heard. Even though they named me Mark, I was never called by my name. I was the "Little Boy" At every interval I heard sounds of the little boy being physically and verbally abused by his alcoholic dad, being told repeatedly that he should have been aborted. Intimidation plastered his mom's face as she too was afraid for the little boy, and her life. Occasionally, I peek into a little room and there is the little boy curled up in a fetal position in the dark, sniffling and wiping his eyes.

Reason 15 - Homosexuality

A more significant portion of hidden memories come flooding in; things become more evident. I see the little boy being taken away from home to stay with family friends, and sometimes with an uncle until his mom got back from work. Mom worked two, sometimes three jobs to support the children, and her alcoholic husband. With feelings of rejection and abandonment, the little boy asks, "Why do I have to leave home, and my sisters stay home?" Shortly after the little boy arrived at the family friend's house, the rain came down. Unable to go outside, hide and seek was played inside. When the little boy was found, he was fondled, kissed, and groped by his friend's older brother. Fighting back the tears, panic, and disbelief warps his face.

Would I be treated this way if I was a girl? My sisters are not being yelled at or being beaten. They don't have to leave the house when mom is not home, why me? The most painful memory was revealed. The little boy got the biggest shock of his life when he was left in his uncle's care. Numerous times he was sexually molested by his uncle, who told him not to say a word. Being in pain, and feeling confused and ashamed, the little boy did not eat for days. He became an introvert. His school work suffered and relationships with everyone came to a screeching halt.

Secretly, he began to wear his sister's dresses. Suffering in silence for so long, he tried to numb the pain by pretending to be a comedian to get a laugh. He openly put on his sister's dresses, makeup, along with other pieces of her clothing and everyone laughed. The little boy struggled with his identity. At age twelve, the tug-of-war began in his mind and body. His major struggle was being attracted to the same sex but still wanting to be with females. Unsuccessfully, he fought the feelings every step of the way.

Fast forward to adulthood, after the meeting with the little boy inside I realize that the same things that caused me pain and discomfort were the same things I desired while being married to my amazing wife. I thought being married to a woman would have erased these strange desires of wanting to be intimate with someone of the same sex, but I found out that it was just a camouflage for me to hide my inner struggles.

A man of uncertainty and lost identity is not who I am or am supposed to be; something or someone interfered with my will. If that is the case, why do I still feel uncomfortable, miserable, and lonely after leaving my wife to live with my male partner? Even though I partake in the act, I will not accept or embrace that this is who I am or suppose to be. This behavior is the manifestation of the negative seeds that were planted within me by my uncle and the family friend. I feel strongly in my spirit that this is not the right way to live; I want to be delivered from this inner turmoil. There has to be a better way. I will continue to fight for my deliverance from this spirit.

Dear beloved, the American Psychological Association says that "Homosexuality is not a mental disorder, and thus there is no need for a cure." I, too, agree that it is not a mental disorder and, therefore, cannot be physically treated. I believe homosexuality is a spiritual attack on God's creation, and thus, there is a need for deliverance. Many homosexuals say they were created that way, but I beg to differ. In my opinion, there was a spiritual interference instigated by satan and his demons somewhere between conception and delivery, whether in the womb or through the birth canal.

Many practice this behavior out of curiosity, while some are confused and are struggling to identify with their identity. Still, some have encountered tragic sexual experiences such as rape or even betrayal from their heterosexual relationship and, as a result, choose to enter into this lifestyle. It is important to note that God loves you, despite your sexual preferences, but He hates your immoral sinful deeds. Like any other sin, homosexuality carries with it a death penalty if there is no repentance.

Whenever we participate in the things that God forbids, He will not turn a blind eye. His heart breaks to hear us say, "God understands, and God is not like that; He is merciful." Reader, God does not understand disobedience (sin). Hence He will not let it slide except when we seek forgiveness. In the eyes of God, there is neither big

Reason 15 - Homosexuality

nor small sin. No matter what our sin may be, there will be severe punishment, if we do not repent. My friend, make your salvation count. It is my sincere prayer that after reading this book, you will identify the areas in your life that need radical change, a change that will guarantee you eternal life and a secured VIP seat In heaven.

Below are some scriptures to open your awareness about what God said about this behavior.

^{25}*Who changed the truth of God into a lie, and worshipped and served the creature more than the Creator, who is blessed forever. Amen.*

^{26}*For this cause God gave them up unto vile affections: for even their women did change the natural use into that which is against nature (lesbian)*

^{27}*And likewise also the men, leaving the natural use of the woman, burned in their lust one toward another; men with men working that which is unseemly, and receiving in themselves that recompense of their error which was meet. (gay)*

^{28}*And even as they did not like to retain God in their knowledge, God gave them over to a reprobate mind, to do those things which are not convenient.... (Romans1:25-28)*

If a man also lie with mankind, as he lieth with a woman, both of them have committed an abomination: they shall surely be put to death; their blood shall be open on them. (Leviticus 20: 13)

Before one of my word pass away heaven and earth will. (Matthew 24:35)

There is a way that seems right to a man but the end is destruction. (Proverbs 14:12)

This I say then, Walk in the Spirit, and ye shall not fulfill the lust of the flesh. (Galatians 5:16)

Prayer

Lord, I appreciate you; I love you and I adore you. Lord, thank you for looking beyond my faults and seeing my needs. Lord, while you were on the cross, I was on your mind; thank you for dying for my sins. Thank you for your redemptive power that has come to redeem me from satan's vicious attacks on my life. Lord, I have done an abominable thing in your sight, thank you for not condemning me as many people do. Thank you for not giving me over to a reprobate mind or looking down on me in disgust, but reaching down with your hand of mercy to deliver me from myself and my sinful habits.

My father and my fighter, you said that your strength would make perfect in my weakness. With your strength, I bind every foul spirit that attached itself to me since childhood days through fondling or sexual molestation by either a cousin, sister, brother, uncle, aunt, neighbor, father, mother or pastor, in Jesus' mighty name. I curse such a curse in Jesus' mighty name. In the powerful name of Jesus, every gay or lesbian spirit that's been tormenting my mind, I strip you from your assignment right now. Through the power in the blood of Jesus Christ, I disconnect myself from this demonic activity. I break and destroy the stronghold of homosexuality and lesbianism off my life now in Jesus' name. Father God, I renounce, denounce, and destroy every covenant I made with this spirit. In Jesus' name.

You foul spirit, I arrest and strip you from your assignment over my life, mind, and body. I will no longer yield the members of my body to you; my body is the temple of God. I rebuke you in Jesus' name. In the mighty name of Jesus, I dig up the roots and seeds of all homosexual or lesbian spirit that was planted in me now. I close every open door that has given you access to my life. I send the fire of God to destroy your powers and stronghold over my life. I deactivate you, I take dominion over you and I terminate your works, in Jesus' name. I cast you out into outer darkness and dry places now, in the name of Jesus Christ. Amen.

You shall not lie with a male as with a woman. It is an abomination. (Leviticus 18:22-23)

Reason 15 - Homosexuality

When Jesus willingly gave His life on the cross, He didn't do it for the Baptist, Adventist, Pentecostal, Catholic or the tongue speaking, bible preaching, church going individuals.

He gave His life for the liar, murderer, witchcraft worker, thief, gossiper, and those who are struggling with jealousy, envy, and homosexuality.

God is not mad at you; He is crazy about you. He wants what is best for you, hence, He hates the sinful acts in which you participate.

Regardless of the sin, it can drive a wedge between you and the daddy who loves you endlessly.
Listen to His calm whisper redirecting you to make a a U-turn back to Him.
I came not to call the righteous, but sinners to repentance.
(Luke 5:32)

"Hypocrisy is saying one thing and doing the opposite. It allows you to feel justified with your double-dealing, two-facedness, and dishonesty."

Reason 16

***

Hypocrisy

So you must be careful to do everything they tell you. But do not do what they do, for they do not practice what they preach.
(Matthew 23:3, NIV)

I will bet you're saying, "I don't get it. How is it possible for hypocrisy to prevent my prayers from being answered?" Follow me closely.

Hypocrisy exhibits self-righteousness and comes off as being sanctimonious but operates, deceptively, at the same time. How can one identify the manifestation of hypocrisy? For one, if you are adamant about not gossiping but you find yourself tearing down a sister or a brother, that is hypocrisy. If you encourage others to forgive no matter what, but you refuse to talk to your family members or a sister or brother because of something you heard that he or she said, of which you have no proof, that is hypocrisy. Another common manifestation of hypocrisy is hearing an individual saying, "Me? Oh, No! I will never do that"; but, then, he or she does, precisely, that regularly. That is hypocrisy.

Hypocrisy is saying one thing and doing the opposite. It allows you to feel justified with your double-dealing, two-facedness, and dishonesty. The Bible clearly states that *"There is a way which seemeth right unto a man, but the end thereof are the ways of death." (Proverbs 14:12)* Perhaps what you have done feels and sounds right to you, as a result, you refuse to repent. For that reason, you are living and walking around with unrepented sin. According to Psalm 66:18, *"If I regard iniquity in my heart, the Lord will not hear me."*

Dear beloved, let us humble ourselves before God and man and examine our lives and behavior. Let us discard the holier than thou attitude. Furthermore, we are not perfect; so, do not condemn anyone for making irrational decisions that cause them to fall or mess up. Their sin is not bigger than ours. In fact, sin has no color, gender, or size. It's one size fits all. The penalty and consequence are the same. Did you know hypocrisy can cause you to kill, hate, and lie? It is time for us to practice and live what we preach as we live a life that is pleasing to God.

Prayer

Father, forgive me for all the sin I have committed. Forgive me for the cumbersome loads that I have placed on others. Lord, please forgive me for the awkward and unmanageable situations that I have caused your people to suffer. I surrender my mind, heart, and soul to you. Wash me one more time with your blood.

Father God, many times I praise you with my lips, but my heart is far from you. Lord, I am guilty of saying one thing and doing the opposite. I am guilty of judging and condemning others for the same things that I am doing. Father, according to your words, I agree with the adversary, quickly, that I am a hypocrite who is in need of deliverance.

Deliver me, O God, from the foul spirit of hypocrisy and release me from its deadly grip. Spirit of hypocrisy, I rebuke you and denounce you, in the name of Jesus.

Lord, hide me in the cleft of the rock from the spirit of hypocrisy. I surrender to you my holier-than-thou behavior, my self-righteous attitude, and my deceptive actions. I will no longer entertain these behaviors.

Lord, I permit you to strip me of every attachment to hypocrisy. Erase every hypocritical thought from my mind as I thoroughly examine

Reason 16 - Hypocrisy

my ways and my spiritual foundation. Lord, let me not think of myself higher than anyone else. Remove from me the sanctimonious attitude and replace it with sincerity and fairness. In Jesus' name. Amen.

They tie up heavy, cumbersome loads and put them on other people's shoulders, but they themselves are not willing to lift a finger to move them. (Matthew 23: 3-4, NIV)

"An idol is that which we give excessive devotion and reverence, and, in so doing, forget God, as our Source. An idol may take the form of a person, our job, house, car, TV show, leisure activity, social media."

Reason 17

✶✶✶

Idolatry

Do not turn away after useless idols. They can do you no good, nor can they rescue you, because they are useless. (1 Samuel 12:21, NIV)

*D*uring courtship, Maria never left my side. She was always available for phone conversations, lunch dates, strolls in the park and on the beach, without us crossing the line. After marriage, the affection and attention grew stronger. The intimacy was phenomenal.

Seeing her potential, I encouraged and assisted her to further her education; and, her honors and distinctions were displayed, proudly, in the corridors as she glided down the aisle at her graduation. Shortly after that, our conversations became few and far between. Like two ships passing in the night, so we were. Our time together diminished; intimacy had to be scheduled; walks in the park or on the beach had become things of the past, as if they had never existed.

Maria became so distanced. I competed daily with her job, friends, and social media for my wife's attention and affection. I no longer fit into her life or her schedule. Material things and her friends had become her priority. Jealousy consumed me. Oh yes, I felt shut out, rejected, and ignored. Nevertheless, I am still head-over-heels with her. I will never stop loving her despite the many idols she chose over me.

Dear reader, can you see yourself in this story? Is this the way you treat God? Where is He on your priority list? Did you place Him in a competition for your attention? Has He become second best in your life, or no longer a part of your being? How would you feel if your spouse refused to establish or build a relationship with you, except when he wants a favor or sex? Would you feel used? What would your reaction be if you knew that your spouse was involved in extramarital affairs? Jealous, right? Idolatry is the act of worshiping our possessions, or an image, or other things, and allowing them to take preeminence in our lives.

Moreover, we have permitted them to take the place of God in our hearts. An idol is that which we give excessive devotion and reverence, and, in so doing, forget God, as our Source. An idol may take the form of a person, our job, house, car, TV show, leisure activity, social media. As absurd as it may seem, doing the work of God can consume us to the point where it becomes our idol. You grow so consumed with "doing" for God that you miss out on the stillness and intimacy of God. Can you imagine someone saying, "I don't get much time to spend with God because of my job?" Or "I am not able to attend church because I have only one day off from work, and I have to mow my lawn, paint my house, wash my car, and spend time with my kids." Anything that consumes our time or takes us away from spending time with God is an idol in our lives. Just think about how God feels when we choose people or things over Him.

When God says He is a jealous God, this does not mean that He is envious or covetous. His jealousy is a form of protection. He is fully aware of the outcome of creating and embracing idols. He knows that once we give ourselves over to something, other than Him, we are prone to be hurt and disappointed. Without God being in control of our lives, our spiritual ears are clogged, and our spiritual eyes are blinded. Consume your idols before they consume you! As of today, pledge that you will spend more time with God, learn His perfect will for your life, and allow Him to be your friend. I promise you, you won't regret it.

I will expose your righteousness and your works, and they will not benefit you. [13] When you cry out for help, let your collection of idols save you! The wind will carry all of them off, a mere breath will blow them

Reason 17 - Idolatry

away. But whoever takes refuge in me will inherit the land and possess my holy mountain. (Isaiah 57:12-13, NIV) [4]*Their idols are silver and gold, the work of men's hands.* [5]*They have mouths, but they speak not: eyes have they, but they see not:* [6]*They have ears, but they hear not: noses have they, but they smell not:* [7]*They have hands, but they handle not: feet have they, but they walk not: neither speak they through their throat.* [8]*They that make them are like unto them; so is every one that trusteth in them. (Psalm 115:4-8)*

Prayer

O covenant-keeping God, have mercy on me. Forgive me for creating idols that take your place. God, I have sinned against you. I have ignored your commandments and allowed many idols to control my life. Lord, I have broken the covenant between us. Please, forgive me. Sprit of Idolatry, I command you to bow to Jesus Christ right now. I decree and declare all idols in my life to be destroyed by fire. Lord, I denounce and renounce every idol that I have permitted to be a part of my life.

Father God, I break every and any generational or bloodline curse of idolatry in my life. I release myself from any bondage from my parents or forbearers that may be affecting my life today. Through the power of the Holy Ghost, I reclaim any virtues stolen from me by idols. Lord, I know that my collections of gods cannot save me. May the wind blow them away and carry them to the bottomless pit. I refuse to bow to any more gods of my parents, ancestors, forbearers, or my own.

Lord, I reconfirm my vows to you. I rededicate my life to you. I choose you to be my God. I take refuge in you, O God. My God and my King, I will forever hide in your secret place away from all idols. In Jesus' name. Amen.

³Thou shalt have no other gods before me. ⁴Thou shalt not make unto thee any graven image, or any likeness of anything that is in heaven above, or that is in the earth beneath, or that is in the water under the earth. ⁵Thou shalt not bow down thyself to them, nor serve them: for I the Lord thy God am a jealous God, visiting the iniquity of the fathers upon the children unto the third and fourth generation of them that hate me.... (Exodus 20:3-5)

Reason 17 - Idolatry

"If you love anything better than God you are idolaters: if there is anything you would not give up for God it is your idol: if there is anything that you seek with greater fervor than you seek the glory of God, that is your idol, and conversion means a turning from every idol."

-Charles Spurgeon

"...God is expecting you to grow both physically and more so, spiritually, but you may have missed God's plan for your life many times because of immaturity."

Reason 18

***

Immaturity

For though by this time you ought to be teachers, you have need again for someone to teach you the elementary principles of the oracles of God, and you have come to need milk and not solid food.
(Hebrews 5:12)

*I*mmaturity can refer to projects, fruits, plants, animals, or people. Immaturity signifies that something or someone is not ready for its intended use or purpose. In reference to the subject at hand, reasons why our prayers are not answered, let's focus on immaturity in humans.

According to Dr. Thomas Armstrong Ph.D. from the American Institute for Learning and Human Development, there are twelve stages of life in the human development cycle: Prebirth, birth, infancy (Ages 0-3), early childhood (Ages 3-6), middle childhood (Ages 6-8), late childhood (Ages 9-11), adolescence (Ages 12-20), early adulthood (Ages 20-35), midlife (Ages 35-50), mature adulthood (Ages 50-80), late adulthood (Age 80+), and death & dying. Others refer to four, five, seven, and eight stages. Regardless, as you grow and age, you are expected to do better at each stage. Sadly, some adults still express childish behavior in so many ways. It's unbelievable. Exhibiting an immature attitude can prevent you from receiving God's plan for your life.

When I was a child, I talked like a child, I thought like a child, I reasoned like a child. When I became a man, I put the ways of childhood behind me. (1 Corinthians 13:11, NIV)

As you grow, you are expected to think more rationally, speak sensibly, and reason intelligently. If these attributes or characteristics are missing, it is possible that you may get mistreated or ignored by other persons. Likewise, God is expecting you to grow both physically and more so, spiritually, but you may have missed God's plan for your life many times because of immaturity.

When God said, His plan for you is to have peace, comfort, happiness, security, hope, and excellent health (well-being) instead of disaster and evil, He meant every word. Even though that is His desire for you, you have to want the same things for yourself. You need to spend time in the Word of God, delight yourself in Him and make Him your priority. You must be positioned in a place of maturity and show that you are ready to receive God's plan and that you are responsible enough to handle the kind of blessing and prosperity that comes with fulfilling God's purpose for you. Bear in mind that prosperity comes in many different ways and not only in monetary ways.

And he shall be like a tree planted by the rivers of water, that bringeth forth his fruit in his season; his leaf also shall not wither, and whatsoever he doeth shall prosper." (Psalm 1:3)

"I know the plans and thoughts that I have for you," says the Lord, "plans for peace and well-being and not for disaster, to give you a future and a hope." (Jeremiah 29:11, GW)

Signs of Maturity

A spiritually mature person is dead to the works of the flesh. When you are spiritually mature, you are not easily offended. You will overlook the ignorance of the individual, who is attacking you or doing you displeasure. You will be sympathetic and understanding to those, whom you believe should know better, but who don't. For such a person, a mature individual will go beyond the call of duty to help them and see them through God's eyes. The spiritually mature individual will know that they may have been attacked by principalities, powers, rulers of darkness, and spiritual wickedness in high places. Your assignment, as the more mature and stronger individual, is to uplift and encourage the immature. Many times, God strategically places individuals in our path and under our umbrella so we can teach, feed, and push them to the next level in God-so they can exercise their full potential. *Brethren, if a man be overtaken in a fault, ye which are spiritual, restore such an one in the spirit of meekness; considering thyself, lest thou also be tempted. (Galatians 6:1)*

When you are fully mature, no matter how negative someone speaks to you or about you, you will never engage in a quarrel or express outbursts of anger. You would rather wait for a more quiet and convenient time to address the situation. You will listen, attentively, to the other person speaking instead of being judgmental, hostile, or interruptive. You will be the first to quash any dispute or discord.

Maturity, in God, will make you shun selfish ambition. You will try to avoid the spotlight and resist drawing attention to yourself. It will be a pleasure for you to promote others before yourself without self-seeking. Once you are mature and you understand the Word of God, you will never be jealous of any one's growth or success but instead, you will celebrate them. As seen above, physically, the various stages of life don't happen overnight. It's a process, as so it is with becoming spiritually mature. It will not happen in an instant. It will take some time, but it all depends on you, not God.

According to Galatians 5:20 (NLT), the works of the flesh are *idolatry, sorcery, hostility, quarreling, jealousy, outbursts of anger, selfish ambition, dissension, division....*

Immaturity is one of the root causes of all offenses.

Avoiding needed discussion about a situation at home, on the job, or in the workplace doesn't mean maturity. Perhaps, you are afraid of confrontation. Just remember, if you don't confront, you cannot conquer. Ask God to show you when, where, and how to address the issue. Be sure to approach the individual or individuals with wisdom and a tempered spirit. You should first minister to yourself that no matter the reaction, you will not be saddened or offended. Again, see people as God sees you when you are in your folly. If God sees that you are stagnant in your spiritual growth– that you're still drinking milk when you should be eating solid food, He will allow someone to offend you to reveal this reality to you so you can let it go or "die to self" and grow spiritually.

Unless you allow your flesh to die, you will continuously react irrationally and ungodly to everything that challenges your physicality, no matter how simple. Anything dead has no feelings; therefore, it cannot act one way or the other.

How do you kill the flesh? Revisit your mission and vision for your life. Ask yourself pertinent questions about your desire and destiny as a born-again Christian. Turn off the television. Get off social media. Stay away from anything that will distract you or take you out of the presence of God. Because of the busyness of life and the many things that have come to occupy your time, you will have to force yourself to spend time reading the Bible, fasting, praying, praising, and worshipping even when it seems impossible. Feeding your spirit man will definitely cause the flesh to die.

The Prodigal Son demanded and got his inheritance prematurely. With such a sudden overflow of wealth, his friends multiplied. Perhaps partying and fine dining with friends was in order. Within a short period, all his money was gone and his friends slowly drifted away. As he stared into space, wondering where his next meal was coming from, he must have pondered how embarrassing it would be to go back home. He asked himself, "How will I survive out here without resources?" And then, "Back home, I was being served, and now, I have become a servant to pigs." As his stomach growled, he reminisced on the days of fine dining and life at home. I can only imagine, with every passing moment, the growling in his stomach got louder and louder. Being caught in a desperate, life-threatening situation, he began eating the pigs' food. Oh, what immaturity, impatience, rebellion, and pride can do to our destiny. You may read the story in its entirety in Luke 15:11-32.

Reason 18 - Immaturity

Dear reader, the things that you desire to elevate you to the next level, propel you into your destiny, and make you happy, can be the same things that cause stagnancy, sadness, and sometimes destruction, if you acquire them prematurely. Perhaps, poor money management is the reason you haven't become a millionaire, as yet. Maybe, lacking responsibility hinders you from becoming a homeowner. It's also possible that lacking compassion, wisdom, and maturity may have prevented you from being a wife or a husband, though likely not the only reason.

Most of the things you are praying for are already placed in trust for you, but you are not mature enough to handle them. Both David and Joseph had an inclination in the teenage years of their future but did not walk in their calling until they were in their thirties.

Would you allow your ten-year-old child to manage your finances? Even though you said that your 2020 Benz belongs to your ten-year-old daughter, would you give her the keys, at this age, and tell her it's okay to drive it now?

Beloved, God is waiting for you to grow up. He is waiting for you to get rid of your negative belief; change the way you speak; renew your mind; and, think, positively, at all times. He is waiting for you to learn how to address unfavorable situations, in a Godly way–not as the scribes and Pharisees, but like the way God would have. My friend, If you want to make heaven your home, you must think like God, see others the way God sees them, and love and treat people the way God loves and treats you. If you desire to walk in the power of God, put away petty things; esteem others more highly than yourself; kill the flesh; and, abandon selfishness and carnality.

Think of it this way. If a father dies and leaves an inheritance for his young children, those children are not much better off than slaves until they grow up, even though they actually own everything their father had. 2They have to obey their guardians until they reach whatever age their father set. (Galatians 4:1-2, NLT)

According to this Scripture, immaturity has a time limit. If you refuse to grow up, you will continue to be a slave, irrespective of the inheritance that was left for you. In other words, you may continue to take orders from others and be enslaved. You may remain in a caterpillar state, being satisfied with crawling and nibbling on leaves instead of becoming the butterfly you were meant to be, spreading your wings and soaring and exploring the unknown.

Your immaturity expiration date is fast approaching. Until you show signs of maturity and responsibility, you may never experience God's plan, promise, and best in your present needs and for your future.

30 Signs of Immaturity

1. You're easily offended.
2. You refuse to change or grow.
3. You refuse to take responsibility for your actions.
4. You are a spendthrift.
5. You are afraid of commitment.
6. You call the other person names during a disagreement.
7. Your life lacks fruit and productivity.
8. You refuse to admit that you are wrong.
9. Your emotions are often uncontrollable.
10. You're insensitive and ignore the feelings of others when they are hurting.
11. You are double-minded.
12. There is instability in all aspects of life.
13. You repeat negative cycles.

Reason 18 - Immaturity

14. You always want to be seen and heard.
15. You feel entitled.
16. You don't handle disappointment well.
17. You turn the slightest discussion into an argument.
18. You bottle your emotions inside instead of expressing yourself in a calm manner.
19. You are easily angered.
20. You are quick to quarrel rather than reason out the issue.
21. Distinct traits of jealousy and envy can be seen in your actions.
22. You are always making excuses for your failure.
23. You're dependent on others and refusing to share what you have.
24. You're quick to highlight another person's faults, shortcomings, and weaknesses.
25. You are always playing the victim card.
26. You still think negatively and believe the worst.
27. You are always seeking to compete with someone.
28. You run with another person's idea and draw attention to yourself as if you thought of it.
29. You wait for a dispute so you can spill your harbored hostility.
30. You exhibit other childish behaviors.

Below are some scriptures on how God views immaturity.

Dear brothers and sisters, when I was with you I couldn't talk to you as I would to spiritual people. I had to talk as though you belonged to this world or as though you were infants in Christ. ²I had to feed you with milk, not with solid food, because you weren't ready for anything stronger. And you still aren't ready, ³for you are still controlled by your sinful nature. You are jealous of one another and quarrel with each other. Doesn't that prove you are controlled by your sinful nature? Aren't you living like people of the world?(1 Corinthians 3:1-3, NLT)

Think of it this way. If a father dies and leaves an inheritance for his young children, those children are not much better off than slaves until they grow up, even though they actually own everything their father had. 2They have to obey their guardians until they reach whatever age their father set. (Galatians 4:1-2, NLT)

¹³Anyone who has to drink milk is still a baby, without experience in applying the Word about righteousness. ¹⁴But solid food is for the mature, for those whose faculties have been trained by continuous exercise to distinguish good from evil. (Hebrews 5:13-14, CJB)

¹³For everyone who lives on milk is [doctrinally inexperienced and] unskilled in the word of righteousness, since he is a spiritual infant. ¹⁴But solid food is for the [spiritually] mature, whose senses are trained by practice to distinguish between what is morally good and what is evil. (Hebrews 5:13-14, AMP)

²I fed you with milk, not solid food; for you were not yet able to receive it. Even now you are still not ready. (1 Corinthians 3:2, AMP)

Prayer

O Glory to God. Lord, I praise you. I worship you. I adore you. Lord, you have been a shield for me and the lifter of my head. Thank you, Lord, for surrounding me as the mountain surrounds Jerusalem.

Reason 18 - Immaturity

Holy Spirit, enlighten me with your words. Thank you for being my shield and buckler.

Father, I acknowledge and confess that I am immature in areas of my life. Father, please forgive me for being easily offended. Pardon me for my outbursts of anger, hostility, and unfriendly tone of voice. Lord, please cleanse me from every trace of jealousy, laziness, selfish-ambition, and uncontrollable emotions. Almighty God, uproot any judgmental spirit, and destroy every quarrelsome spirit from within me.

Lord, after walking with you for so many years as a born-again Christian, like electricity, your power and anointing should be flowing through me. Father, I should be way more advanced in ministering and dissecting your words to your people, winning souls, healing the sick and discerning the next plan of the enemy, but instead, I am the one who still needs to be taught. Lord, I know you are disappointed to see me still being unskilled in the word of righteousness like babes in Christ. I know you desire to see me grow in all aspects of life and discern right from wrong as do the mature.

Lord, my immaturity has caused me much pain, embarrassment, and uneasiness because at this stage, I am just learning the fundamentals of salvation that I should have known. O God, help me to stop drinking milk and start eating solid food. Father God, I am grateful for the pastors, the teachers, and mentors that you have assigned to assist me along my spiritual journey. Lord, grant me a teachable and humble spirit as I sit at their feet. Help me not to lean on my own understanding but to acknowledge you in all my actions. Father, please reveal to me any other areas in my life that need to change and be matured, physically and spiritually. Lord Jesus, help me to live by your Spirit and put the deeds of the flesh to death so that I can live peacefully with you and all men.

Thank you, Jesus, for helping me to move away, daily, from drinking milk to eating solid food. Thank you, Mighty God, for granting me the desire of my heart to mature physically, mentally, emotionally, and spiritually. Thank you, Lord, for teaching me how to manage my money well. Thank you for delivering me from the spendthrift spirit. Thank you for allowing me to become an excellent steward and a great business owner.

O God, help me to wait on you and not run ahead and abort that which is rightfully mine.

In Jesus' name. Amen.

I have yet many things to say unto you, but ye cannot bear them now. (John16:12)

Reason 18 - Immaturity

"Your immaturity expiration date is fast approaching. Until you show signs of maturity and responsibility, you may never experience God's plan, promise, and best in your present needs and for your future. Unless you allow your flesh to die, you will continuously react irrationally and ungodly to everything that challenges your physicality, no matter how simple."

"Satan, himself, targeted you. He is intimidated by the greatness bubbling within you, so he called a conference against your purpose and your destiny. His sole intention is to inflict pain and destruction upon you."

Reason 19

✱✱✱

Incest

You must never have sexual relations with a close relative, for I am the Lord. (Leviticus 18:6)

*B*eloved, this is a very sensitive topic; but, please, don't bypass it. I send courage and strength to you, right now, to read to the end. Please, pray the prayer of deliverance by faith; and receive your deliverance.

"Shh. Don't say a word. Sarah, I have something to share with you. Please, promise me that you will not repeat it to anyone," said a broken and shattered young man.

"What is it?", she asked.

With tears streaming down his face, and in a trembling voice, he answered, "I just found out that my daughter's mother is my aunt, and my father is my brother."

"What!" Sarah gasped. "I'm stunned. I don't know what to say. I am so sorry."

"It's much more complicated than that. I wish I had never been born."

"Oh, Roy, don't say that. I can only imagine your feeling of despair; but, regardless of the way you were conceived, God wants you to be here. He has a great plan for your life. Don't you ever forget that. Your mom could have aborted or given you up for adoption, when she found out that she was pregnant by her son; but, she didn't. Despite the ridicule and disgrace, she gave you a chance at life.

"But, I don't want to seem insensitive to your situation. Please, have a seat and feel free to express your hurt and concerns," Sarah said.

"Sarah, you don't understand. This has been going on for generations. When will it end? My sisters were also molested by their father since they were five years old; and, it continued into their adulthood. Isn't that sick? The sad part?–Everyone was told not to say anything. Keep it as a secret. It's like sworn secrecy.

"The most embarrassing part is that my children and I are a part of this demonic, infested turmoil. What do I tell my children? How do I break this heart-rending, devastating news to them? I am afraid that they will not forgive me and develop resentment and anger towards me. As traumatic as it is, I have to tell them. I refuse for my children to be prey for these vultures. They will not fall into their snare.

"I have confronted a few of the family members about it, some denied it; and, others think they have done nothing wrong. It's normal. I am sure other family members are suffering in silence; but, it makes no sense to tell anyone because they will not believe them. The victims will be blamed for putting it in the culprits' way. My family doesn't care. They are already doomed and on their way to Hell. For one, they refuse to acknowledge their wicked deeds, and they refuse to repent. As a matter of fact, I don't care if they repent or not. I want them all to go to Hell."

"Roy, I hear you, and my heart goes out to you and your family. As disgusting as the behavior is, if they repent and turn away from partaking in incest, they won't have to go to Hell. Incest is driven by a demonic spirit and has attacked your bloodline and generation. It can be destroyed through the power of prayer and fasting.

"Roy, I know the wound is fresh. I know your mind, body, and soul are hurting right now. It's okay to take some time and grieve. However, don't sit and linger in pain for too long because it will do more harm than good. I heard you venting and spewing out hate and anger. It is perfectly fine to be angry but sin not in your anger. However, when hatred and unforgiveness get a hold of your heart, the whole dynamics change.

"Yes, whenever another person hurts us, revenge is the first thing that comes to mind. Roy, leave all vengeance to God. He will avenge you.

"Don't allow the spirit of hate, anger, and unforgiveness to consume you. If you do not find it in your heart to forgive the ones who hurt you, you will be forever in pain and turmoil. Forgiveness is not easy; however, it is doable and it is a requirement for your freedom from bondage, guilt, and shame. God will give you the strength to get through this devastating blow.

"Count me in. I am your cheerleader. You will rise above this and will be able to help others who may be going through this same thing. You must declare the Word of God to those who need guidance and be someone to whom they can vent. I hope and pray that your family knows that this practice is a sin. I guess they haven't heard or read what the Bible says about sleeping with your next of kin."

Beloved, you may know of someone who has been molested by a family member or is a product of incest. Maybe you are the result of incest. Perhaps, you have been sexually molested by a family member. For all you know, it could have happened just once or multiple times.

Satan, himself, targeted you. He is intimidated by the greatness bubbling within you; so, he called a conference against your purpose and your destiny. His sole intention is to inflict pain and destruction upon you. If he is unable to destroy you, then he will go to any lengths to make sure that you do not enjoy life and make you miserable instead. The fact that you are reading this book tells you there is still hope for your freedom. I encourage you to be the best person you can be. Don't allow this negative situation to impede you from living a full, productive, and positive life.

Incest is a curse that enters the bloodline, causing a domino effect from generation to generation. Nothing takes God by surprise. The fact that you were born into this family and not another, could it be that you are the one to destroy the curse once and for all–to expose the demons and reveal the secrets? Like Roy, you could be or have been the one to say, "Enough is enough. This curse stops here, and will not attach itself to my children or their children."

Listed below are some Bible verses that speak against the act of incest.

Leviticus 18: 6-19 NLT

[6]"You must never have sexual relations with a close relative, for I am the Lord.

[7]"Do not violate your father by having sexual relations with your mother. She is your mother; you must not have sexual relations with her.

[8]"Do not have sexual relations with any of your father's wives, for this would violate your father.

[9]"Do not have sexual relations with your sister or half sister, whether she is your father's daughter or your mother's daughter, whether she was born into your household or someone else's.

[10]"Do not have sexual relations with your granddaughter, whether she is your son's daughter or your daughter's daughter, for this would violate yourself.

[11]"Do not have sexual relations with your stepsister, the daughter of any of your father's wives, for she is your sister.

[12]"Do not have sexual relations with your father's sister, for she is your father's close relative.

[13]"Do not have sexual relations with your mother's sister, for she is your mother's close relative.

¹⁴"Do not violate your uncle, your father's brother, by having sexual relations with his wife, for she is your aunt.

¹⁵"Do not have sexual relations with your daughter-in-law; she is your son's wife, so you must not have sexual relations with her.

¹⁶"Do not have sexual relations with your brother's wife, for this would violate your brother.

¹⁷"Do not have sexual relations with both a woman and her daughter. And do not take[a] her granddaughter, whether her son's daughter or her daughter's daughter, and have sexual relations with her. They are close relatives, and this would be a wicked act.

¹⁸"While your wife is living, do not marry her sister and have sexual relations with her, for they would be rivals.

¹⁹"Do not have sexual relations with a woman during her period of menstrual impurity...."

Prayer

O God, you are my God. You are my strength. You are my rock and my fortress. Lord, I love you. Had it not been for you, O God, where would I be? Thank you, Lord, for preserving me. Thank you for being my buckler and my salvation. O mighty God, in you I put my trust.

My God, I confess that I have committed and engaged in incest. Lord, I repent from such hideous lawlessness. Please forgive me for desecrating your temple and disobeying your words. O miracle-working God, I stand in need of healing and deliverance from the spirit of incest. Heal my hurting heart, O God, from its crippling memory. Decontaminate my entire body and systems in the mighty name of Jesus Christ.

O God, you have seen the abuse that I have suffered at the hands of my _____. Inject your red rich blood into my veins and flush out every residue and contamination of this toxin. Deliver me, O God, from the generational and bloodline curse of incest. Lord, this demonic spirit has been plaguing my family from generation to generation to the point of shame and disgrace. Lord, I crave your amazing grace and tender mercy to erase the feeling of worthlessness, low self-esteem, guilt, fear, anger, and hatred. Lord, I will no longer blame myself for the wickedness that was done to my family and me. Deliver us from the victim mentality. Father God, I refuse to succumb to the wound and pain inflicted upon me by this foul spirit. Dear God, help me to forgive those who have taken my innocence, abused my body, and sabotaged my self-esteem through incest.

In the mighty name of Jesus Christ, I renounce, denounce, and reject every foul spirit that is operating behind this spirit of incest. In the name of Jesus, I tear down every stronghold and bind the strongman of all sexual abuse from family members right now, in Jesus' name. I send the fire of God to destroy every demonic activity that is operating through incest. Through the power in the blood of Jesus Christ, I cripple your operations and command you not to function in my life anymore. Spirit of incest, I cut you off and strip you of any authority you may have to afflict the minds of my family and me. I cast you out into outer darkness and dry places, in the mighty name of Jesus.

Thank you, Lord, for the deliverance and your healing virtue that is penetrating my mind, body, and soul right now. You are awesome, mighty God. Amen.

Reason 19 - Incest

Prayer

If you are pregnant as a result of incest

Father in heaven, have mercy upon me.

Lord, I am not proud of my involvement in incest. I am rather embarrassed and ashamed because I have done wrong in your sight. Please forgive. Lord, I have been encouraged to abort this child that I am carrying, so I can protect my name and character, but I refused, despite how it was conceived. Lord, I am being ridiculed, mocked, and jeered; nonetheless, I will not give in to the pressure.

Lord, when I think of the many individuals who would like to have children but can't, I consider myself blessed to be able to bring life, another human into this world. Lord, you knew how this child was conceived, yet you still allowed life to begin in my womb. Then, who am I to undo what you have done?

Father, you gave me life. You kept me through the many devastating life challenges that I have encountered. Therefore, I will allow this child to enjoy the life you have given to him/her.

Lord, I humbly ask you to protect this innocent child from retardation, deformity, sickness, promiscuity, vulnerability, that may be the result of the curse of incest. May this curse stop, with me, and never attach itself to my children or grandchildren. In Jesus' mighty name. Amen.

"...jealousy respects no one. It is the offspring of envy and covetousness. Stay clear. Jealousy exhibits irrational behavior compounded with pain, sadness, low self-esteem, and inferiority–always wanting and wishing to have what someone else has or to do what someone else does or better."

Reason 20

***

Jealousy

Anger is cruel and fury overwhelming, but who can stand before jealousy? (Proverbs 27:4, NIV)

As human beings, we all tend to exhibit jealousy, whether it's over someone else's success, achievement, accolades, relationships, or their possessions. The list is extensive. Jealousy is a form of admiration but in a covetous manner and should not be swept under the rug or taken lightly. The Bible says that jealousy rots the bones. Jealousy is one of the outrageously wicked spirits. It leads the pack, opens the door for many other spirits to invade your mind, and enslaves you. Later in this chapter, I will list some of the spirits for which jealousy opens the door.

I stumbled upon Bishop TD Jakes being interviewed by Maria Shriver on YouTube. During the interview, he shared his story about feeling jealous of his friend's success. He said, around the time he released his movie, "Woman thou art Loose," a friend of his also released a movie. Bishop Jakes stated that his movie didn't do badly, but according to moviegoers, his friend's movie made a home run.

"Each time I heard someone say how good his movie was, I felt *funny*," Bishop Jakes said.

"Was funny the word?" Maria asked.

"Yes, it was funny to me because I have never felt that feeling before, and I was not happy with that kind of feeling," he replied. "I was ashamed for allowing myself to feel that way. I had to look myself in the face and say, you are jealous!"

Bishop Jakes explained further, "I don't want that in my heart so what I did was, I got behind my friend and pushed his movie. I sold tickets for it. I put on events for it; and, everyone thinks I was just pushing his movie; but, I was really pushing jealousy out of my heart. I don't want that in me. After I began helping my friend to promote his movie, I felt a sense of relief from that so-called funny feeling. Shortly after that, the Lord began to bless my movie...."

Dear reader, jealousy respects no one. It is the offspring of envy and covetousness. Stay clear. Jealousy exhibits irrational behavior compounded with pain, sadness, low self-esteem, and inferiority–always wanting and wishing to have what someone else has or to do what someone else does or better. Jealousy will cause you to lose focus on you and who you were created to become while also distorting your understanding of reality.

Not everyone was born a visionary or to be a leader or has creative ideas; therefore, it is ok to emulate others and be zealous after good things but not in a negative, competitive, deceptive, or undermining way. If, at first glance, you cannot, sincerely, compliment your friends or family members on their accomplishments or possessions or their appearance, and respect them for that, but, instead, make negative comments such as, "I can do it better" or "I should and must have that too," or "You are just showing off," or "It doesn't take all that," you are, definitely, experiencing and entertaining the spirit of jealousy. Another sign of jealousy is if you are always trying to out-do the person you say you admire. If you possess these traits, quickly acknowledge them and do your utmost best to expel them out of your heart and spirit.

Here is another scenario where jealousy is present. If you always find yourself saying, "I am not jealous of Muriel. How can I be jealous of her? She is a hard worker and a go-getter. It would be unfair for me to be jealous of her." It merely means that you are wrestling with the

Reason 20 - Jealousy

feeling of jealousy but fighting hard against it becoming a stronghold in your life. If that is the case, then you are in a perfect place because you've identified the spirit of jealousy creeping in; and you are trying your best to kill the seed and the root before it becomes a huge tree.

However, if the thought crosses your mind that Muriel doesn't deserve the blessings and favors she receives; and instead, you think that it should have been you in her position, you are jealous. If your initial response to Muriel's testimony of blessing and favor is, "Wow, that's great! I am so happy for you", but, there is a feeling of uneasiness in your belly and, in your mind, you think or mutter under your breath, "Why are you telling me? I don't need to hear your business. You just want to brag."; and you can't wait for her to stop sharing, the spirit of jealousy is embedded in your spirit.

As Bishop Jakes did, you should quickly identify and acknowledge the unwanted spirit of jealousy lurking around. My friend, it takes a mature and big person to admit that he experiences feelings of jealousy. After Bishop Jakes detected that the funny feeling was jealousy, he denounced it immediately.

Beloved, if you harbor the spirit of jealousy, you will be walking around physically free but spiritually and mentally bound. There will be no peace in your mind because you don't know and haven't learned how to be satisfied and embrace what you already have. Instead, you will find yourself moving mountains so that you can have the same thing that your friend or family member has. The Bishop said when you see those weeds growing in your garden, uproot them immediately. Kill them.

Get yourself together. Be sold out to the Holy Spirit with your mind, body, and spirit. There will be no limit to what you can do or achieve. Learn to appreciate and be satisfied with what God has entrusted to you. When you uproot the seeds of jealousy, you will discover your purpose. Your potential will be unveiled; and your gift and talent will make room for you. You will begin to thrive; and nothing can, successfully, impede God's plan for your destiny. You never know what a person does or has done to achieve what he or she has. It could have been an honest investment or through hard work. Perhaps, it's immoral involvement. Or, maybe, he or she sold his or her soul to satan. Either way, are you willing to pay the price to get what they have? Regardless of how the success is achieved, don't get distracted by jealousy. Just bless them, wholeheartedly, and wait for your seasons for blessing and favor. Though your vision tarries, wait for it. It will come to fruition.

How to get rid of jealousy

My friend, yes, jealousy can prevent your prayers from being answered, not because of the jealousy, per se, but because of what it does to your heart–especially in those moments, when it seems as if someone is climbing the ladder of success and getting ahead of you. To get rid of jealousy, ask the Holy Spirit to give you a spiritual heart transplant–a heart that is filled with genuine love–a heart that is sincerely willing to serve others.

Quit comparing yourself to others. Reassure yourself that you are more than enough; and rebuke the spirit of inadequacy. Stare intensely in the mirror and speak these words into your life daily: "I was created to be more, do more, give more, and love more. I am a motivator. I am a leader. I am born to transform lives and propel individuals into their purpose."

Begin to encourage those whom you envied to continue to do their best and be great at what they do. Uplift their spirit by sincerely ministering to them. Be their cheerleader and cheer them onto excellence. Share their pain in the moment of defeat and help them strategize and make a victorious comeback. This new lifestyle change may not be easy, but if you genuinely desire to be free from this spirit, you must continue to be open and honest with God and reprimand yourself. If you fall, of course, get up and continue the journey of healing.

Reason 20 - Jealousy

If you are consistent, you will experience God's loyalty as you behold His glory, and you will begin to see life in its purest form. Each time you encourage, uplift, or inspire someone, you will discover that you are benefiting even more. The second and final coming of Jesus Christ is fast approaching our doorsteps. Don't allow jealousy to prevent you from inheriting the kingdom of God. Get your house in order. Don't get left behind.

As promised, here are some of the spirits that accompany jealousy, of which we may be unaware, and how they operate.

Resentment is a constant tension between you and another person.

Hatred is a strong feeling of dislike and disgust, especially at the sight of the person or the mention of their name.

Opposition is when you constantly try to object and oppose every effort the person makes, expressing resistance with hostility.

Conflict is a disagreement or dispute between both individuals.

Greed/Lust is an unsatisfied spirit that wants everything in sight to use, abuse, and refuse.

Envy will make you do the unthinkable to achieve what others have.

Covetousness means if you can't get it or have it, then they shouldn't have it either.

Destruction is when you secretly hope that what a particular person has will come to naught.

Rivalry means you're always trying to compete to show that you are better than someone else.

Selfishness ambition is when someone is self-centered and always trying to draw attention to themselves, and one who couldn't care less if others are struggling.

Malice is when you seek to cause pain or suffering on others without remorse.

Anger is a spirit that can disguise itself very well but lashes out at the least amount of confrontation or simple discussion with the person of whom they are jealous.

Division is when you try to recruit individuals to agree with your assumptions and seek to turn their minds against the individual of whom you are jealous.

Slander/Lying is when someone attempts to assassinate the character and discredit another person's credibility and integrity.

Murder is literally wanting the person to die, not so that the murderer can have the possessions of the deceased, but so that they know that the person of whom they are jealous is hidden underground so they won't have to see that person evolve into greatness in front of their eyes.

You desire and do not have, so you murder. You covet and cannot obtain, so you fight and quarrel. You do not have, because you do not ask. 3You ask and do not receive, because you ask wrongly, to spend it on your passions. (James 4:2-3, ESV)

Prayer

What a friend we have in Jesus, all our sins and grief to bear... All because we do not carry everything to God in prayer.

Heavenly Father, I thank you for the privilege of being able to carry everything to you in prayer. It is so sweet to put my trust in you and take you at your word. Thank you, Lord, for fulfilling your promises to me. Thank you for your immeasurable love. Thank you for standing by me and for restoring the spirit of genuineness within my heart.

Reason 20 - Jealousy

Everlasting Father, I am struggling with jealousy to the point where I get carried away with the negative desires–craving that which someone else has. Lord, there is a feeling of uneasiness and discomfort when others around me are being blessed with the things that I think I should have. God, I am dissatisfied with my blessings because of jealousy. Help me, O God! Deliver me from the jealous thoughts that are trying to consume my mind. God, I am so disappointed with myself for harboring jealousy in my heart.

Father God, come into my heart, forgive and replace the spirit of jealousy with your peace, love, and kindness. Lord, I desire to be holy, pure, sanctified, and be set apart so you can use me unlimitedly.

Father, according to James 3:16, *...where jealousy and selfish ambition exist, there is disorder [unrest, rebellion] and every evil thing and morally degrading practice.* Spirit of jealousy, in the mighty name of Jesus Christ I rebuke you and eject you out of my heart. As of today, I will no longer allow you to cause selfish ambition, rebellion, morally degrading practices to show up in my actions. I bind you, in the name of Jesus, and cast you out into outer darkness and dry places. In the mighty name of Jesus, I take authority over my heart and my emotions. I will not fight or quarrel with anyone because of their achievements or favor. By God's amazing grace and his unlimited mercy, I will not murder anyone physically, emotionally, mentally, verbally, or spiritually because of jealousy. Lord, I surrender my heart to you.

O Mighty God, if my desires are not being met, teach me how to be still and wait patiently on you. Oh, Sovereign God, thank you for delivering me from the spirit of jealousy; thank you for cleansing me thoroughly. Father God, thank you for teaching me how to be genuinely happy for my sisters' or brothers' breakthroughs, successes, blessings, and favor without being a hypocrite or feeling uneasy. O God, I thank you for showing me how to actively wait for my breakthrough and blessing to overtake me.

In Jesus' name. Amen.

¹⁴But if you have bitter jealousy and selfish ambition in your hearts, do not be arrogant, and [as a result] be in defiance of the truth. ¹⁵This [superficial] wisdom is not that which comes down from above, but is earthly (secular), natural (unspiritual), even demonic. (James 3:14-15, AMP)

Reason 20 - Jealousy

"Jealousy will cause you to lose focus on you and who you were created to become while also distorting your understanding of reality. Not everyone was born a visionary or to be a leader or has creative ideas; If you are tested positive for Jealousy, you may want to quarantine in the arms of Jesus. If you are willing to accept being injected with His blood, it is available."

"Many individuals who struggle with the spirit of lust lack compassion, emotion, sincerity, and loyalty towards anyone. Sometimes, such an individual is not able to commit to a serious relationship."

Reason 21

***

Lust

But every man is tempted, when he is drawn away of his own lust, and enticed. 15 Then when lust hath conceived, it bringeth forth sin: and sin, when it is finished, bringeth forth death. (James 1:14-15)

What is lust? Lust is a strong, intense desire for something that does not belong to you. Your eyes have seen it, and, now you are captivated by what you have seen and purpose in your heart that you must have it. One can lust for food, power, or another person, along with other things. The Bible speaks about the lust of the eyes, the lust of the flesh, and the pride of life. However, let's talk about the lust of the flesh.

Lust, also called lasciviousness, is defined as a strong, intense sexual desire. This kind of passion is the most dangerous because it doesn't only affect the luster, it also affects the person who is lusted after–friends, and families. A dissatisfied spirit of greed drives lust. Like every other sin, lust is dangerous to your health because of its deceptive characteristics. It appears to be genuine, but beware, it is a silent destroyer.

What does it do?

Whenever lust enters and operates through a person, it can disrupt marriages, displace children, distort families, and interfere with the relationship between God and that individual. If not careful, lust will cloud your judgment, blind your eyes to reality, alter your personality, and cause you to be cold and insensitive to the feelings of your spouse or others. If you allow the spirit of lust to overtake you, your eyes, mind, and spirit will be closed to the Word of God, the conviction of the Holy Spirit, and your heart will be desensitized to its pain. You will always try to justify your actions and make excuses for your lustful conduct. Hence, you twist the Word of God to fit your lewd behavior.

Many individuals who struggle with the spirit of lust lack compassion, emotion, sincerity, and loyalty towards anyone. Sometimes, such an individual is not able to commit to a serious relationship. They may say the right things, but their words do not match their action. It has been noted that infatuation can last anywhere from one to thirty-six months. This crush or passion, which is driven by lust, always competes with real love but eventually lends itself to unfaithfulness and disobedience to God.

Lust will cause you to lie to your spouse or to the people who care about you. You will find yourself continuously defending your action or explaining your behavior. Before you know it, you become unbearable to the folks who genuinely love you. Perhaps you tell yourself that you don't like confrontation and so you begin to drift away from your family, friends, and God. You begin to avoid church folks and stray from the faith. Consequently, you have tarnished your character and your integrity and many lose respect for you.

Do not let your heart turn aside to her ways; do not stray into her [evil, immoral] paths. (Proverbs 7:25, AMP)

Before I was afflicted, I went astray, but now I obey your word. (Psalm 119:67, NIV)

The Acronym for LUST

L – Lie

U – Unbearable

S – Stray from God & your Partner

T – Tarnish your character / Integrity

Reason 21 - Lust

How does it operate?

Persons who are struggling with the spirit of lust can be very deceptive as they approach you to offer assistance. The spirit behind this appetite drives them to be cunning, manipulative, tricky, and appear to be innocent. If lust doesn't get its way, it can also turn to blackmail, as did Tamar to her father-in-law, Judah.

Tamar disguised herself as a prostitute and sat in wait of Judah. Not knowing she was his daughter-in-law, Judah approached her and asked her to be intimate with him.

"What will you give me if I sleep with you?" she asked.

"I will send you a young goat from my flock," Judah replied.

"May I have something else to hold onto until you send the goat?" she asked.

"What would you like me to give you," Judah inquired. Tamar requested his staff, ring, and the cord that was in his hand, and he gave them to her. As promised, Judah sent back the goat to the young lady, but she was nowhere to be found. No one had ever seen or heard of a prostitute being in that area.

Three months later, residents, from the district in which Tamar lived, sent a message to Judah stating that Tamar is guilty of prostitution because she is pregnant. Judah commanded that she be brought out and burned to death. Tamar sent the staff, ring, and the cord to Judah.

"I am pregnant for the man who owns these. See if you can identify them," Tamar said.

You may read the entire story in Genesis 38:1-27.

A lustful person will wait as long as he or she has to and go any distance to get that particular prey. Because lust is always craving for the things it cannot or shouldn't have, it will allow the person through whom it is operating to believe the grass is greener on the other side. The spirit deceives the individual into believing that he or she, whom he or she is pursuing, is better than their wife or husband at home.

But lust never satisfies. Once the spirit of lust attaches itself to you, you may find yourself going from partner to partner, and being indecisive about with whom you would like to settle. You may experience feelings of confusion or frustration when it comes to choosing a mate. Before you know it, you are expressing a strong desire for Brandon, whom you thought was a Godsend; and, then, after being with Harvey, suddenly, you can't tolerate him anymore. Then there's Kevin, who promises you the world. Overflowing with excitement, you shout, "Yes! He is the one. We are compatible in so many ways, it's unbelievable." Shortly after, though, Kevin gets on your nerves as well and you dumped him and declare, "The devil is a liar. I know those previous men were blessing blockers. They came to prevent my Boaz from locating me." Next comes Howell. "Oh, without a doubt, he is a Godsend. Words can't explain this beautiful soul."

Listen, lust is afraid of commitment and refuses to settle down. It will disguise itself as real love, causing you to marry the wrong person. For you to have a Godly and successful marriage, you must fight, denounce, and reject the spirit of lust. Most importantly, you must avoid temptations, especially those that will trigger lustful feelings, which will cause you to be unfaithful.

What happens when lust is activated or entertained?

When lust is entertained, it opens doors for other spirits to invade your temple, such as fornication, masturbation, adultery, lying, greed, disobedience, along with the spirit of incubus and succubus, which are sex demons that engage in sexual activities with individuals while they are sleeping. The practice of fornication, especially with multiple partners, may also create open doors for your body to be afflicted physically and spiritually, which can cause a negative domino effect in your immediate family and generations to come.

REASON 21 - LUST

How can the spirit of lust invade your temple?

Spirits are transferable. Believe it or not, they can enter your body or your home through various channels such as watching pornography, sexual movies, listening to seductive music, reading books that have explicit sexual content, being engaged in conversations about sexual acts and intentions. The spirit of lust can also invade your mind through dreams. Have you ever dreamt of having sex with your spouse or someone from your past?

Whenever you encounter such dreams, it's a possibility that a fallen angel took on the form of your spouse or the person from your past to accomplish its assignment against you successfully. That is known as a familiar spirit. Having sex in your dream signifies that you are being molested by the sex demons (incubus: male) or (succubus: female). Be it known that the same manner in which angels have names, so do demons.

What we referred to as demons are actually fallen angels. Even though the word "Fallen Angel" is not written in the Bible, it is used to describe those angels who rebelled against God and were thrown out of heaven along with satan. *"For if God spared not the angels that sinned, but cast them down to hell, and delivered them into chains of darkness, to be reserved unto judgment…." (2 Peter. 2:4)*

Some of these fallen angels are now being used by human beings and satan himself to carry out evil assignments. In the passage below, "the sons of God" refers to the fallen angels, and "the daughters of men" refers to humans.

That the sons of God saw the daughters of men that they were fair; and they took them wives of all which they chose. ³And the LORD said, "My spirit shall not always strive with man, for that he also is flesh: yet his days shall be a hundred and twenty years." ⁴There were giants in the earth in those days; and also after that, when the sons of God came in unto the daughters of men, and they bare children to them, the same became mighty men which were of old, men of renown. ⁵And

God saw that the wickedness of man was great in the earth, and that every imagination of the thoughts of his heart was only evil continually. (Genesis 6:2-5)

I am not a sex therapist, psychologist, or expert on what I am about to bring to your attention. Perhaps you are more knowledgeable about it than I am; or you may not be familiar.

Last but not least, the spirit of lust, along with many other spirits, can be transferred to you via sexual intercourse, kissing, oral sex, and even caressing. Yes, sex is pleasurable. We can all agree as we understand it to be so; however, there is a negative side to it, apart from sexually transmitted diseases (STD).

You may have heard about airborne diseases such as tuberculosis (TB), flu, chickenpox, measles, valley fever, and anthrax. They are called airborne because they travel by air into the human body and animals as well through their breathing. For example, if an individual who is infected with TB sneezes in aisle one of the supermarket, even though you're in aisle ten, you can still be infected by breathing in that which was expelled from the infected person. It is said that a sneeze can travel up to 200 ft, at a speed of 100 miles per hour, and lingers in the air for approximately 45 minutes. All of that is to say that, if one can succumb to illness through mere breathing even though there was no physical touch from the host (the affected person), how about the penetration of the body during intimacy?

After being involved in an intimate relationship, you may discover that you have become emotionally unavailable to anyone else even though you know that there won't be a serious relationship between you and the individual with whom you had a casual affair. Although it was established from the beginning that there are no strings attached, you, especially the female, are yearning after this person, always.

Most individuals who sexually give their bodies to someone, other than their husband or wife, may have unexplainable occurrences or situations in their lives but never stop to think that it could have been from their sexual partners. Some individuals may testify that their finances came under attack, their personality changed, or their tolerance level diminished. Others may say that they found themselves getting, unusually, angry over simple things and start using foul language. Some people may testify that, suddenly, they experienced feelings of hate or a strong dislike towards other individuals, or they couldn't stand being around others. At the same time, others may realize that they have developed an unusual craving for sex, perhaps being attracted to the same sex. Or they may even experience sickness, abdominal pain, suicidal thoughts, or a strong dislike for sex. Unfortunately, some individuals may never get married, and, if they do marry, there may be a lack of happiness, joy, peace, or faithfulness in the marital home.

If you should inquire, secretly, about the individual or individuals you've been with if they are experiencing any of the above, there is a 99% chance that you will find that yes, they are or have been in the past.

So, what happens, then? Your soul has encountered a transference of spirit. You have adopted their negative ways or their struggles. Some may refer to it as soul-tie.

Make no friendship with an angry man; and with a furious man, thou shalt not go: Lest thou learn his ways, and get a snare to thy soul. (Proverbs 22:24-2)

God knows more than we do. He sees miles and years ahead of us. He knows the consequences and the price we will pay when we partake or indulge in certain behaviors. To protect us from unnecessary pain and suffering, He encourages us multiple times in His Word to walk in the Spirit so we won't fulfill the lust of the flesh. Temptation comes in attractive and beautiful packages of all sizes, from various angles and can catch us off guard. Be watchful.

Generational curses of lust

- **Judah**, 4th son of Jacob, slept with his daughter-in-law Tamar after mistaking her for a harlot. (Genesis 38:1-27) Lust will blind you.

- David, from the tribe of **Judah**, slept with Bathsheeba who was another man's wife. (2 Samuel 11: 2-4)

- Amnon, **David's** son, slept with his sister, Tamar. (2 Samuel 13:1-39) Lust can affect the whole family.

- Solomon, **David's** 17th son, had 700 wives and 300 concubines. Because of his lust for women from lands where they worshipped others gods, against which God had instructed him, Solomon's heart was turned away from God to idolatry. (1 Kings 11)

- Reuben, Judah's brother, was cursed by his dad, Jacob, after Reuben lay with Jacob's concubine Bilhah. This was considered adultery, and he lost his father's respect. Reuben further disrupted the marriage bed by overturning Bilhah's bed after she became his father's primary following the death of Judah's wife, Reuben's mother. *"Unstable as water thou shalt not excel; because thou wentest up to thy father's bed then thou defilest it." (Genesis 35:22; 49:4)*

Lust is not just a male thing. Both men and women are affected by this spirit of lasciviousness. Unfortunately, women may experience the brunt of it more than men because most women enter relationships with their emotions while some men appear cold and callous, emotionally undisturbed. Because women are easily attached and sometimes appear clingy, they have a higher expectation when it comes to intimate relationships, which may leave them emotionally attached to a fantasy.

Did you know that lust can deceive you into believing that, because your dad and other family members struggled with lust and it appears to run in your family and you were born that way, you can't change? Do not listen to that lie. *"Therefore if any man be in Christ, he is a new creature: old things are passed away; behold, all things are become new." (2 Corinthians 5:17)*

Reason 21 - Lust

How to be delivered from the spirit of lust?

Lust, like any other spirit, has come to steal your joy, kill your potential, and destroy your future. To be delivered from the spirit of lust, you must first acknowledge that you have a lust problem. It will be tremendously helpful if you can identify the root cause of this presumptuous spirit, which can become a stronghold in one's life as a result of rape, incest, multiple sex partners, flirting, and other indulgences, as mentioned earlier. You may, also, want to find out when this unusual craving for sex began. Was it in your childhood years? Teenage years? Young adult years? Or adult years? Gathering information from your past, which has influenced and formed the person you have become, will assist you in attacking and destroying the right source. If lust is a fruit, then, most naturally, a seed was planted from which many roots were developed.

If flirting or sexual encounters causes you to lust, stay clear of the things or persons who will lure you into the sinful act. If you are one who likes and is easily persuaded by flirty jokes, disconnect yourself from the company of flirters. Try your best to avoid individuals to whom you are attracted. Shut down every sexual pass or compliment made towards you. Avoid listening to seductive music or watching anything that promotes sex.

Because lust is driven by a spirit, you will not be able to destroy it with physical weapons. Develop a prayer and fasting relationship with God. *But this kind of demon does not go out except by prayer and fasting.* (Matthew17:21, AMP). God is your source of strength when you are weak. It is not His will for you to die from the invasion of this manipulating spirit. If you lack wisdom or understanding, let your request be known unto God. He will grant it unto you. Receive it by faith.

And Jesus said unto them, "Because of your unbelief: for verily I say unto you, If ye have faith as a grain of mustard seed, ye shall say unto this mountain, Remove hence to yonder place; and it shall remove; and nothing shall be impossible unto you." (Matthew 17:20)

Hear what the Bible says about lust

[13] Meats for the belly, and the belly for meats: but God shall destroy both it and them. Now the body is not for fornication, but for the Lord; and the Lord for the body.

[15] Know ye not that your bodies are the members of Christ? Shall I then take the members of Christ, and make them the members of an harlot? God forbid.

[16] What? Know ye not that he which is joined to an harlot is one body? For two, saith he, shall be one flesh.

[17] But he that is joined unto the Lord is one spirit.

[18] Flee fornication. Every sin that a man doeth is without the body; but he that committeth fornication sinneth against his own body.

[19] What? Know ye not that your body is the temple of the Holy Ghost which is in you, which ye have of God, and ye are not your own?

[20] For ye are bought with a price: therefore glorify God in your body, and in your spirit, which are God's. (1 Corinthians 6:13 & 15-20)

And he called the name of that place Kibrothhattaavah: because there they buried the people that lusted. (Numbers 11:34)

But among you there must not be even a hint of sexual immorality, or of any kind of impurity, or of greed, because these are improper for God's holy people. (Ephesians 5:3, NIV)

Prayer

Heavenly Father, I appreciate you. I love you; I adore you; and, I bow down before you. Thank you, Lord, for being a comfort to me in times of trouble. Lord, you have been so good to me. Words are not enough to explain. You are superb. You are excellent in all your ways. You are magnificent. I revere you, O God. I exalt your name above every other name.

Reason 21 - Lust

Father, your Word says that your strength is made perfect in my weakness. Father, I come boldly before your throne of mercy, seeking your strength to overcome this spirit of lust. Lord, I confess that I have opened many doors, causing the spirit of lust to enter and hold me hostage. I am drawn away by the desire of my eyes and my flesh. Please forgive me.

Father God, my mind is willing to do the right thing, but my flesh is in a tug-of-war. Deliver me, O God. Help me to submit myself to you that I can resist any flirting and temptations of the devil. Lord, I cast my burden upon you because I know you will sustain me and restrain the spirit that is trying to destroy my relationship with you. O God, give me the tenacity to withstand the schemes and conspiracy of the devil and not be ignorant of his tactics.

My Father and my fighter, you told me in Luke 10:19 that you have given me power and authority over all the powers of satan, you have given me the ability to trample serpent and scorpion, and they can never hurt me. According to Psalm 91:13, you have empowered me to stomp upon lions, snake, the young lion, and dragons.

Satan, with the power vested in me, I bind up your works of wickedness against my mind, body, and soul in the mighty name of Jesus. I take authority over your schemes, every principality, powers, rulers of darkness, and spiritual wickedness in high places and low places. In the name of Jesus, I paralyze every demonic activity in my life. I am aware that my fight is not physical; therefore, I draw for my spiritual weapon of prayer, praise, and worship to defeat you in the mighty name of Jesus.

Glory be to God for his grace and mercy. Thank you, Jesus.

Lord, I acknowledge that I am not my own, and my body is the temple in which you dwell. Forgive me for abusing your temple. In the mighty name of Jesus Christ, as of today, I surrender my body as a living sacrifice unto the Holy Spirit. Spirit of lust, I will not allow you to ruin or dictate my life anymore. You are not welcome in my life. I denounce, renounce, and reject every lustful spirit, ungodly soul ties, fornication, adultery, lasciviousness, all sexual immorality, and any other spirits that are involved. You foul spirit, I render you powerless. I strip you from all your assignments to destroy my home, family, and friends. In Jesus' name, I cast you out into outer darkness and dry places.

Father God, reveal to me any triggers that can cause me to fall prey to this spirit again. I destroy every lingering residue of lust and greed. I erase every memory, concerning infidelity and immorality from my emotions, my will, and my spirit. Jesus Christ of Nazareth, I rejoice in knowing that your uncontaminated blood sanctifies, cleanses, and covers me. Lord, help me not to entangle myself again with this deceptive, deadly spirit or any other ungodly spirit.

In Jesus' name. Amen

Reason 21 - Lust

Listen. Lust is afraid of commitment and refuses to settle down. It will disguise itself as real love, causing you to marry the wrong person.
For you to have a Godly and successful marriage, you must fight denounce, and reject the spirit of lust. Most importantly, you must avoid temptations, especially those that will trigger lustful feelings, which will cause you to be unfaithful.

The Acronym for LUST
L – Lie
U – Unbearable
S – Stray from God & your Partner
T – Tarnish your character / Integrity

"Deception is the sin of misleading by a false appearance or statement. It is so cunning that it is not exactly telling a blatant lie but making an incomplete statement or withholding essential information that misleads an individual into believing something other than the truth."

Reason 22

***

Lying/Deception

A false witness shall not be unpunished, and he that speaketh lies shall perish.... The desire of a man is his kindness: and a poor man is better than a liar. (Proverbs 19:9, 22)

To many, lying feels like just another normal part of life. Some individuals lie just for conversation's sake. Some lie to be seen and heard, while others lie to exalt themselves so they can look and sound extraordinary. And, some are habitual liars. Habitual liars will stare you straight in the face, tell lies about you, and deliberately send the innocent to jail without remorse. Even though lying is an apparent reason for unanswered prayers, from another angle, I would like to share with you how we casually allow lying to become part of our daily lives without paying attention to the devastating effect it can have on our salvation.

During tax season, for example, some individuals may file for another person's children as their own. (Lie number one) After receiving the tax return check, instead of disclosing to the parent of the children, the correct amount received because the children were added, one-third of the amount was quoted and then divided into two. (Lie number two)

Some individuals have the habit of lateness, so they tend to create situations or a mishap in their mind to cover their late pattern, which causes them to lie. For instance, whenever they are late, it's either they were stuck in traffic, or the car had a flat tire, or the babysitter or the relief didn't show up on time, or they couldn't find their keys—there is always an excuse for the tardiness. (Lie number three)

Others may call in sick to work because they want to go on a trip, to a game, or other such event. (Lie number four) Many added to the length of time at their current address and report that they are earning more income than they actually are, in order to be qualified for a job or mortgage or lease or credit cards. (Lie number five) Being annoyed by the continuous ringing of the phone and not in the mood to talk, you ask someone, "Please answer that phone and tell them that I am not here." (Lie number six)

These are just a few of the things we lie about. Sadly, because they seem so insignificant and harmless, we forget to repent of them.

But Peter said, "Ananias, why hath Satan filled thine heart to lie to the Holy Ghost, and to keep back part of the price of the land? 4Whiles it remained, was it not thine own? and after it was sold, was it not in thine own power? why hast thou conceived this thing in thine heart? thou hast not lied unto men, but unto God." (Acts 5:3-4)

Deception

As I began to ponder what to write about the concept and spirit of deception, the Lord reminded me of a time when I was deceptive. He said, "I want you to tell that story in this book, as an example of deception." Ouch! Now, I have to put myself out there; but that is okay because we all need spiritual healing and deliverance from the small things that are preventing our prayers from being answered.

A few years ago, someone reached out to me but I didn't respond right away. This is a copy of the actual email I sent when I finally did respond.

Hi Margret, I am sorry I missed you. You were right, about the number of clients. You won't have access to me before June twenty-eight. My mom passed away in Jamaica.

Reason 22 - Lying/Deception

Yes, my mom did pass away in Jamaica, but was that the reason she would not have access to or be able to reach me? Was that the reason I didn't respond to her immediately? No, it was not. What was deceptive about mentioning my mom's death and Jamaica in the same email, immediately her mind thought, "Oh, she is in Jamaica that's why I couldn't reach her." See, that is what she was led to believe–that I was in Jamaica for my mom's funeral and that's the reason she was unable to reach me on that particular day, which wasn't the truth. She tried to contact me *before* I went to Jamaica. Immediately after I sent the email, the Holy Spirit called me out on it. Oh yes, I was deeply convicted about this deceptive action and intent.

Deception is the sin of misleading by a false appearance or statement. It is so cunning that it is not exactly telling a blatant lie but making an incomplete statement or withholding essential information that misleads an individual into believing something other than the truth. It is an appearance of fact but far from the reality of the truth. Deception comes from the word deceit, which is defined as lying, fraudulent, cheating, and mystification. It is the intention to conceal, camouflage, and distract. Deception violates trust and gives birth to feelings of betrayal and anger. *I urge you, brothers and sisters, to watch out for those who cause divisions and put obstacles in your way that are contrary to the teaching you have learned. Keep away from them; for such people are not serving our Lord Christ, but their own appetites. By smooth talk and flattery,* **they deceive the minds of naïve people.** *(Romans 16:17-18, NIV)*

Beloved, indeed, these are the little foxes that spoil the vine, according to Song of Solomon. If you search deep within you, you may find other areas in which you've lied and forgotten to seek forgiveness. Since you are reading this book, you still have time to repent. We don't have to sin, but if we do, remember that we have an advocate who is pleading our case. *My little children (believers, dear ones), I am writing you these things so that you will not sin and violate God's law. And if anyone sins, we have an Advocate [who will intercede for us] with the Father: Jesus Christ the righteous [the upright, the just One, who conforms to the Father's will in every way—purpose, thought, and action]. (1 John 2:1, AMP)*

These six things the Lord hates, indeed, seven are an abomination to Him;... A proud look [the spirit that makes one overestimate himself and underestimate others], a lying tongue, and hands that shed innocent blood... A heart that manufactures wicked thoughts and plans, feet that are swift in running to evil, A false witness who breathes out lies [even under oath], and he who sows discord among his brethren. (Proverbs 6:16-19, AMP)

Prayer

Lord, you are my light and my salvation. How precious is your name, O God. You are marvelous, magnificent, ever-loving, and kind. I praise your name. I worship and adore you. Thank you, Lord, for being my help and my salvation and the strength of my life.

Father, I know how much you detest lying. I know it is the number one thing named among the abominations that you despise. O God, I confess that I have lied, sometimes unnecessarily. Lying has become a habitual thing in my daily life. I have been a false witness. I have sown seeds of discord; and, I made mischief–all with my lying tongue. God! My soul cries out in agony. Hear my cry of torment; and send me help from your sanctuary. Father, no matter how hard I try to speak the truth, the spirit of lying seeks to attach itself to it. Lord, I am tormented daily with guilt because I know I am hurting you. O God, I feel helpless. Help me, Jesus, to stop lying.

El Emet, you are the God of truth. Forgive me for disregarding your commandment. Forgive me for practicing lies, and for lending my tongue to be used deceitfully by satan. Lord, like a spear and arrow, I've allowed lies to pierce my soul. God, each time I lie, it feels as if a dagger penetrates my heart because I am aware of the anguish and disappointment you feel. Forgive me and have mercy on me, O God. In the mighty name of Jesus, deliver me from lying. Please, don't put me away in your anger and hide not your face from me, O God. Father God, the things that I don't want to do, I keep on doing, and

Reason 22 - Lying/Deception

it's so challenging to do the things that I should do. *(Romans 7:19-25)* Lord, I submit and surrender my sinful nature unto you. I am no longer a slave to sin, but a freeman "man" in you.

El Elyon, the Most High God, I gird my loins with the belt of truth so that the spirit of lies and deception will have no power over me. In the mighty name of Jesus, I denounce, renounce, and reject every spirit of lies within me. I will not allow you to hinder me from inheriting eternal life. You lying spirit, I bind you and cast you out into outer darkness and dry places, in the name of Jesus. I command you never to speak through my mouth again. You are no longer welcome in my life, and you cannot manipulate my spirit anymore. My tongue is off-limits to you and your cohorts. I will use my tongue to testify of God's goodness, witness to others, decree, and declare God's Word. I will speak the truth no matter what the consequence.

Lord, inject me with your blood and flush out every residue of lies from my heart. Father God, as of today, I will bind your commandment to my heart, mind, and spirit. I will allow it to lead and direct my actions. It will keep me even while I am sleeping. When I'm awake, it will speak for me continually. O mighty God, your commandment will be as a lamp that guides me through the darkness and keeps me from lying to you, others, and myself. Continue to teach me your ways, O Lord, and lead me in a plain path of righteousness in Jesus' name. Amen.

But have renounced the hidden things of dishonesty, not walking in craftiness, nor handling the word of God deceitfully; but by manifestation of the truth commending ourselves to every man's conscience in the sight of God. 2 Corinthians 4:2

"Beloved, malice can be compared to a disease of the heart. It is, entirely, a heart issue. Take Cain, for example. Jealousy triggered his malice to the point where he stole his brother's life and destiny."

Reason 23

***

Malice

Wherefore laying aside all malice, and all guile, and hypocrisies, and envies, and all evil speaking. (1 Peter 2:1)

When I was a child, the word malice was thrown around so lightly. It was often used in reference to two individuals not talking to each other for a long time. When I learned of its true meaning, I was shocked. Malice is generally defined as the intention or desire to harm someone; to do evil; strong hostility or animosity. Now, I see and understand, that, because of the evil intention and desire to harm or inflict pain on the individual whom you hate and despise, resentment incubates within you, which will prevent you from speaking to that person.

I have never seen so much malice in my lifetime. I didn't even know such malice existed. After carefully observing the hate crimes against individuals because of their race, the color of their skin, religion, sexual preferences, culture, nationality or ethnicity, it is evident that malice is rampant in today's society. Malice contributes to fighting, quarreling, and even murder. The Pharisees and Scribes were perfect examples of malicious, spiteful people.

An individual who harbors malice may be struggling with inner turmoil. He or she may be dealing with unresolved conflicts and has decided that he or she will not suffer the anguish alone. The burning of churches, the prejudice, and the bloodshed around the world tell us that malice is very much alive. Many individuals argue and are even at odds with each other about what they should and shouldn't eat as born-again Christians. Some are ready to condemn those who are eating forbidden foods, but remember, *It is not what goes into the mouth that defiles a person, but what comes out of the mouth; this defiles a person. (Matthew 15:11, ESV)*

Beloved, malice can be compared to a disease of the heart. It is entirely a heart issue. Take Cain, for example. Jealousy triggered his malice to the point where he stole his brother's life and destiny. Out of the abundance of the heart, the mouth speaks. (Matthew 12:34) What is coming out of your heart through your mouth? Is it love and good wishes for your sisters and brothers? Or, are you spewing out venom towards them so you can rejoice over their downfall and demise?

The enemy enjoys manipulating the mind, allowing you to believe that the other person is your enemy. By doing so, malice can build up within you, causing you to act out of character and displease God. Victory can be yours if you dwell in God's secret place and pray for those whom you dislike or resent. Don't allow your feelings of wanting to repay evil for evil to get to the point of malice. You can get rid of malice by guarding your mind with the helmet of salvation, protecting your heart with the breastplate of righteousness, and wrapping your bowels with compassion and the belt of truth.

My sister or brother, think about the reason you became a born-again Christian. I assume it was because you don't want to live a sinful life anymore, that you love God, and you want to do the right thing at all times. You want to make heaven your final home, and you pledged that you would not go to Hell with the wicked. Am I right? Don't lose that vision! Exhibit sincere love towards each other the way you would like to be loved; and treat each other with respect in the same manner in which you would like to be esteemed.

Jesus came and paid for your freedom with His life, so you are free to embrace and celebrate each other, regardless of race, gender, nationality, religious or sexual preference, or skin color. Our mandate is to pray without ceasing for those who are different, love them,

Reason 23 - Malice

and make them feel that someone cares. Yes, Jesus called us to be fishers of all men, not some men. And by all means, we should not be silent about wickedness or be intimidated by evil but resist injustice, denounce, rebuke, and reject it from its core.

Prayer

Draw me closer to you, O God. Let me feel your heartbeat once again. Lord, as the deer panteth for the water, so my soul cries out for you. O, mighty God, you reign King over the universe. You are my God. You are my everlasting King. You are my soap that cleanses me from the spirit of malice. Thank you for your extended mercy towards me, O God.

Father, according to Job 9:30-31, no amount of snow or cleansing agent can cleanse me from the iniquity of malice. Unless I surrender my heart to you, even my clothes will reject me; and you would plunge me in the pit. Wash the evil of malice away from my heart, O God, so that I may be saved.

Lord, I have harbored wicked thoughts within me for a long time. I know your eyes are watching all my ways, and nothing is hidden from your face. Father God, I confess that I am guilty of malice. Be my refining fire and my soap, O God, and burn every seed, residue, and debris of malice out of my heart. Then, cleanse me thoroughly. Lord, I desire to see and spend eternity with you. Here are my hands; clean them. Here is my heart; make it pure. Forgive me, Lord, for allowing my heart to be a home for resentment, hatred, jealousy, and unforgiveness, which gave birth to malice. I repent of the monstrous sin, in Jesus' name.

In the mighty name of Jesus, I rebuke, renounce, and reject the spirit of malice. I eject you from my heart, you wicked spirit of malice. I shoot arrows of fire into your place of gathering, where you are conspiring against me and my destiny. I bind you, in the name of Jesus and cast you out into outer darkness and dry places. I destroy your works and assignments, and I take authority over my heart and my mind in Jesus' name. Lord, come into my heart and be Lord over my thoughts and actions. Father God, replant the seed of love within me and continue to water it daily. Thank you, Lord, for delivering me from malice and all the attached spirits, in Jesus' mighty name. Amen

But who may abide the day of his coming? and who shall stand when he appeareth? for he is like a refiner's fire, and like fullers' soap. (Malachi 3:2, KJV)

Although you wash yourself with soap and use an abundance of cleansing powder, the stain of your guilt is still before me," declares the Sovereign LORD. (Jeremiah 2:22, NIV)

If I should wash myself with snow and cleanse my hands with lye, ³¹then You would plunge me into the pit, and even my own clothes would despise me! (Job 9:30-31, Berean Study Bible)

For mine eyes are upon all their ways: they are not hid from my face, neither is their iniquity hid from mine eyes. (Jeremiah 16:17)

For we ourselves also were sometimes foolish, disobedient, deceived, serving diverse lusts and pleasures, living in malice and envy, hateful, and hating one another. (Titus 3:3)

Reason 23 - Malice

"Victory can be yours, if you dwell in God's secret place and pray for those, whom you dislike or resent. Don't allow your feelings of wanting to repay evil for evil to get to the point of malice. You can get rid of malice by guarding your mind with the helmet of salvation, protecting your heart with the breastplate of righteousness, and wrapping your bowels with compassion and the belt of truth that Jesus Christ is Lord."

"Jesus, clearly, stated in the Scripture above that God is a master and so is mammon; but, we must choose which master to serve. We cannot serve both, simultaneously."

Reason 24

***

Mammon

No man can serve two masters: for either he will hate the one, and love the other; or else he will hold to the one, and despise the other. Ye cannot serve God and mammon. (Matthew 6:24)

*Y*ou may have heard the word mammon before. Many believe that mammon means money. It doesn't, actually, but they are closely connected to each other. This subject is rarely preached upon or spoken about from the pulpit. Mammon is one of the most subtle and dangerous spirits attacking society today, especially the body of Christ. Lack of knowledge of its existence, power, and capabilities makes us ill-equipped to fight and defeat it; and, hence, it appears to be victorious from generation to generation.

How does God feel about us having money?

Before I get into what mammon is and how it operates, may I declare that money is an essential commodity. Money is not bad or evil. Money is a necessity of life. It is one of God's greatest desires to see His children with excess wealth so they can help those in need. If not, how and what will we lend and not borrow? (Deuteronomy 28:11-13) How can we occupy until he comes? (Luke 19:13) He wishes for us to prosper spiritually, physically, mentally, and financially. (3 John 2) God wants us to build His kingdom, honor Him with our wealth, and swim in the ocean of abundance.

Honor the Lord with your wealth And with the first fruits of all your crops (income); Then your barns will be abundantly filled And your vats will overflow with new wine. (Proverbs 3: 9-10, AMP)

The money belongs to God, not satan. (Haggai 2:12) As a matter of fact, the entire world and its contents belong to God. (Psalm 24:1 & Psalm 50:10-12) Therefore, if we are His heirs and joint-heirs with Jesus, then everything on earth should be readily accessible to us, His children. So, as His children, why are we struggling so much? Why does it appear as if we are in a perpetual financial drought and famine? I would be happy to shed some light and share some vital information about the culprit that is sabotaging and holding our finances hostage.

What is mammon?

Jesus clearly stated in the Scripture above that God is a master and so is mammon; but, we must choose which master to serve. We cannot serve both, simultaneously. As already mentioned, mammon does not mean money. It is actually the master, the god that rules over money. It's an evil spirit, assigned by satan to govern and control cash and, in turn, enslave those who choose it to be their master. Mammon is a master manipulating spirit with extraordinary power and authority to dictate the world's currency—who gets it, who should have it, and who will not enjoy a dime.

How does mammon operate?

As a master, it tries extremely hard to control the world's wealth and resources, and favors whoever will bow and sell their soul for material gain. Satan, being the god of this world, tends to use money and material things as bait to lure weak, double-minded, materialistic people into his snare. He creates systems that can easily blind our eyes and shift our focus, and dependency on God, to depending upon his systems and the help of man. And even if our gospel is veiled, it is veiled to those who are perishing. **The god of this age has blinded the minds of unbelievers** *so that they cannot see the light of the gospel that displays the glory of Christ, who is the image of God.* (2 Corinthians 4:3-4, NIV). Besides, don't forget that "...*vain is the help of man.*" (Psalm 60:11)

Like a bully, mammon consistently plagues the lives of those who are waiting patiently, and depending on God, while standing, firmly, on

Reason 24 - Mammon

His words. It steals and withholds their finances, afflicts their health, breaks up marriages, and causes children to be rebellious. Mammon seeks to manipulate us into feeling like an unsuccessful outcast, wanting us to believe that we are inferior because we are not among the elite with millions of dollars, multiple cars, the penthouse, or in the spotlight. Mammon appears innocent, and without the spirit of discernment, we can be tricked into believing that all that glitters is gold, with nothing to fear. It will try to mimic the character of God, but there is always something that exposes its deceptive plans.

If I should give mammon a surname, it would be "Mammon More." Mammon inveigles individuals to get more, crave more, and hunt for more material things hoping to fill the void they feel inside. It whispers continuously in the ear of its victims, saying, if you get a little more money, your problems will be solved. If you get a second job, you will be able to afford your dream car. If you implement a plan that will increase your cash flow, your marriage will be better. With more overtime at your job, you will be much happier. I guarantee that if you join this particular organization, money won't be an issue anymore, and you'll be more recognized and respected. Most importantly, there will be no more lack. You will be able to afford all that your children need.

Signs of Mammon Being Present

When mammon wheedles its way in our lives, our priorities change. Our desire to get rich and become a millionaire suddenly increases. We compromise our integrity by entering into ungodly relationships just to change our appearance and financial status. To satisfy the sudden urge, we tend to take on extra projects, work excessively, and sometimes entertain company and rub shoulders with individuals with whom we have or should have nothing in common. We may start visiting places that are off-limits to us. Instead of us being the leader and influencer, we are being led and influenced by the children of darkness.

Another sign of mammon being present is staying awake during the night, trying to find ways how to make money and become rich. If you are constantly arguing, getting angry, and miserable with your spouse because you are not getting enough money and have decided to walk away for someone else who is wealthy, you have entertained and succumbed to the spirit of mammon.

Today, the spirit of mammon is very much alive in our homes, churches, and lives. It has driven individuals to call their backyard pool "the pool of Bethesda," charging the sick and afflicted thousands of dollars to enter the pool, promising them instant healing. The spirit of mammon influences men to prostitute the gospel and sell pieces of cloth and bottles of water, as healing agents, for hundreds of dollars. The spirit of mammon operates through greed, and the individuals, through which this spirit operates, will squeeze out your last dime to meet their needs and couldn't care-less if you are evicted from your home tomorrow, or die of hunger.

Which Master Will You Choose?

God or Mammon? My friend, the spirit of mammon, is here to deplete us physically and spiritually. To those of us who have decided to stay loyal to God, the Creator of the universe, mammon does everything within its power to ensure that we live in lack if we refuse to make it our master. Sadly, due to the lack we face, or think we face, we tend to hold back on giving God our time, tithes, and offering, thinking we do not have enough to give. Hence, we struggle physically. Bear in mind, although we may be physically weak, we are a spiritual powerhouse.

Individuals who are willing to compromise and choose mammon to be their god and master will, physically, flourish and may never experience lack. Mammon makes sure they are satisfied so there will be no need to turn and choose Jesus Christ.

It has been said that many people believe that once they are financially, secure, they don't need God or salvation. Mammon servants may be giants physically or financially, but spiritually, they are but an ant; they are spiritually poor and depleted. Mammon encourages us to store up treasures on earth and set our hearts on them, leaving no

Reason 24 - Mammon

room for the Holy Spirit to minister to our minds. Individuals who have allowed money to be their idol and the only source may testify that they experience sleepless nights, discomfort, and fear. They are afraid of losing their cash, earthly possessions, and investments. *Lay not up for yourselves treasures upon earth, where moth and rust doth corrupt, and where thieves break through and steal: But lay up for yourselves treasures in heaven, where neither moth nor rust doth corrupt, and where thieves do not break through nor steal: For where your treasure is, there will your heart be also. (Matthew 6:19-21)*

Listen to what Jesus said about those who are controlled by the spirit of mammon in Mark 10:17, 21-25:

[17]And when he was gone forth into the way, there came one running, and kneeled to him, and asked him, "Good Master, what shall I do that I may inherit eternal life?"

[21]Then Jesus beholding him loved him, and said unto him, "One thing thou lackest: go thy way, sell whatsoever thou hast, and give to the poor, and thou shalt have treasure in heaven: and come, take up the cross, and follow me."

[22]And he was sad at that saying, and went away grieved: for he had great possessions.

[23]And Jesus looked round about, and saith unto his disciples, "How hardly shall they that have riches enter into the kingdom of God!

[25]"It is easier for a camel to go through the eye of a needle than for a rich man to enter into the kingdom of God."

The scripture clearly states that you cannot serve two masters because it's impossible to be equally loyal to both at the same time. Eventually, one will be disappointed. Of the two masters who are ruling simultaneously, which one will you permit to dominate your life and become your master? Think of a house or a piece of land that is being captured by an intruder who, after capturing it, lives in the house, and mines the property. Does that mean he owns the property? Absolutely not! If the property had been left vacant and he seized the opportunity to live freely, then, certainly. But, if the rightful owner returned for his property, showing legitimate proof of ownership, then, the squatter would have to vacate the premises.

With that said, even though satan and his demons may seek to rule over money, that doesn't mean it's theirs. As the peculiar royal heirs of God that we are, when we show up, mammon and it's imps must hand our inheritance over to us. Satan wants us to bow and surrender ourselves to him, as he tried before with Jesus, not because he cares for our well-being, but because his goal is to get back at God and destroy us in the process. *All these things will I give thee, if thou wilt fall down and worship me."* (Matthew 4:9)

Of course, we know that Jesus did not bow. For one, what satan offered to Jesus, was created and owned by Jesus Himself. Likewise, whatever mammon is offering us today, we were given dominion over since creation. Satan is doing all that he can through the spirit of mammon to keep money away from the sincere, sold-out saints of God. He's determined to bring us to a breaking point to distrust and disobey God. Don't let him be victorious over you.

Unfortunately, there are individuals whose foundation is weakened; and, they're unable to resist or withstand the temptation, and they, eventually, allow mammon to deceive them. Hence, they are drawn away by the exceptional love for money. Unaware, we sometimes open doors giving satan permission to interfere with our finances and, as a result, it can hinder God's divine intervention on our behalf. Most situations in which we find ourselves could have been prevented if we only follow God's ways of living. Look at what God says in Deuteronomy 28:13: *And the Lord shall make thee the head, and not the tail; and thou shalt be above only, and thou shalt not be beneath;* ***if that thou hearken unto the commandments of the Lord thy God, which I command thee this day, to observe and to do them....***

How to destroy the spirit of mammon

Remember, mammon always pressures individuals to get more and hold on to it, or withhold it from others. Either way, a simple way to destroy the stronghold of mammon in our lives is by **GIVING**. If I have a seed and tightly clutch it in my hand, it will remain a seed; however, if I open my hand and release or plant that seed, it will become a mighty fruit-bearing tree, and I will reap a mighty harvest. *"Give, and it shall be given unto you; good measure, pressed down, and shaken together, and **running over, shall men give into your bosom**. For with the same measure that ye mete withal it shall be measured to you again." (Luke 6 :38)*

Opening our hands to bless others will bring back unlimited blessings to us and to whom we are closely connected. Giving to charities or ministries that are making a difference and changing lives locally or internationally is an excellent way to make giving a lifestyle, or perhaps starting a charity or ministry in your community to assist the needy! Never believe that you don't have anything to give or share. Seek God's direction. He will work with what you have—with what He's already equipped you for. Remember, little is much when God is in it.

Giving out of your abundance may not move God because there was no true sacrifice or it didn't jolt or deprive you. When you make a sacrifice to lend a helping hand, I promise you, it will not go unnoticed. You will be like the widow who gave her last and was blessed tremendously. Giving takes selflessness and discipline. You cannot out-give God and you will never give towards the work of God or feed the less-fortunate and not be rewarded.

[29]And Jesus answered and said, "Verily I say unto you, there is no man that hath left house, or brethren, or sisters, or father, or mother, or wife, or children, or lands, for my sake, and the gospel's, 30But he shall receive an hundredfold now in this time, houses, and brethren, and sisters, and mothers, and children, and lands, with persecutions; and in the world to come eternal life. (Mark 10:29-30)

Beloved, man shall not live by material things only. We would, likely, be surprised to find out the many things to which we are attached, but can live without. Breaking and destroying the spirit of mammon also takes faith, trust, and obedience to the Word of God, which most of us find it difficult to obey and apply. Even though we do not see or understand how God is working things out, by **faith**, we must believe that it is done. We must **trust** Him to fulfill His promises and do the impossible. **Obey and follow His** commands.

We often get frustrated and confused because we are constantly leaping ahead without God's permission and doing the opposite of what He commissioned us to do during the waiting process. Jesus asked us to seek Him, first, before we attempt to seek help or ideas from man or material things. He encouraged us not to worry about what to eat, drink, or wear, but instead, seek Him first. Seek to do the right thing, at all times; and whatever we need will be given to us who obey and seek Him diligently.

My friend, don't forget, as with any other spirit or powers, we were given power over mammon as well. Let us trample and paralyze its power in Jesus' name and watch your finances multiply and stay with you. *"But seek ye first the kingdom of God, and his righteousness; and all these things shall be added unto you." (Matthew 6:33)* You can find more in Deuteronomy 28:11-13.

Prayer

Father in heaven, I glorify you. I adore you and bless your name. God, you are my source. Jehovah Jireh, thank you for your power of provision. Jehovah Nissi, thank you for wrapping your arms around me. Jehovah Shalom, thank you for keeping me in perfect peace.

Almighty God, out of lack of knowledge, I have entertained the spirit of mammon, allowing it to become my master. God, I have succumbed to its manipulating action. O God, I am deceived into thinking that, if my finances increase, I will be happier and more comfortable, but the opposite is true. Father, I have abandoned our relationship for the love of money. Lord, please forgive me for choosing money and material things instead of you. Father God, I realize that my craving for money has taken the place of my first Love for You. Lord, I am guilty of spiritual adultery. I am guilty of

Reason 24 - Mammon

selfishness and of trying to hoard and hold on to everything I have and still hunting for more.

Dear God, I seek your hand to deliver me from this manipulating spirit, hallelujah! Reach down your strong, mighty arms and pull me out of the deadly grip of mammon. O God, I have signed a spiritual death warrant with mammon for my soul. Help me get back on the path of righteousness. Lord, because I have turned away from you towards mammon, my ministry is struggling spiritually, and my sheep have been wounded and gone astray. My home is in turmoil; and my health is failing. God, I have been trying to fill the void in my life with material things and the busyness of life-pushing you away from me and my affairs, and putting you in reserve. Forgive me, O God.

In the mighty name of Jesus Christ, I bind up the strongman that is governing mammon. I break and destroy the stronghold of mammon over my life and finances. I command all powers and principalities, influencing the spirit of mammon, to be stripped from their assignment, in Jesus' mighty name. Through the power of the Holy Ghost, I command you to abandon your assignment for my soul and my relationship with God. May the spirit of frustration and confusion invade the camps of the enemy and frustrate those who take counsel against me, in Jesus' mighty name.

My Father and my fighter, I seek your permission to release your warrior angels Michael, Gabriel, and Uriel, to destroy the spirit of mammon and all agents of satan, who have taken counsel to dictate my life, manipulate my finances, and sabotage my relationship with you.

Spirit of mammon, I chose Jesus Christ to be the Master over my soul. I rebuke you, in the name of Jesus. I detach myself from your charm and render you powerless, in Jesus' name. I strip you of your power and authority to manipulate my affairs. I reject and denounce you. You will no longer get the opportunity to control my actions. In Jesus' mighty name. Amen.

Labour not to be rich: cease from thine own wisdom. ⁵Wilt thou set thine eyes upon that which is not? for riches certainly make themselves wings; they fly away as an eagle toward heaven. (Proverbs 23:4-5)

Reason 24 - Mammon

"Individuals, who are willing to compromise and choose mammon to be their god and master will physically flourish and may never experience lack, but will be spiritually malnourished. Mammon servants may be giants physically or financially, but spiritually, they are but an ant. They are spiritually poor and depleted."

"Masturbation is a sinful work of darkness. If you are one who believes that nothing is wrong with it, how does it make you feel after you are finished? Do you feel dirty? Guilty? Ashamed?"

Reason 25

***

Masturbation

¹⁸*Run away from sexual immorality [in any form, whether thought or behavior, whether visual or written]. Every other sin that a man commits is outside the body, but the one who is sexually immoral sins against his own body. (1 Corinthians 6:18, AMP)*

It is God's will that you should be sanctified: that you should avoid sexual immorality....

(1 Thessalonians 4-3, NIV)

Is masturbation a sin? Many have argued and continue to argue that it is not. Unfortunately, masturbation is an addiction that plagues so many born-again Christians and forces them to indulge, secretly, in the act. Many are bothered by mere participation, while others think nothing is wrong with releasing and pleasing yourself. Those who are bothered by the involvement have tried various ways to overcome but to no avail. They are left with feelings of embarrassment, guilt, helplessness, and frustration. Surprisingly, married individuals are not exempt from this spiritual attack and many participate in this behavior.

First and foremost, the word masturbation is not written in the Bible, and I agree it was never said, "thou shalt not masturbate." However, many Scriptures imply that it is a sin. It's like talking about the "rapture." The word rapture is not written in the Bible, but there are scriptures that indicate that we will be caught up (raptured) to meet Him in the air. (1 Thessalonians 4:17)

For you to get to the act of masturbation, there is a feeling of sexual desire that overwhelms you beyond your control. Perhaps, the memory of the past flashes across your mind. Maybe you have seen a commercial, a movie, or a book with sexual connotations, or you may have smelled a perfume or cologne that triggers the desire. It could have been that your hand passed over your chest or private areas triggering the appetite. Either way, one of your five senses were activated by something or someone. Hence, the stimulation of the genitals begins.

When you think of the process, it is impossible to have a blank mind, as many people argued. Because masturbation is rooted in lust, it cannot be done without imagining a person or having some fantasy. Your actions are the manifestation of your thoughts and feelings being activated by what you see, hear, feel, touch, and smell. Yes, masturbation is a sin.

Individuals whose conscience is already seared with a hot iron, may choose not to regard right from wrong, and prefer to keep on living in sin and make excuses to justify their immorality. Therefore, to them, masturbation feels normal, and there is no remorse or repentance. They are quick to tell you the act of masturbation is not a sin, and you are not doing anything wrong. An evangelist once said to me that it is not a sin to be intimate with your own body, and furthermore, if the opportunity arose, she would teach young people that it is better to masturbate than to commit fornication or adultery. "I strongly believe that nothing is wrong with it. For one, whenever I am engaged in the act, my mind is blank. I am not thinking about anyone or anything," she said.

Listen, my friends, this is more than just another way of releasing oneself and enjoying the pleasure without the pain, and this is why Jesus said in Matthew 5:28, *"by **looking** lustfully at a woman, you already committed adultery (sin) in your heart?"* A mere look is innocent and far different from a look that is laced with lust. When "just a look" becomes lustful, it means that you are already visualizing a sexual action from beginning to end your mind. So, if

Reason 25 - Masturbation

looking lustfully at someone is a sin, how will He view the actual participation in fondling your private body parts to the point of orgasm?

Masturbation is a sinful work of darkness. If you are one, who believes that nothing is wrong with it, how does it make you feel after you are finished? Do you feel dirty? Guilty? Ashamed? The sexual act, on the whole, is a private matter and should stay in the bedroom or where ever it's done.

Nonetheless, if there's an awkwardness when the topic arises, and you're embarrassed to mention that you participate in it freely, –that you are secretly indulging in the behavior and pretending as if you are against it. You know it is wrong. Do you believe it is holy and acceptable to God? *"I beseech you therefore, brethren, by the mercies of God, that ye present your bodies a living sacrifice,* **holy, acceptable unto God***, which is your reasonable service." (Romans:1:12)* It is immoral.

Beloved, the enemy of our soul is very subtle and deceptive. Stay close to God and His Word. Build a unique relationship with Him; and ask Him to order your steps as well as your actions. Seeking God's direction will help you to walk blameless before Him. There is an uncleanness about masturbation. What is your conscience saying? Whatever you do, you should do unto the Lord. Does masturbation glorify God? Do you think He is pleased with you during and after your indulgence? If you are burning with sexual desires and can't resist the temptation of sinning against God's temple, allow God to choose a mate for you and get married.

If you are married and your spouse is not meeting your sexual needs, this is not a license to sin. This is why you need to build a unique relationship and fear for God so that, when your flesh wants to rebel against God's instruction, your love and fear for Him won't allow you to. You must see this act the same way God sees it and rebuke it each time it creeps up on you. *What shall we say then? Shall we continue in sin, that grace may abound? God forbid. How shall we, that are dead to sin, live any longer therein? (Romans 6:1-2)*

Whatever you make the focus of your life, or continuously think about, and pay more attention to, may dwell in you and become your reality. Be careful with what you feed your mind or how you allow it to stray. You will attract what you think about even though you may not want it to be a part of your life. *For the thing which I greatly feared is come upon me, and that which I was afraid of is come unto me.* (Job 3:25)

Participating in masturbation can be as deadly as any other sin. It opens the door to the spirit of addiction, along with many other foul spirits to enter your body. Do your best to avoid the triggers and disconnect from anything that will activate this spirit. Much like lust, you should triple padlock the point of entry through which they come. If it's through your eyes, stop looking at sexually laced movies or books. If it's through your hearing, quit listening to sexually driven conversations or music. Take control of your emotions. Cast down every imagination and everything that tries to exalt itself against the Word and the power of God. In other words, resist it as soon as the thought enters your mind by rebuking and denouncing it immediately.

And I heard a loud voice saying in heaven, *"Now is come salvation, and strength, and the kingdom of our God, and the power of his Christ:* **for the accuser of our brethren is cast down, which accused them before our God day and night."** *(Revelation 12:10)*

My friends, don't allow satan to condemn or accuse you. He is waiting for you to nudge the door ajar, permitting him to wreak havoc in your life. Do not give him ammunition to shoot you. Acknowledge your weaknesses, and take it to God in prayer. Ask God to extend His grace towards you and let His strength be your strength. Remember, God promises that His strength will be made perfect in your weakness. I guarantee you, if you seek to establish an in-depth relationship with God and search for Him wholeheartedly, masturbation will have no place in your heart, mind, or spirit. *"Then shall ye call upon me, and ye shall go and pray unto me, and I will hearken unto you. And ye shall*

Reason 25 - Masturbation

seek me, and find me, when ye shall search for me with all your heart." (Jeremiah 29:12-13)

My sisters and brothers, Just keep your mind on Jesus. *"Take heed unto thyself, and unto the doctrine; continue in them: for in doing this thou shalt both save thyself, and them that hear thee." (1 Timothy 4:16)*

Below are a few Bible verses supporting that masturbation is sexual immorality.

Let us walk properly as in the daytime, not in orgies and drunkenness, not in sexual immorality and sensuality, not in quarreling and jealousy. ¹⁴But put on the Lord Jesus Christ, and make no provision for the flesh, to gratify its desires.(Romans 13:13, ESV)

But because of the temptation to sexual immorality, each man should have his own wife and each woman her own husband. *(1 Corinthians 7:2, ESV)*

Do not present your members to sin as instruments for unrighteousness, but present yourselves to God as those who have been brought from death to life, and your members to God as instruments for righteousness. (Romans 6:13, ESV)

Flee also youthful lusts; but pursue righteousness, faith, love, peace with those who call on the Lord out of a pure heart. ²³But avoid foolish and ignorant disputes, knowing that they generate strife. ²⁴And a servant of the Lord must not quarrel but be gentle to all, able to teach.... (2 Timothy 2:22-24, NKJV)

³For this is the will of God, that you be sanctified [separated and set apart from sin]: that you abstain and back away from sexual immorality.... *(1 Thessalonians 4:3, AMP)*

Put to death, therefore, whatever belongs to your earthly nature: sexual immorality, impurity, lust, evil desires and greed, which is idolatry. (Colossians 3:5, NIV)

Prayer

O sovereign God, you rule triumphant over my life. Lord, I bless your holy name. I command everything in me to praise and worship you. Lord, I acknowledge you as my source of strength, my helper, my redeemer, and my savior.

"If we confess our sins, he is faithful and just to forgive us our sins, and to cleanse us from all unrighteousness." (1 John 1:9) Heavenly Father, you promised me if I confess my sins to you, you will forgive and cleanse me. Father, please forgive me for indulging in masturbation and any other sexual immorality. Lord, my iniquities are before you, my secret sins are in the light of your presence. Hide your face from my sin, O God. Lord, I confess that I have delighted myself in the pleasure of masturbation without thinking of the ramifications. Forgive me for presenting my body parts as an instrument of unrighteousness. Everything is uncovered and exposed before your eyes. Cleanse me, O God. Purify and purge me from this iniquity.

Lord, I am weak and vulnerable to the stimulation of my body. Deliver me, O God, and blot out my iniquity. Let your strength be my strength so I may flee sexual immorality and pursue righteousness. Sanctify me, O God, that I may abstain and be separated from sin. In the mighty name of Jesus, help me to walk holy before you, as as I bring my struggles under subjection to your name. Lord, by myself, I cannot win this war that is fighting in my flesh, but with your sufficient grace, I will overcome. Send me a surplus grace and endurance, O God. Bring my conscience under conviction whenever the thought of entertaining or participating in masturbation invades my mind and my thoughts.

In the mighty name of Jesus Christ, I bind every spirit of sexual perversion seeking to control my life. I revoke and loose myself from any covenant or contract that I may have signed, knowingly or unknowingly, with any sex demons, incubus or succubus. Through the power of the Holy Ghost, I forbid you from tormenting my mind. I close every open door that allows you foul spirits to enter my environment.

Reason 25 - Masturbation

Lord, I surrender my mind, body, and spirit to you right now, protect me from every polluting fantasy, in Jesus' name. Amen.

Nothing in all creation is hidden from God's sight of Him to whom we must give account. (Hebrews 4:13)

For the eyes of the LORD roam to and fro over all the earth, to show Himself strong on behalf of those whose heart is fully devoted to Him. You have acted foolishly in this matter. From now on, therefore, you will be at war. (2 Chronicles 16:9)

For His eyes are on the ways of man, and He sees his every step. (Job 34:21)

"Hide Your face from my sins and blot out all my iniquities." (Psalm 51:9)

"Thou hast set our iniquities before thee, our secret sins in the light of thy countenance." (Psalm 90:8)

"Murmuring and complaining ties God's hands, causing Him to get angry and take drastic measures like He demonstrated with the children of Israel when they allowed doubters (the ten spies) to instill fear in them, which prevented them from possessing the Promised Land."

Reason 26

***

Murmuring

Neither murmur ye, as some of them also murmured, and were destroyed of the destroyer. (1Corinthians 10:10)

As I gazed at the beautiful sunset, within arm's length sat four attractive ladies waiting for the commencement of our friend's wedding reception. Oh, what a breathtaking moment, watching the sophisticated guests as they strolled into the elegantly decorated hall. As the stunningly adorned bride made her entrance, the atmosphere was illuminated with smiles and applause from the attendees. Then suddenly, one of the ladies exclaimed, "Oh no! Our evening is ruined! Pamela (Pam) is here." Unfortunately, Pam made her way to their table. Without asking if that seat was reserved for someone, she pulled out the chair and sat. Unable to switch to another table, they were stuck with her for the remainder of the evening.

Before Pamela could get settled in, she started complaining about the decor, the lighting in the room, and that the air conditioning was too cold. As one of the ladies handed Pamela her scarf from around her neck, Pamela stated, "This scarf doesn't match my clothes, and it's a bit too thick. As the waitress approached their table, one of the ladies whispered, "Pam, please be specific with your food choice." Some attractive mouth-watering dishes arrived at the table. Pam began to tear apart the contents of her plate with her eyes. As a food judge would, she began tasting each item with reservations. With her first bite, she began to complain, and from the expression on the other ladies' faces it was evident that they had lost their appetite.

As always, after the reception, a group of people stood outside, reminiscing about the evening's event. Suddenly, everyone started scrambling and headed hastily towards their cars. To my surprise, they were running away from Pam. People are afraid to ask Pam how she is doing because she is known to be a consistent complainer. Because of her murmuring and complaining attitude, her friends continuously avoid her and her telephone calls.

Dear reader, perhaps you are not aware that your continuous complaints and murmuring may have caused your friends to avoid your phone calls, or run in the other direction when they see you or refuse to spend time in your company. If you have experienced such behavior, you may want to do some self-examination, and try to get rid of the murmuring and complaining spirits.

Are you hard to please and never satisfied? Are you the person who never sees the good in anyone or anything that's been done for you? Do you exhibit the spirit of ungratefulness and unthankfulness?

If you can feel so frustrated and annoyed with someone's consistent complaints, can you imagine how God feels when we exhibit a spirit of ungratefulness, murmuring, and complaining? How many times do we tend to grumble and complain about what God is not doing now, and conveniently forget all He had done the days, weeks, months, years before.

Murmuring and complaining ties God's hands, causing Him to get angry and take drastic measures like He demonstrated with the children of Israel when they allowed doubters (the ten spies) to instill fear in them, which prevented them from possessing the Promised Land. Murmuring is a sin that is similar to the sin of ungratefulness. Because we spend more time focusing on the negative things around us, our eyes are blinded to reality. Hence, the constant murmuring and bickering about what is not going right in our lives drains our energy and that of those around us. It causes us to arrive at wrong conclusions based on poor judgment. We misinterpret God's

Reason 26 - Murmuring

deliverance power for hatred, and call good evil, and evil good. Being afraid of the unknown can prevent us from moving forward to get things done, and as a result, we blanket the atmosphere with murmuring and complaining.

It is unfortunate how we turn against God when life becomes challenging and times get hard. In those moments, we doubt His potential to fix our situation and His capacity to understand what we are going through. We ignore His promises, criticize and question His way of doing things, and rebel against His plan for our lives. No matter how many times we see God work miracles on our behalf and turn things around in our favor, we still find a reason to complain and doubt Him. One minute, we rejoice and testify about His goodness, and the next, we ask, "God, where are you? Why me, Lord? God, I cannot take it anymore." Some may have even gone as far as to say, "I should have never been born."

My sisters and brothers, I know it can be frustrating when you have no idea how you will get through a particular situation, but reflect on your past for a minute. Can you identify at least one dilemma from which God rescued you? Can you remember Him showing up at the last minute when things were about to crumble? Some individuals find it hard to give thanks when their life is not going as planned. Put the book down for a quick second, grab a pen and a piece of paper and make a list of all the good things that God has done for you from birth until now, then start a praise party. When you begin to give thanks and shout praises despite the negative situations, depression, fear, loneliness, lack, and the spirit of sadness cannot stay in that Holy Ghost charged atmosphere. They will have to take their flight.

God does not suffer from amnesia or dementia. He knows what you need, and when it's needed. Quit murmuring and complaining, and watch God move on your behalf. The children of Israel were supposed to be in the wilderness for only forty days, but their murmuring and ungratefulness kept them an extra forty years. Listen to the instruction and direction of God and not your friends or family. They will shift you out of the perfect will of God, causing you to miss

His plan for your life, eventually leaving you on your own to die.

I encourage you to read Deuteronomy chapter one in its entirety.

²⁷You grumbled in your tents and said, "The Lord hates us; so he brought us out of Egypt to deliver us into the hands of the Amorites to destroy us... ³¹ and in the wilderness. There you saw how the Lord your God carried you, as a father carries his son, all the way you went until you reached this place." ³² In spite of this, you did not trust in the Lord your God, ³³ who went ahead of you on your journey, in fire by night and in a cloud by day, to search out places for you to camp and to show you the way you should go. (Deuteronomy 1:27-33, NIV)

Prayer

Lord, I appreciate you. I adore you. You are awesome in my life. O sovereign God, you are my King. You are my Lord and Savior. I praise your name, O God. I command my heart to worship you. I command my mouth to sing praises to you, and I command my spirit to honor you. Hallelujah!

Father God, I am guilty of murmuring and complaining. I am guilty of impatience and ungratefulness. I am guilty of dissatisfaction and discontentment with all you have done in my life. God, I have questioned and doubted your capacity to help me despite your assurance in Your words. Almighty God, I know your ways are higher than mine, yet I rebel against your will as the Israelites did. I ignore your plan of salvation by criticizing my waiting process. I belittle your potential to give me the best and protect me as the ten spies did. Lord, please forgive me. Lord, I promise I will quit hosting pity parties and feeling sorry for myself.

Lord, I surrender my murmuring and complaining attitude to you. I bind up every murmuring spirit and render it powerless, in Jesus' mighty name. No longer will I allow my mouth or my flesh to get in the way of what you are doing in my ministry, home, marriage,

Reason 26 - Murmuring

health, children, and my life. Father God, even though I don't know which way you are taking me, lead and I will follow without a murmur. Father, the path on which you may take me may not be my choice, but I trust you with all of my heart. I know that all things will work together for my good because I love you, and you called me to work for you. Glory to God.

Thank you, Holy Spirit, for taking me through the wilderness, the Red Sea, and the Jordan. Thank you for taking me out of the fiery furnace and the lion's den. Lord, thank you for redeeming my soul from Hell. Thank you for your salvation. Amen

Do all things without murmurings and disputings. (Philippians 2:14)

"Despite God showing us the warning signs, setting off our inner alarm, and sending us messages, we purposely choose to ignore Him. We continuously rebel and disobey the unction of the Holy Spirit and are compelled to do our own thing."

Reason 27

***

Not God's Will

For ye have need of patience, that, after ye have done the will of God, ye might receive the promise. (Hebrews 10:36)

As Bethany laid still, the deafening scream of loneliness torments her night and day. They argued, they fought, they make up, they cuddled. And, as she stared at the blank walls of her room, she wondered what it would feel like to hear the echo of another human's voice on the other side. There is an emptiness within that she tried so hard to fill, to no avail.

The thought of approaching the age of 40 without a partner or soulmate scared her. As she pondered her future, she vented to her friends, "I have a great career. I own my home. I am financially stable. My car is paid for in full, and if I may say so myself, I am a beautiful and attractive young lady. So what's wrong with me? Why am I still single? I believe if I find a husband, I will be happy and complete."

In the summer of 2010, Bethany was invited to her first singles retreat. At first, she was a bit skeptical of course, but to her astonishment, it was more than she anticipated. "The laughter, the fun, and the decor were extraordinary. It was worth the sacrifice of my time and money," she bragged to her friends. As she strode with her single colleagues into the candle-lit dining room, they were mesmerized by the relaxed ambiance. As she took her seat, her eyes began to search the room. At a glance, her eyes collided with the most attractive gentleman, sitting alone, directly across from their table. There was instant chemistry, albeit nonverbal and surrendered to fleeting mutual stares. Like a magnet, she felt pulled towards him as he continued to stare at her intensely. With his captivating smile, it was impossible to ignore what she felt even though she tried very hard to disguise it. With a chuckle, one of the ladies said, "Hmm, someone seems a little distracted here!" Grinning from ear to ear, Bethany replied, "The Lord is my shepherd, I see what I want."

Dontae invited Bethany to dine with him at his table, and as they grew acquainted with each other, they exchanged numbers. Like a telephone operator, they were always on the phone, and, the two love birds seemed inseparable.

"I couldn't ask for a better man," she pondered. He treated her like a queen. Her needs were met even before they were verbalized. "Thank you, Jesus. I finally found the man of my dreams." She gushed in relief. During one of their dates at Donatello's Fine Italian Restaurant, they dived into a deep conversation around marriage, family, and other life topics.

After three beautiful months of dating, Bethany began to notice that the tone of Dontae's voice had shifted. His once charming tease had now surged into impatience, and he was often very curt and short with his answers whenever she tried to indulge in conversation. Nonetheless, like a speeding car, she accelerated through the flashing yellow lights, the stop signs, and the red lights and warning signs that were evident in Dontae's actions. As time progressed, Bethany's restlessness became increasingly unbearable. Everything in her began to scream, "The grass is not greener on the other side. He is not your husband. Do not marry him." The more she saw the wild side of him and heard the inner voice saying, "End the relationship," the more she ignored the voice, thinking it was just a phase and it would pass.

As disbelief warped her face, she would mutter, "This is unbelievable. I can't believe how such a handsome, caring man who portrayed such great qualities could behave in such manner. Maybe he is

Reason 27 - Not God's Will

depressed." She kept thinking, "I know when we get married, he will change." Shortly after the wedding, the rejection, cheating, abuse, and humiliation began. Her tears gushed like the falling water from Niagara Falls. Misery became her housemate and sleep was something of a treat. Regrettably, the situation got worse and plummeted downhill rather quickly. Bethany became furious and angry with God for allowing this man to mistreat her. With a voice of disappointment, she screamed, as she sobbed uncontrollably, "God! How could you do this to me? I will not go back to church! I want nothing to do with you anymore!"

Beloved, many times, we pray and badger God for something or someone to satisfy our fleshly desires, not concerned about the side effects or the consequences. We fast and pray, we kick and scream, and most of the time, we start negotiating with God to get our way. Despite God showing us the warning signs, setting off our inner alarm, and sending us messages, we purposely choose to ignore Him. We continuously rebel and disobey the unction of the Holy Spirit and are compelled to do our own thing. God repeatedly told Bethany, "Daughter, that which you desire will only cause you more pain and sorrow than satisfaction and gratification. He is not the husband I created for you. I have someone more compatible with you spiritually, physically, and emotionally but YOU MUST WAIT."

Can you identify with Bethany? Your situation may not be a marriage, but it may well have been. Perhaps, it's buying a house, a car, a business, a potential relationship, or any other major decision. I encourage you to submit your flesh under the mighty hand of God and wait for His perfect will for your life. Doing so will help you avoid picking up unwanted baggage and subjecting yourself to unnecessary spiritual warfare. My sister, my brother, wait patiently on God. You are worth the wait. When we ask outside of God's will, our hearts are filled with selfish desires. As my friend and spiritual father, Pastor Amoah stated, "Perhaps the reason we pray outside of God's will is because we are unsure of His will. Until God's sovereign will becomes our perfect wish, our prayer life will be unplugged from its very power supply."

14And this is the confidence that we have in him, that, if we ask anything according to his will, he heareth us: 15And if we know that he hear us, whatsoever we ask, we know that we have the petitions that we desired of him. (1 John 5:14-15)

Prayer

Glory, Hallelujah! You are Lord. You have risen from the dead so that I can have an extraordinary life. Glory to God, Lord, you are superb. Lord, I thank you for all that you have done for me--some of which I don't deserve. You are my rock, my sword, and my shield. Thank you for the unlimited protection. Hallelujah!

Father God, you have endured a lot of heartache from me. Lord, I blamed you for the unnecessary trouble I brought upon myself. I rebelled against your warnings and walked contrary to your perfect will for my life. Like a child, I throw temper tantrums so that I can have my way. Lord, you know me better than I know myself. You know that I am strong-willed and determined, but I realize that I am creating more harm for me than good. Father, there are times, when I know that someone or something is not right for me, but I refuse to pray for Your perfect will to be established in my life, because I know or am afraid you are going to say No, and I want it regardless. Forgive me, Lord.

Master, as of today, I cast all my cares upon you, because I know you care for me and my well-being. I surrender my will to you, and I will wait for you to bring to fruition that, which is in your perfect plan for my life. Lord, no matter how I beg and plead, kick and scream, don't allow me to have anything that will be detrimental to my spirit and physical body. Lord, if I desire something that's not in your perfect will for me, erect a mountain so vast that I can't get around it, so high that I can't get over it, and send it deep into the ground that I can't get under it, no matter how I try. May that obstacle prevent me from embarrassing myself in the future.

Reason 27 - Not God's Will

Father, even though it may be painful and disappointing not having my desire, I trust you with my heart. I know you will give me peace that passes all understanding. Lord, I will humble and submit myself under your mighty hand so that you may exalt me in due time. Hallelujah!

He has shown you, O mortal, what is good. And what does the LORD require of you? To act justly and to love mercy and to walk humbly with your God. (Micah 6:8, NIV)

"Pride is a disease of the heart. The heart, being the core of our emotions, intellect, and spiritual base, we have the choice to pursue good and evil. With pride anchored so deeply within our hearts, we tend to make choices that please the flesh, exalt us, and blow the trumpet indicating that we are here!"

Reason 28

✸✸✸

Pride

Haughty and arrogant eyes and a proud heart, The lamp of the wicked [their self-centered pride], is sin [in the eyes of God].
(Proverbs 21:4, AMP)

*I*s there anything positive about pride? Can it be good? Are there times when pride becomes necessary? We have and continue to read about pride in the newspaper, magazines, and storybooks. From the pulpit, preachers sound the alarm about it. Numerous accounts of its molestation are outlined in the Bible. We are quick to identify it in others and likewise to express our views about it, but ignore the fact that we are drowning in pride ourselves.

Let's take a look at these three definitions of pride according to the Oxford dictionary: (A) A feeling of gratification arising from association with something good; (B) Self-respect; (C) Arrogant behavior or conduct. In its simplest term, the word pride suggests being "boastful or proud of." According to these definitions, it is safe to say, pride can be good as well as bad. Good pride will allow us to acknowledge God as the ultimate source of all our blessings, success, and favor, not the resource.

Since we are talking about the reason for unanswered prayers, let us zoom in on the third definition: "Arrogant behavior or conduct." Pride does not discriminate in the persons it selects to afflict. At one time or another, we all have struggled with pride. The spirit of pride daringly seeks to take up continuous residency in the heart. If we don't pay attention, it will take us off guard with its silent crafty leaps.

As we carefully analyze this definition, we realize that pride explores the extremity of selfishness. It blocks the vision of dependency on God, causing us to think that our accomplishments are solely the result of our own effort, as it attributes the praise and glory to self.

Where does pride come from?

Pride is a disease of the heart, the heart being the core of our emotions, intellect, and spiritual base, we have the choice to pursue good and evil. With pride anchored so deeply within our hearts, we tend to make choices that please the flesh, exalt us, and blow the trumpet indicating that we are here! We seek satisfaction for and through our selfish decisions. Since this kind of pride is ego-centric behavior, no one else matters. As descendants of Adam, we have inherited his sinful nature after he disobeyed God and fell from grace in the Garden of Eden. Adam had a choice, emotions, and free will to choose but chose the wrong path.

God resists the proud

Like Adam, we too have free will to choose. Sadly, we tend to choose the wrong path because we were born in sin and shaped in iniquity. Pride is explicitly selfish. It erects an idol in the heart, which compels us to take an interest only in self. If there is any glory to be given, it goes to self; and, anything left over still goes to self. The Bible speaks about numerous people whose hearts were lifted with pride and suffered the consequences thereof. Because of pride's destructive nature, God warns us, repeatedly, to reject it so we can avoid its wrath.

Pride opens the door for its by-products, such as attributing God's glory to ourselves, unforgiveness, partiality, a judgmental spirit, hatred, revenge, hypocrisy, and self-righteousness, along with being vain and self-centered. If any of the above is left unchecked, it can lead to destruction. Pride cost satan the splendor of heaven. Pride cost Nebuchadnezzar his dignity. Pride allowed Samson to take God's glory and boasted about his victory over the Philistines: Then Samson said, *"With a donkey's jawbone I have made donkeys*

Reason 28 - Pride

of them. With a donkey's jawbone, I have killed a thousand men." (Judges 15:16 NIV) Pride made the Scribes and Pharisees exhibit an enormous degree of self-righteousness as well as jealousy, rage, and anger towards Jesus, His teachings, and miracles. *For it is not he who commends and praises himself who is approved [by God], but it is the one whom the Lord commends and praises. (2 Corinthians 10:18, AMP)*

Beloved, the spirit of pride respects no one–not age, race, gender, or the complexion of your skin. It ambushes its prey anytime, anywhere. There is absolutely nothing wrong with feeling a sense of accomplishment or satisfaction, but we should not fail to recognize God, from whom our help comes. Everyone desires an enjoyable life, but, when it creates enmity between God and us, we are, definitely, treading on dangerous ground. A prideful heart angers God, but a humble and teachable spirit move His hands towards helping us: *Has not my hand made all these things, and so they came into being? These are the ones I look on with favor: those who are humble and contrite in spirit, and who tremble at my word. (Isaiah 66:2, NIV)*

It's only through humility that our hearts can be totally devoted to God, so it's in our best interests to humble ourselves, both physically and spiritually. Submitting ourselves to the Holy Spirit is the master key to defeating the spirit of pride.

How many times have we, like Samson, boasted about our accomplishments, without honoring God, who endowed us with the strength, effort, and ability? Failing to honor and give God the glory was one of the many reasons Nebuchadnezzar went down onto his hands and feet like that of a four-footed beast, eating grass for years. *For everyone who exalts himself will be humbled [before others], and he who habitually humbles himself (keeps a realistic self-view) will be exalted." (Luke 14:11, AMP)* My friend, don't allow the Lord to humble you; instead, humble yourself, and receive more grace.

Is pride preventing you from acknowledging God as your only Source, and accepting Jesus Christ as your Lord and Savior? Is it preventing you from forgiving others or asking for forgiveness? Is pride causing you to serve your own interests instead of God's? Are you engrossed with pride to the point where revenge is all you can think about? Is pride the reason you never admit when you are wrong? Does pride cause you to refuse Godly counsel and get offended, when you are corrected? Entertaining the spirit of pride can be crippling to our growth, spiritually, and mentally.

My friend, loose yourself from the bondage of pride by drawing closer to God in daily in-depth conversations. Building a relationship with God will eradicate all spiritual toxins from your mind and body. You do not have to remain defeated by pride. Once we were born again in the family of Christ, we became more than conquerors and set FREE by the blood of Jesus Christ. Ask God to teach you how to become child-like. *Stand fast therefore in the liberty wherewith Christ hath made us free, and be not entangled again with the yoke of bondage. (Galatians 5:1)*

Prayer

Preserve me, O God, for in you I put my trust. Lord, You are my tower of strength. You are my fortress. I worship and adore you. Lord, I magnify your holy name in all the earth. Master, you are amazing and I love you.

Heavenly Father, I have sinned and continue to do so by entertaining the spirit of pride. I confess that my heart is filled with false pride. Lord, I admit that there is no humility in my action or my words. Pride has become a normal part of my life and has blinded my eyes to its destructive nature. Father, because of pride, I refuse to forgive those who hurt me. Because of pride, I've ignored salvation. Because of pride, I never apologize or admit when I am wrong. Lord, because of pride, I think that I have arrived and that I am invincible, indispensable, and untouchable.

REASON 28 - PRIDE

Lord, I repent of my sins. Please remove the sin of pride from my life, O God. Lord, I humbly ask you to deliver me from the spirit of pride and self-centeredness. Forgive me for exalting myself. Forgive my arrogance. Forgive me for mistreating and looking down on others. Lord, grant me your wisdom. I know you despise a proud look and a heart that is lifted up. Help me, O God, to be and remain humble, in Jesus' name.

Thank you, Jesus, for healing my heart and for delivering me from the spirit of pride. Spirit of pride, I renounce, denounce, and reject you from my life. You will not exalt yourself through me, anymore. My heart belongs to the Holy Spirit.

Take a seat in my heart, O God, and never leave my side. Father God, let not the foot of pride come against me, anymore, and let not the hand of the wicked remove me from my rightful place. In Jesus' precious name, I ask. Amen.

By your great wisdom and by your trade you have increased your riches and power, and your heart is proud and arrogant because of your wealth.... (Ezekiel 28:5, AMP)

"My friend, we are battling rebellious spirits all around us, whether it's in the home, workplace, church house, or the White House. It is a spirit that is not afraid to attach itself or operate through anyone. It is self-seeking, always wanting to usurp authority."

Reason 29

***

Rebellion

For rebellion [disobedience] is as the sin of witchcraft, and stubbornness is as iniquity and idolatry. Because thou hast rejected the word of the Lord, he hath also rejected thee from being King.
(1 Samuel 15:23, AMP)

Rebellion is a willful act of disobedience. With our minds already made up, we insist on going ahead with our plans no matter what the ramifications and with total disregard for instruction or direction. One who exhibits a stubborn attitude with the notion of "it's their way or no way" is held captive by the spirit of rebellion. Even though we may not verbalize it, our actions blatantly tell God, "I heard you, but I will not obey. I do not care what you want to do because I am going to please my flesh."

Together, the words rebel and rebellion are mentioned 98 times in the Bible. Most of those times refer to men rebelling against God or His instructions. Refusing to come under the authority of someone, who is set over us is straight out rebellion. God hates rebellion so much that He compares it to witchcraft. Rebellion grieves the Holy Spirit. *But they rebelled, and vexed his holy Spirit: Therefore he was turned to be their enemy, and he fought against them. (Isaiah 63:10)*

We were all born with a rebellious nature–a nature that doesn't like being told what to do by anyone. Let's take a look at some of the ways we express our rebellious attitudes. Take babies and toddlers, for instance. Even though their understanding is not fully developed, they know how to say, "No", to their parents, when they don't want to do something. Defiant teenagers rebel against the instruction of their teachers and parents. The little miss-independent wife refuses to submit to the authority of her husband. Stubborn employees disrespect the authority of their employer. Spiteful church members disobey the direction of their pastor.

All these actions show some of the many ways that we allow the spirit of rebelliousness to operate in our lives and against those whom we rebel. Not in all cases, but one of the root causes of rebellion can stem from jealousy. A few typical examples are: William thought he should have gotten the supervisor position instead of Robert, so William ignores Robert's instructions. Arlene thought she should have been ordained instead of Beverly, so Arlene decides to tune out Beverly's sermons. Brenda believed she should be earning more money than her husband so she refused to contribute to the overhead or food for the house.

An individual who manifests the spirit of rebellion may say, "I am a grown man/woman. I don't take orders from anyone," or "I can do whatever I want to. No one will control my life." God wants to help us out of this rebellious state, but we keep ignoring His commands. *Many times He would deliver them; They, however, were rebellious in their counsel, and so sank down in their iniquity. (Psalm 106:3)*

Throughout the Bible, many rebelled against God and suffered drastic consequences. The most rebellious was Lucifer before he became satan. According to Ezekiel 28:14-15, *Thou art the anointed cherub that covereth; and I have set thee so: thou wast upon the holy mountain of God; thou hast walked up and down in the midst of the stones of fire. Thou wast perfect in thy ways from the day that thou wast created, till iniquity was found in thee.*

Lucifer was a cherub, the highest in the hierarchy of angels–the honor guard, who was responsible for covering and protecting the glory of God. He was so essential and exceptional that he was covered with every precious stone: *...the sardius, topaz, and the diamond, the beryl, the onyx, and the jasper, the sapphire, the emerald, and the carbuncle,*

Reason 29 - Rebellion

and gold: the workmanship of thy tabrets and of thy pipes was prepared in thee in the day that thou wast created. (Ezekiel 28:13)

Moses disobeyed God's instruction to speak to the rock. Instead he hit the rock and missed his destiny—the Promised Land. Nebuchadnezzar rebelled against God's commandment and built idols, and for that, he was turned into a beast. The Bible recounts that he went on his hands and knees like an animal, eating grass for many years. King Saul disregarded Gods' instruction to slay all the animals and Amalekite people he conquered, and lost his throne to David. David took another man's wife and had the woman's husband killed. The first child from that union, a son, died. It doesn't matter who we are or how much He called us friends or uses us to perform never-before-seen miracles, if we rebel against His words we will be sitting in darkness according to Psalm 107:10-11: *Such as sit in darkness and in the shadow of death, being bound in affliction and iron; 11Because they rebelled against the words of God, And contemned the counsel of the most high.*

Nebuchadnezzar, David, and Saul were all kings who had done amazing things in God's name and for God's cause. Moses had been God's instrument for bringing the Israelites out of slavery in Egypt and parting the Red Sea. None of those amazing deeds left these leaders exempt from the consequences of their rebellion against God.

My friend, we are battling rebellious spirits all around us, whether it's in the home, workplace, church house, or the White House. It is a spirit that is not afraid to attach itself or operate through anyone. It is self-seeking, always wanting to usurp authority. Unless we bring the spirit of rebellion under the obedience of Christ, we won't be able to overcome or proclaim victory. Sadly, our children, the generation to come, will suffer the plight.

For though we walk in the flesh, we do not war after the flesh: For the weapons of our warfare are not carnal, but mighty through God to the pulling down of strong holds. Casting down imaginations, and every high thing that exalteth itself against the knowledge of God, and bringing into captivity every thought to the obedience of Christ; ***And having in a readiness to revenge all disobedience, when your obedience is fulfilled.*** *(2 Corinthians 10:1-6)*

Being rebellious towards God or our fellow brothers and sisters will prevent our prayers from being answered. Let us break up our fallow ground and aim to please God. Jesus is coming soon. Will you hear, "Well done" or "Depart from me I never knew you?" You have a choice. Don't get left behind.

Obey them that have the rule over you, and submit yourselves: for they watch for your souls, as they that must give account, that they may do it with joy, and not with grief: for that is unprofitable for you. (Hebrews 13:17)

Prayer

O sovereign God, I bless your name. My soul magnifies you and my soul worships you. Everything in me gives honor to you, O God. Lord, how excellent are your works. Thank you, Lord, you for continuously watching over us.

Lord, you left the courts of glory to dwell amongst a rebellious people in spite of our disgusting rebellious attitudes. Lord, I confess that I am rebellious. I have been entertaining the spirit of rebellion far too long. Father, rebelliousness has altered my divine purpose and destiny, which has hindered my success because I refused to honor those in authority. Because of pride, I refuse to listen and follow instructions from those who are set over me and watch over my soul.

My Father and my fighter, I repent of the sin of rebellion. O, mighty God, dismantle and destroy anything that was orchestrated in the spirit realm that has caused me to rebel against you and those in authority. Holy Spirit, purge my mind of this foul spirit, in Jesus' name. I strip and loose myself from under the spell of rebellion. Spirit of rebellion, I bind you in the mighty name of Jesus and cast

Reason 29 - Rebellion

you into outer darkness and dry places. I strip you of your power and your assignment for my life. Rebellion, I bring you into captivity and command you to bow to the power and name of Jesus Christ. You will not attack my family or me anymore.

The blood of Jesus Christ redeems me. I am purged and set free by the power of the Holy Ghost. Satan, I know that I am wrestling with you and your cohorts, but I cast down your works, and every high thing that exalts itself against me, my purpose, my destiny, and my relationship with God. Lord, thank you for delivering me from the spirit of rebellion. You rebellious spirit, the Lord rebukes you, and I reject and renounce you in Jesus' name. Amen.

But they rebelled against me and were not willing to listen to me; they did not cast away the detestable things of their eyes, nor did they forsake the idols of Egypt. Then I resolved to pour out my wrath on them, to accomplish my anger against them in the midst of the land of Egypt. (Ezekiel 20:8)

"Even though rejection is somewhat similar to rebellion, a person exhibiting rejection is less adamant about what they will not do versus an individual expressing rebelliousness. Whenever we are instructed by God to carry out a specific duty, He is expecting total obedience."

Reason 30

✳✳✳

Rejection

He that turneth away his ear from hearing the law, even his prayer shall be abomination. (Proverbs 28:9)

*H*ow can rejection prevent my prayers from being answered? Are you saying that, if someone has rejected me or I rejected them, my prayers will not be answered? According to the Scriptures, there are many ways in which we express rejection. However, I will share with you three simple ones that we so often overlook, which, as a result, our prayers may have gone unanswered.

Rejecting God's instruction

Even though rejection is somewhat similar to rebellion, a person exhibiting rejection is less adamant about what they will not do versus an individual expressing rebelliousness. Whenever we are instructed by God to carry out a specific duty, He is expecting total obedience. By doing otherwise, according to the leading of our flesh, we deliberately ignore His request and reject His instruction. In addition to discarding His words, we eventually made matters worse by lying about what we did. When we are caught in the lie, we make excuses and try to justify why we disobeyed God's direction. Therefore, rejecting God's instruction and His words and refusing to repent will lead to unanswered prayers. We all have sinned. *Whoever rejects Me and refuses to accept my teachings, has one who judges him; the very word that I spoke will judge and condemn him on the last day. (John 12:48, AMP)*

Rejecting Jesus Christ

What is the opposite of rejection? Yes, acceptance. You may have heard that Peter was one of Jesus' favorite disciples. He was a part of Jesus' inner circle. Peter would have done anything to protect Jesus, and even cut off another man's ear to prove his loyalty. However, there came a time when Peter's back was against the wall. He was trapped in a life or death situation. Once cornered, Peter denied knowing Jesus. Fortunately, for Peter, he repented and continued with Jesus, stronger than before.

Today, many people classify themselves as atheists; they don't believe God exists. Some who once walked with Christ but have backslidden; they crucify Him all over again. And Jesus said unto him, *"No man, having put his hand to the plough, and looking back, is fit for the kingdom of God." (James 9:62) He came to his own people, and even they rejected him. (John 1:11, NLT)*

If they shall fall away, to renew them again unto repentance; seeing they crucify to themselves the Son of God afresh, and put him to an open shame. (Hebrews 6:6)

In a nutshell, they have rejected Jesus Christ as Lord and Savior. They have rejected Him as the only way, the truth, and the life. Beloved, if we refuse to accept Jesus here on earth because He doesn't meet our intellectual standard, or because of what our friends might say or think about us, or we don't believe in Him, He will not force Himself on us. Neither will He force us to accept Him. How can we receive what we don't recognize?

But whosoever shall deny me before men, him also will I deny before my father which is in heaven. (Matthew 10:33)

Rejecting the cry of the poor

Too many times have I seen individuals who have forgotten where they came from, how they struggled in the past, and how they overcame. Some individuals enjoy looking down on another person

Reason 30 - Rejection

who is not in their league or doesn't meet their standard of life. I watched a skit where this man, Bob, took his date, Melissa, to a top-of-the-line restaurant. Throughout the evening, he bragged about his accomplishments, his many cars, and his wealth. He ordered bottles of champagne one after the other. Being so self-absorbed, he didn't realize that Melissa did not even have a sip, he drank them all by himself. When the waiter handed him the check, he chuckled and repeated, "Five hundred dollars? That's nothing. Here is your tip." He tipped the waiter one hundred dollars. A look of disgust and disappointment veiled Melissa's face throughout the entire evening.

Upon leaving the restaurant, they were approached by a young man who was selling flowers.

"Flowers for the lady?" the young man asked.

"How much?" asked Bob.

"Twenty dollars."

"Twenty dollars for this?! I will give you fifteen," Bob said.

"Sir, you see, I am just trying to buy dinner for my children and me, so I will take whatever you have," the young man said.

Bob chuckled and said, "Oh, here, since it's like that, I will give you five dollars for the bunch." Bob took the flowers from the young man and handed them to Melissa. With a look of scorn, she refused the flowers and walked away.

My point is, Bob had no problem impressing the bartender by spending six hundred dollars for champagne and tip but then robbed the young man fifteen dollars and turned a deaf ear and rejected his cry for help for him and his children. *Whoso stoppeth his ears at the cry of the poor, he also will cry himself, but shall not be heard. (Proverbs 21:13)*

My friends, be careful how you treat each other. In God's eyes, there are no celebrities. Your wealth, accolades, and accomplishments do not impress God. Your possessions won't entitle you to VIP treatment from Him. He won't ignore the less fortunate and pay more attention to you. Please, don't forget that the size of everyone's grave will be the same. We will all be squeezed into a tiny box and buried beneath the earth or our cremated remains placed in an urn.

Be sure to follow God's instructions and never reject His words. Rejecting God's unconditional love through His act of unselfish death for us means we reject Him as the supplier, the savior, the teacher, the ultimate source, and our guidance counselor. It also means that we reject prayer, worship, assembling ourselves, and we reject the command to seek God first. Listen, it is time to get ready to meet the bridegroom. There is no time for backsliding or to be playing church. Hold onto Jesus. At the end of the day, what or who you may have traded Jesus for cannot help or save you. Jesus is all you have. He is the only one who can give you everlasting joy and everlasting life.

Then the King will turn to those on the left and say, "Away with you, you cursed ones, into the eternal fire prepared for the devil and his demons. [42] For I was hungry, and you didn't feed me. I was thirsty, and you didn't give me a drink. [43] I was a stranger, and you didn't invite me into your home. I was naked, and you didn't give me clothing. I was sick and in prison, and you didn't visit me."

[44]Then they will reply, "Lord, when did we ever see you hungry or thirsty or a stranger or naked or sick or in prison, and not help you?"

[45]And he will answer, "I tell you the truth, when you refused to help the least of these my brothers and sisters, you were refusing to help me." (Matthew 25:41-45)

Do not withhold good from those to whom it is due, when it is in your power to act. [28]Do not say to your neighbor, "Come back tomorrow and I'll give it to you"— when you already have it with you. (Proverbs 3:27-28, NIV)

Reason 30 - Rejection

Prayer

Blessed be the Lord my strength, my redeemer, and my strong tower. Praise be to you, Lord, for your unconditional love towards me. Bless the Lord, oh my soul, and all that is within me, bless His holy name.

Lord, please forgive me for rejecting you, your instruction, and those who require my help. Out of ignorance, I walked in my own understanding and refused to allow you to direct my path. Lord, I have rejected your teachings, warnings, and your love. Forgive me, O mighty God. Lord, thank you for never withholding your precious love from me, your servant. Thank you, Jesus, for not rejecting me in my folly.

In the mighty name of Jesus, I break and destroy the spirit of rejection off of my life. Place the right spirit within me, O God. Lord, Cain asked you if he was his brother's keeper–implying that he is not responsible for his brother's whereabouts because he was not his brother's babysitter. But, today, I declare that I am my brothers' and sisters' keeper. Lord, I am reminded that the least I do unto others I do unto you. Help me not to turn and look the other way but make the less fortunate my priority as I do the best I can to meet their needs.

Lord, I promise, as of today, I will treat people with love and give them the respect they deserve. My Father, strengthen my discernment so I can quickly identify when someone requires help. Let me be more sensitive to their situation; and, fill me with compassion. Grant me wisdom, knowledge, and understanding to be a better ambassador for you.

Thank you, Lord, for hearing and answering prayer speedily. Amen.

Therefore, anyone who rejects this instruction does not reject a human being but God, the very God who gives you his Holy Spirit. (1 Thessalonians 4:8, NIV)

"Selfishness, like a tsunami or creeping lava from an erupting volcano, will destroy everything in its path. Individuals who manifest the spirit of selfishness tend to be unfriendly, and don't care if anyone has, as long as they have. It doesn't matter who gets as long as they get."

Reason 31

***

Selfishness

Do nothing out of selfish ambition or vain conceit. Rather, in humility value others above yourselves. (Philippians 2:3, NIV)

*N*umerous Scriptures address the topic of selfishness. They offer wisdom and warning about the danger of being self-absorbed and ignoring the needs of others. We are reminded in Proverbs 11:25 (AMP), *The generous man [is a source of blessing and] shall be prosperous and enriched, And he who waters will himself be watered [reaping the generosity he has sown].*

Some individuals strongly believe that mental and personality disorders can contribute to selfishness. It is possible. However, from my observation, selfishness is the offspring of a narcissist– always overindulging in oneself and disregarding the desires of another. I believe it can also be a learned behavior. Selfishness is a debilitating sickness of the heart and mind, which may be caused by childhood trauma, lack of money, or the fear of losing what you have. Selfishness can be triggered by greed, pride, and lust for material things. It definitely comes with readily identifiable symptoms, which are usually uttered in phrases like "me," "myself," and "I."

Selfishness can be expressed in various ways. Sometimes, even those, who mean well, behave selfishly without being conscious of what they are doing, while others know and are proud to be selfish; and they don't care. The Bible does not say seek SELF first, but seek first, the kingdom of God and His righteousness.

How does it operate?

Selfishness, like a tsunami or creeping lava from an erupting volcano, will destroy everything in its path. Individuals who manifest the spirit of selfishness tend to be unfriendly, and don't care if anyone has, as long as they have. It doesn't matter who gets as long as they get. Once they are safe, they couldn't care less about who gets hurt. They believe they are God's gift to men or women, and life revolves around them and no one else. They will do whatever it takes to achieve their goal, irrespective of who gets trampled on in the process. Selfishness can cause them to be angry and disappointed to the point where they are plunged into a deep depression when things don't go as planned or they can't have it their way. *Unfriendly people care only about themselves; they lash out at common sense. (Proverbs 18:1, NLT)* For selfish individuals, giving or sharing with others is like extracting a tooth–extremely hard to do–unless they are benefiting greatly, thrust into the spotlight, praised, and their good deed noised abroad.

Selfishness doesn't only affect the person manifesting it, but multiple people. Look at those who are selfish with their time. It is the family who usually suffers the most because a selfish person rarely has the time to call or spend time with their loved ones. They are generally too busy and pre-occupied with their own schedules to care enough to consider someone else's time. If they are married, their marriages tend to suffer and sometimes suffocate to death because one spouse never takes the feelings of the other into consideration. One spouse wants to be waited on, hand and foot. As he or she begins to turn a deaf ear and blind eye to the scream for affection and attention of the other spouse, also ignoring physical and financial needs. If children are involved, the children are sometimes forgotten or ignored.

Self-centeredness is also a manifestation of selfishness, which can make you behave as if you are the center of the universe and as if there is no one as intellectual, self-sufficient, or independent as you are. You are not bothered or moved with compassion towards another person, who may be facing hardship or challenges and you refuse to listen to anyone's concerns. Instead, you continuously interrupt the

Reason 31 - Selfishness

conversation to get your point across, ranting and raving about your needs, all that you have done, and your achievements. Selfishness will make you refuse to give a ride home to someone who is desperately in need of a car. It can make you deprive an individual of food, as well as withhold much-needed information that could enhance or elevate someone else.

Sadly, I firmly believe that selfishness can also cause individuals to entertain suicidal thoughts or commit suicide. Let me expound a little more on what I mean by this. First, if the thought of suicide is bombarding your mind right now, I feel your pain. I am so sorry. My heart goes out to you. Perhaps you feel as if suicide is the only way out of your pain and struggles, and if you entertain the concept, you will be better off than you are now.

I sincerely pray that you will think long and hard about the people, who love and care for you. Think twice about the many lives you were sent on earth to impact and make a significant difference for. I know it may not feel like you're having much of an impact now; and you don't want to deal with heartache. You may feel like no one will notice your absence or will care that you're gone, but the exact opposite is true. The people you left behind will experience great loss, pain, and heartache, because you have really impacted their lives in ways you can't see. They will face questions that will remain unanswered, for the rest of their lives, about why you killed yourself and about what they could have done to keep you with them. And, most importantly, if you kill yourself, you will never fulfill the purpose for which God chose you.

Many have attempted suicide and have come very close to dying; but, God intervened; and, they are still here today. Some have testified that they are extremely happy that the attempt was unsuccessful because of the major impact they have on their communities and the world, today. Others may not have shared their testimony, but I'm sure they would tell you they are ecstatic to be here, based on what they are doing and whose lives they are influencing.

Committing suicide is a sin that no one will get forgiveness for, simply because the person who is dead can no longer say, "Lord, have mercy" or repent. Again, nothing is worth losing your eternal life. Put the book down for a minute and begin to talk to God, in your own words; and think about your family, friends, and your purpose. Maybe, even this journey, to the brink of suicide, can be turned into a story to help talk someone else down off their ledge.

How to get rid of Selfishness

As always, you must first admit that you are selfish or have the tendency to be selfish. Then, identify and denounce all traits of selfishness within you, and acknowledge that it is a sin. Take responsibility for your selfish actions without playing the blame card. Repent. Be willing and ready to starve yourself of the attention you crave. Forgive yourself for hoarding everything for yourself; and, make amends with those, whom you deprived of assistance. Begin to see your possessions as gifts and tools from God to help those who are in need.

Again, the Bible didn't say seek SELF first, but rather, seek, first, the kingdom of God and his righteousness. *O Lord, I know that the way of man is not in himself: it is not in man that walketh to direct his steps.* (Jeremiah 10:23)

Defeating self-centeredness demands humility. You must learn to enjoy giving and sharing without expecting to be praised or shoved into the spotlight in return. If your desire is to stand out among the crowd and be impactful in the life of others, you have to portray the attribute and character of Christ. *[A]nd whoever wishes to be first and most important among you must be slave of all. For even the Son of Man did not come to be served, but to serve, and to give His life as a ransom for many.* (Mark 10:44-45)

Beloved, selfishness is not a stepping stone to happiness or success but, instead, a stumbling block to promise and purpose. If you continue to entertain the spirit of selfishness, you may experience loneliness, despair, isolation, and misery. Unless you are connected to God and start building a relationship with Jesus Christ, there will be a feeling of abandonment. You may believe that the entire world is against you, but selfishness has blinded you to the fact that the world's attitude towards you is actually the result of your attitude and, in fact, in essence self-inflicted.

Start embracing and believing the Word of God so you can expel the darkness of selfishness. Below, I share with you **26 Traits of Selfishness**. If you can identify with any of them, surrender them to God and seek His deliverance power to help you get rid of these foul spirits. Jesus loves unconditionally. It is not His will for anyone to perish but for us to change, turn away from the things that are harmful to us physically, but more so spiritually. He desires to have us reign with Him in the afterlife here, on earth. (2 Peter 3:9)

26 Traits of Selfishness

- Lack of compassion and empathy
- Quick to put others down so self can be exalted
- Manipulative and tendency to use others
- Likes to be in control
- Hates to be corrected
- Will not admit or acknowledge when they are wrong
- Enjoys looking down on others
- Fears being devalued, lacks self-worth
- Has a form of entitlement as if they deserve it all
- Expects others to go above and beyond to meet their needs
- Expects a slap on the wrist but wishes severe punishments for others for lesser or similar infractions

38 Reasons For Unanswered Prayers

- Refuses to listen to reasoning if they don't agree with it
- Intimidated by the intelligence and maturity of others
- Refuses to compromise
- Lacks vision
- Always craves attention
- Always criticizes others
- Judgmental, egotistical, narcissistic, arrogant
- Lacks humility
- Vengeful
- Enjoys taking credit for a successful group project
- Prefers to stay in the shadow when things are not working in their favor
- Refuses to take risks, runs away from hard work, but won't hesitate to criticize those who tried but didn't achieve their expected goal
- Easily angered
- Struggles with low self-esteem
- Suicide

Reason 31 - Selfishness

Prayer

Great and loving savior, you are the lover of my soul. You are awesome. You are magnificent. You are incomparable. Lord, how marvelous are the works of your hands. Hallelujah! Almighty God, thanks for loving me beyond measure.

O God, selfishness has become my norm. Lord, I think about no one else but myself. God, I am self-centered, conceited, and strive for self-gratification. I am always seeking attention. I am controlling and full of myself. Father God, I have become a lover of pleasure and self more than I am of you and people. Deliver me and forgive me for my self-absorbant attitude. Deliver me from the critical spirit. O mighty God, liberate me from the judgmental, egotistical, narcissistic, arrogant spirit that uses me daily to make others feel inferior and saddened.

Lord, I know that I deserve your wrath and fury because I disobeyed the truth of righteousness and always seek things for myself while ignoring you and the needs of my fellow brothers and sisters. Lord, I realize that the spirit of selfishness has opened the door for the spirit of jealousy, covetousness, vile practices, and pride to enter my heart; but, in the mighty name of Jesus, I seek your deliverance power to invade my heart and destroy the spirit of selfishness along with every other spirit that is attached.

Lord, I think myself better than everyone else; but, deep within, I am afraid. I have lost self-confidence. I feel intimidated and inferior. Blessed Redeemer, help my hurting heart to rest in you. Help me to trust, obey, and believe that you will meet all my needs and fulfill your promises in my life.

Spirit of selfishness, I rebuke you in the mighty name Jesus. Through the power in the blood of Jesus Christ, I command you to abandon your assignment for my life. I render you powerless. You foul spirits, I renounce, denounce, and nullify any covenant that I have made with you knowingly or unknowingly. Thank you, Jesus, for teaching me how to be humble. Thank you for showing me how to give and share from my heart without looking for anything in return. Thank you for tugging at my heart and my conscience to the point of repentance. Amen.

You shall not covet [that is, desire and seek to acquire] your neighbor's wife, nor desire your neighbor's house, his field, his male servant or his female servant, his ox or his donkey or anything that belongs to your neighbor. (Deuteronomy 5:21, AMP)

But for those who are self-seeking and do not obey the truth, but obey unrighteousness, there will be wrath and fury. (Romans 2:8)

For where jealousy and selfish ambition exist, there will be disorder and every vile practice. (James 3:16, ESV)

Don't be selfish; don't try to impress others. Be humble, thinking of others as better than yourselves. (Philippians 2:3, NLT)

For people will be lovers of self, lovers of money, proud, arrogant, abusive, disobedient to their parents, ungrateful, unholy....(2 Timothy 2:2, ESV)

Reason 31 - Selfishness

"Beloved, selfishness is not a stepping stone to happiness or success but, instead, a stumbling block to promise and purpose. If you continue to entertain the spirit of selfishness, you may experience loneliness, despair, isolation, and misery."

"As a result of seeking help from the sorcerer, you will open the doors for demonic spirits to invade your life, cripple your business, wreak havoc in your home, and cause a financial drought."

Reason 32

***

Sorcery

There shall not be found among you anyone who makes his son or his daughter pass through the fire, one who uses divination, one who practices witchcraft, or one who interprets omens, or a sorcerer. (Deuteronomy 8:10, NAS)

One definition explained that sorcery is the use of power gained from the assistance or control of evil spirits, especially for divining. What is divining? It is the use of magical powers to see into and foretell future events. This means, one has willfully given themselves over to demonic spirits to help or control their undertakings as they exercise magical powers, which they refer to as beneficial magic or black magic. The one who practices sorcery is known as a sorcerer, which can be either male or female.

Sorcerers are deceptive. They deceive individuals into believing that they can give them unlimited powers to do whatever or become whoever they would like. People who are double-minded, desperate, impatient, and wicked may seek the help of sorcerers, who convince them that they can heal and deliver the sick and demon-possessed, when in fact, they cannot.

Hear me well. Seeking the help of a sorcerer or anyone who works with demonic spirits for healing and deliverance is one of the gravest mistakes you can ever make. Upon leaving their place of practice, you will return home with unwanted companies. You will be assigned high-ranking demons to restrain the original, oppressing demons, keeping them quiet, but only for a short period. The demonic spirits will be attached to you and to whatever objects you were given–whether candles, potion, cloth, oil, statues, or the words they told you to repeat during your rituals. Oh, without a doubt, they can affect change. Things will appear calm as if their professed "healing" works; but, shortly after, situations will get worse, because it is not a part of satan's character to do good.

As a result of seeking help from the sorcerer, you will open the doors for demonic spirits to invade your life, cripple your business, wreak havoc in your home, and cause a financial drought. Satan will be entirely satisfied with the door barely ajar. Indeed, he only needs a foothold. Once he gets that foothold, he will upgrade to a stronghold, then to possession. No one can successfully bargain with the devil. You will end up on the losing side. *Can a man take fire in his bosom, and his clothes not be burned? (Proverbs 6:27)* And John 10:10 reminds us that: *"The thief (Satan) comes only to steal and kill and destroy; I have come that they may have life, and have it to the full."*

Trust God and arm yourself with His words, and you will receive the extraordinary power which was already promised to you when you accept Jesus Christ as your personal savior. Eventually, you will overpower and destroy the powers of darkness.

Choosing sorcery over God is an abomination and outright rejection of God's teachings against sorcerers and their deeds. You are inviting the wrath of God upon you and your household. *Whoever rejects Me and refuses to accept my teachings, has one who judges him; the very word that I spoke will judge and condemn him on the last day. (John 12:48, AMP)* You are telling God that you have no confidence in His help. You prefer to lend your ears and heart to the lying, unclean spirits, who tell you to hate your enemy and place a curse or hex on them contrary to God's instructions to love your enemies and pray for them. *But I say to you love [that is, unselfishly seeks the best or higher good for] your enemies and pray for those who persecute you. (Matthew 5:44, AMP)*

Reason 32 - Sorcery

The Spirit of Divination

Divination is the art or practice that seeks to foresee or foretell future events or discover hidden knowledge, usually by the interpretation of omens (sign/signal) or by the aid of supernatural powers, unusual insight, intuitive perception.

Do you know the story in Acts 16:16-22 about the young lady, who followed Paul and Silas everywhere they went to preach? While Paul was preaching, the young lady implored the audience to listen keenly to him because he was real. He was an anointed, mighty man sent by the most-high God to minister to the people so everyone could be saved and have eternal life. She was telling the truth, but Paul discerned a demonic spirit in operation. Disgusted and annoyed with her interference, he stopped and commanded the spirit to get out of her and immediately, she held her peace. This young lady operated as a soothsayer (seer, psychic, fortune-teller) who was prophesying under the influence of the spirit of divination.

The masters for whom she worked, grew angry after realizing that they were no longer benefitting from her prophecies. The men conspired against Paul and Silas, accusing them of brainwashing the residents of the communities with unlawful doctrines and teachings, causing extensive trouble in the city. They dragged Paul and Silas to the rulers and magistrates, who ripped off Paul and Silas's clothing and commanded the entire community to beat them. Paul and Silas suffered such malicious acts because they were sold out for Jesus Christ.

I mention this story to warn you to be watchful. Take heed to whom you listen and allow to speak into your life and your spirit. As you already know, sorcerers, witches, psychics, obeah men, enchanters, and other agents of satan do not seek direction from the true and living God, but demonic spirits. A spirit of divination can operate through anyone who has opened the door. Be observant and guard your mind to those who speak negative words in your spirit about your friends or family members. If you are one who quickly believes the worst, satan will use his demons or agents to feed you negative information, which may cause you to destroy your relationships, health, and mindset single-handedly. Believe it or not, demons will lie about you or about the person whom they want to pull away from you; and, when they do, it appears as if it's the truth.

Beloved, we are God's masterpiece. He created us to have a unique relationship with Him. Think of a parent who is looking forward to honoring their children's requests and meeting their needs. As a parent myself, it is such an incredible feeling when my child comes to me for advice or help, and I can honor his request. However, there were times when he sought help and advice from his friends and other people instead of coming to me. I was furious because he ended up getting the wrong information and followed the wrong path.

I can imagine how God must have felt when He saw His children running to the sorcerers for advice, wisdom, power, and control. He made it clear in James 1:5: *If any of you lacks wisdom, you should ask God, who gives generously to all without finding fault, and it will be given to you. (NIV)* He also warns us in Psalm 60:11: *…vain is the help from man.* And how can you forget Matthew 6:33: *But seek ye first the kingdom of God, and his righteousness; and all these things shall be added unto you.* And further, Psalm 1:1: *Blessed is the man that walketh not in the counsel of the ungodly, nor standeth in the way of sinners, nor sitteth in the seat of the scornful.*

In all these verses, God is saying that you will be prosperous, favored, and protected, if you refuse to take advice and instruction from the ungodly, law-breaking, disobedient people—sorcerers. As a believer in the omnipotence of God, if you continue to search the heart of God, feed on His words, apply His teachings continuously, you will grow spiritually and physically stronger each day. The Word of God will water you consistently. Before you know it, the sorcerers, witches, warlocks, obeah man, and other satan agents will be coming to you for their healing and deliverance.

Reason 32 - Sorcery

Nothing is absolute. Being a loyal, dedicated born-again Christian doesn't negate the fact that you will encounter troubles and challenges along your journey. Remember, we all have a common enemy, who is consistently fighting to keep us in lack, frustrated, and confused so we can give up on God and turn to him, satan. Psalm 1:3 states that the leaves of the tree will not wither. My interpretation: If you will be like the tree planted by the rivers of water and you will bear fruit in your season and your branches will not wither, meaning that regardless of what the enemy tries to do and irrespective of the setbacks, whatever you put your hands to will prosper. When you adhere to God's instructions amidst any virus or chaotic situation, His protection is guaranteed. You don't have to be a casualty of any virus, ill health, failed marriage, unsuccessful business, or financial lack.

God instructed the Israelites to put the blood over their doorpost and wherever He would see the blood, He would pass over. Likewise, everything you do or will be a part of will be covered and protected by the powers of God, despite the many evil counsels taken against you. In Psalm 1:4, God says that the ungodly are like the chaff (unusable bits or trash) which the wind blows away. He is telling you that you should not take advice from the wicked because they are unstable, without value. Ouch! Therefore, the wicked will not go unpunished, and those who practice sin continuously have no place in eternal life with those individuals who lived right, did right, talked right. Again, God knows your innermost thoughts. Please read Psalm one in its entirety. *The blood shall be a sign for you on [the doorposts of] the houses where you live; when I see the blood, I shall pass over you, and no affliction shall happen to you to destroy you when I strike the land of Egypt. (Exodus 12:13, AMP)*

Therefore shall evil come upon thee; thou shalt not know when it riseth: and mischief shall fall upon thee; thou shalt not able to put it off: and desolation shall come upon thee suddenly, which thou shalt not now. [12]*Stand now with thy enchantments, and with the multitude of thy sorceries, wherein thou hast laboured from thy youth; if so be thou shalt be able to profit, if so be thou mayest prevail. ¹³Thou art wearied in the multitude of thy counsels. Let now the astrologers, the stargazers, the monthly prognosticators, stand up, and save thee from these things that shall come upon thee. (Isaiah 47:11-13)*

And never again shall the light of a lamp shine in you, and the voice of bridegroom and bride shall never be heard in you again; for your businessmen were the great and prominent men of the earth, and by your magic spells (sorcery) and poisonous charm all nations were led astray (seduced and deluded). (Revelation 8:23, AMP)

Prayer

Holy Spirit, you are welcome in my life. You are an amazing God. You are the lover of my soul. Precious Lord, take my hand and lead me into the path of righteousness. Hallelujah! Lord, you have shown me your unconditional love continuously despite my sinful deeds. I love you, Lord.

Lord, I have sinned against you. I have turned away from your instruction and embraced the teachings of demons and devils. Lord, I have opened my spirit to sorcery and the spirit of divination, please forgive me. Almighty God, your Word says these things should not be named among me. In the name of Jesus, I renounce and reject all spirits attached to sorcery. I disconnect myself from any covenant or allegiance made to satan and his demons through sorcery. In the mighty name of Jesus, I render all demonic activities through sorcery to be powerless, null, and void. I cast you into outer darkness. Deliver me and cleanse me thoroughly from all evil attachment and engagement, in Jesus' mighty name. Stretch forth your mighty hands and save me, O God, from this death trap. Save me from the darkness that enthralls my existence.

Thank you, Father God, for delivering me from sorcery. I cleanse my hands and my heart from such corruption, in Jesus' name. Help me not to take counsel or advice from the ungodly. May I not stand in the

Reason 32 - Sorcery

way of those sinners nor sit in their congregation. Help me, O God, to delight myself in you and meditate upon your Words day and night. God, I will allow your Words to water my soul continuously. Lord, like a tree planted by the rivers of water, so will I be strengthened in you. Keep me in the stream of that continuous flow. Let nothing uproot me, O God, so that whatever I put my hand to will prosper. I will bear unlimited fruit and flourish in my season. I shall not wither, my business will not crumble, my health will not fail, my finances will not disappear, and my Godly relationships will not be cut off. In Jesus' mighty name. Amen

Be sober, be vigilant; because your adversary the devil, as a roaring lion, walketh about, seeking whom he may devour. (1 Peter 5:8)

"There are many things and ways in which we steal and ignore the ramifications, which are endless. Saints of God, it's not only those who break into banks, people's homes, or hold someone at gunpoint who will be facing God's judgment, if they don't repent..."

Reason 33

***

Stealing

²"If anyone sins and is unfaithful to the LORD by deceiving a neighbor about something entrusted to them or left in their care or about something stolen, or if they cheat their neighbor,

³or if they find lost property and lie about it, or if they swear falsely about any such sin that people may commit— ⁴when they sin in any of these ways and realize their guilt, they must return what they have stolen or taken by extortion, or what was entrusted to them, or the lost property they found. (Leviticus 2:2-4, NIV)

𝒲e all know that stealing will prevent our prayers from being answered. Now, allow me to jog your recollection to moments, when you may have stolen, either with or without realizing it, and have failed to ask for forgiveness. I am sure what I am about to mention may seem trivial to you, but do you think stealing is nothing in the eyes of God? He didn't put a value, a size, or an amount on sin. No matter how minute, sin is still a sin in his eyes.

I was engaged in a casual conversation with a husband and wife, Ainsworth and Marlene, about how challenging it is to find good and honest workers. At one point, Ainsworth stated, "It is very rare to find a worker who doesn't steal. As a matter of fact, I had a boss who told me not to work for a company if there is nothing there to steal."

For a moment, I sat there speechless after hearing such a ridiculous statement.

"Why would your boss say such craziness?" I asked.

"My boss said, 'If an employee is being paid $400 per week, that's only a fraction of what he or she could have gotten, so when employees steal from the company they are being compensated for what they should have been paid in the first place. See, most companies underpay their workers because they know that some of them are dishonest and have sticky fingers," Ainsworth explained.

"Yes, it's true," Marlene affirmed. "Being the housekeeping supervisor for many hotels, I have witnessed many workers stealing various items from the hotel rooms."

"Like what?" I asked. She began to list the items: towels, irons/ironing boards, telephones, can openers, televisions, sheets, even mattresses, and the list continues.

I couldn't believe what I was hearing. Unashamedly, some individuals stole things that they didn't even need and bragged about hoarding them in their back yard, garage, or on the porch. Some also expressed how much they look forward to going to work because of what they can steal. When asked why he or she does it, the individual, who is stealing from his or her workplace, will respond, "The company has money. They can afford it, and it will not be missed."

Here is another overlooked area—employees being on their personal phones during working hours. Being on your personal phone for an extensive amount of time talking to your friends, family, or conducting other business is actually stealing your boss' time? These conversations are happening within the hours that you will write down on your timesheet as proof that you worked your full seven hours after your hour-long lunch break.

My friend, what have you taken and thought that it wouldn't be missed and you wouldn't be found out, and, hence didn't think to repent? Did you know that using your neighbor's wifi continuously to avoid being billed by the cable company is stealing? Have you ever taken paper towels, garbage bags, toilet paper, first aid, or office supplies from your workplace for personal use at home? How about something as small and contrite as staples or whiteout? If you did not ask for those items, this is considered stealing. The company did not purchase them with you in mind.

What about watching the cashier not cash-in an item while scanning your merchandise, and you took it and said nothing? Have you ever been given excess money by the bank teller or the cashier at the store and refuse to return it? Remember the children you lied about when filing your taxes? Because they were on it, you received an extra $6,000-$8,000 but gave the parent of the child only $500. That is stealing.

The next one I am about to mention may seem like the norm because it has been done so frequently by many, undisturbed; and, you believe it's no big deal. Going to the movie theatre, recording the movie from the screen, then burning the movie onto DVD and reselling it for a profit. Or duplicating musical CDs for profit (bootlegging). That is stealing. *Food gained dishonestly tastes sweet to a person, but afterwards, his mouth will be filled with gravel. (Proverbs 20:17, GWT)*

There are many things and ways in which we steal and ignore the ramifications, which are endless. Saints of God, it's not only those who break into banks, people's homes, or hold someone at gunpoint who will be facing God's judgment if they don't repent. Those of us who participate in the above-mentioned acts will also be damned, If we refuse to repent. Let us pay close attention to the small things in which we indulge ourselves and see as no big deal. God's eyes are watching our every move and listening to every word, which comes out of our mouth. Let us search ourselves for bad, embarrassing habits that could cost us our salvation.

[A]nd do not go on presenting the members of your body to sin as instruments of unrighteousness; but present yourselves to God as those alive from the dead, and your members as instruments of righteousness to God. (Romans 6:13, NAS)

Prayer

Heavenly Father, I have yielded my mind and hands to satan, permitting him to manipulate me into working for him. As of today, Lord Jesus, I surrender and rededicate my mind and my hands to you. Lord, wash me, cleanse me, and purge me from my iniquities and trespasses. Hear my cry for mercy, O Lord, and deliver me from every immoral, harmful, and illegal thought flooding my mind right now. Lord, please forgive me for embarrassing you and the Holy Ghost. Forgive me for being malicious, greedy, and envious of other people's possessions to the point where I resort to stealing. Father, I regret allowing myself to be a tool in the hand of satan.

Lord, I knowingly and purposely deprived others of their possessions to satisfy my crooked desires. Forgive me, O God. I repent from the sin of stealing. I know your eyes are watching me wherever I go and whatever I do. Nothing that I have done is hidden from you. Thank you, Lord, for not giving up on me. Thank you for convicting me and tugging on my conscience. O God, I realize that I was only thinking about myself and what I needed. My selfish desires blinded my eyes to the feelings of other individuals. O God, my disgusting action spoke aloud that I did not care if anyone was hurt through my envious conniving ways.

God, deliver me from this heartlessness and create in me a clean heart and the right spirit. Lord teach me to be satisfied with what you allow me to have. Through the power of the Holy Ghost, who will enable me, I will not steal anymore. In Jesus' name. Amen.

Let him that stole steal no more: but rather let him labor, working with his hands the thing which is good, that he may have to give to him that needeth. (Ephesians 4:2)

Reason 33 - Stealing

"What a brutish master sin is, taking the joy from one's life, stealing money and health, giving promise of tomorrow's pleasures, and finally leading one onto the rotten planking that overlies the mouth of the pit."

-Jim Elliot

"Forgiveness works both ways. If you have been crying out relentlessly for God to forgive you, it means that you are aware of the importance of forgiveness. So why are you hesitant to forgive the individual or individuals whom you resent and hold hostage?"

Reason 34

✶✶✶

Unforgiveness

14For if ye forgive men their trespasses, your heavenly Father will also forgive you: 15But if he forgive not men their trespasses, neither will your Father forgive your trespasses.

(Matthew 6:14-15)

I heard a story about an older man who testified of his encounter with death and God. "Shortly after my seventy days fasting ended, my time on earth was expired. I met with God, who told me that I was not qualified for eternal life in heaven because I had unforgiveness in my heart against my primary school teacher."

Wow! A sixty-or-more-year-old root of bitterness that he held onto without addressing or resolving it. His flesh had swept it under the rug, so to speak. I assume, over the years, he may have told himself that he didn't remember the incident with his teacher until someone mentioned the teacher's name. Perhaps, he consoled himself by saying that he wasn't hurting--that it was okay, and he had actually forgiven the teacher. The mouth says one thing, but the heart says another. God reads the intent of our hearts. If I compared unforgiveness to a disease, it would be cancer. Unforgiveness, like cancer, can metastasize or spread throughout the entire body undetected for a long time while the body is still functioning. However, there will come a time when the body can no longer withstand the deadly grip.

Some offenses are worthy of jail or prison time or even the death penalty. It is never okay for anyone to inflict physical, emotional, verbal, psychological, or spiritual pain on another individual. Such behavior is unacceptable and inexcusable. Perhaps, you have encountered situations that hurt you deeply, and it feels as if there is no way you can forget or forgive this person. If you say forgiveness is hard, I am in total agreement with you; and, I sympathize with you. For your peace of mind and freedom, I encourage you to seek God's intervention to help you slay this giant. It may be a mountain that you cannot tackle by yourself; but, nothing is impossible with Him.

The destructive nature of unforgiveness will block your prayers from being answered. It can erase your name from the Lamb's book of life, invite all sorts of trouble into your life, and attract demonic spirits to afflict, inflict, and torment your health, marriage, finances, work/career, home-life, and mind. If you, willfully, harbor unforgiveness in your heart and, verbally, tell yourself that you will have nothing to do with the person or persons who hurt you, unfortunately, your fasting, prayers, and sacrifices will be in vain. I am sure you don't want to waste your time and effort. Unforgiveness is a one-way ticket to eternal damnation (Hell). Is that the path you would like to take? Perhaps you are excusing your unforgiveness saying that I have no clue what the individual has done or how bad the offense was. If that is true, you are absolutely right. I don't know; and, I can't begin to imagine; but, I would like to remind you that forgiveness is one of the prerequisites to make heaven your final destination.

Then came Peter to him, and said, Lord, how oft shall my brother sin against me, and I forgive him? till seven times? [22]Jesus saith unto him, I say not unto thee, until seven times: but, until seventy times seven. (Matthew 18:21-22) (unlimitedly; as often as you need to)

Then his lord, after that he had called him, said unto him, "O thou wicked servant, I forgave thee all that debt, because thou desiredst me: [33]Shouldest not thou also have had compassion on thy fellowservant, even as I had pity on thee? [34]And his lord was wroth, and delivered him to the tormentors, till he should pay all that was due unto him. (Matthew 18:35)

Reason 34 - Unforgiveness

This story is about a servant who owed his master 10,000 talents and begged his master to have patience and forgive him. The master forgave him. A few hours later, the same servant saw a fellow-servant who owed him 300 talents. He grabbed him by the throat and demanded his 300 talents. Unable to pay at that time, the fellow-servant fell on his knees and begged him for patience and forgiveness; but, he refused to forgive his fellow-servant and threw him into prison. I encourage you to read the entire story found in Matthew 18:23-35.

When you deliberately decide not to forgive, you are presumptuously saying, "I prefer to live in this sin. I do not care if I go to Hell or not." Consequently, you have relinquished your rights to claim that you are a born-again Christian. Forgiveness works both ways. If you have been crying out relentlessly for God to forgive you, it means that you are aware of the importance of forgiveness. So why are you hesitant to forgive the individual or individuals whom you resent and hold hostage? How many times have you gone to God asking forgiveness for the same thing? Perhaps that offense which you refuse to forgive was simple he said/she said, that may have occurred only once, years ago, yet still, you refuse to forgive?

According to the word of God, the gifts He has given you and the calling to which He's called you are without repentance. So, even though you might be embracing the spirit of unforgiveness, God will still allow you to use your gift to heal the sick, raise the dead, cast out demons, prophesy accurately, speak in tongues, and win millions of souls. However, at the end of your life when you stand before Him, there will be no preferential treatment for anyone who breaks the law of God. He will not compromise or go against His words. Unless you sincerely repent and forgive yourself and the individuals who have hurt you from your heart, you may never get to your promised land. Paul knew that it is possible to use his gifts to win souls for Christ and still be lost, hence he penned this scripture verse. *But I keep under my body and bring it into subjection: lest that by any means, when I have preached to others, I myself should be a castaway. (1 Corinthians 9:27)*

How will you know if you are still carrying the heavy burden of unforgiveness? Many times we say we forgive, but that may be so far from the truth. Our lips say what the outcome should be, but our hearts express the present situation. Remember, God reads the intent of the heart. Out of sight, out of mind, right? It must have been a fantastic feeling in not hearing nor seeing the one who caused you pain. Hence, you believe that you have forgiven that individual. However, the real test comes when you are both sharing the same space or you hear the individual's voice or name. At that moment, if you started to feel the pain or hurt again as if it's a fresh wound, unforgiveness is present. If you are suddenly engulfed with disgust, anger, resentment, or coldness, that is a sign that you have not forgiven that individual. If you think that your evening is ruined and leaving their presence would make you feel better, you are definitely harboring unforgiveness. If there's a tension or awkwardness speaking to the individual, unforgiveness is present.

Did you know that when you refuse to forgive, you are the one being hurt the most? Did you know that unforgiveness can cause significant damage to your organs (heart, lungs, kidneys, liver, and brain) and be the root cause for many illnesses such as high blood pressure, cancer, diabetes, and much more? By carrying around the spirit of unforgiveness, you are holding yourself hostage and in bondage while the individual is free to sleep, be healthy, and live comfortably in peace.

For your salvation's sake, restore your fear and obedience to the voice of God. Forgiveness does not mean you forget the circumstances surrounding your hurt or even place yourself in the same position to get hurt again. It just means that, as your heavenly Father forgave you of many indiscretions, so you need to follow His example and forgive your earthly brothers and sisters. You may have heard the saying unforgiveness is like drinking poison and waiting for the person who offends you to die. The person who holds on to the spirit of unforgiveness will die twice, physically, and spiritually.

Reason 34 - Unforgiveness

Forgiveness doesn't mean that you are weak. It doesn't mean that what happened to you is insignificant. It doesn't mean that you deny the hurt. It doesn't mean that you are ignorant to satan's devices, and leaving open doors for his agents to re-enter. Forgiveness means that you respect and fear God so much that you are willing to obey His words over satan's lies. Forgiveness means exhibiting spiritual maturity, morality, and choosing to do the right thing even when you were wronged. That is taking the high road. You are no longer allowing satan to keep any secret for you or have access to your life through sin.

Matthew 5:43-44 says, Ye have heard that it hath been said, Thou shalt love thy neighbour, and hate thine enemy. But I say unto you, Love your enemies, bless them that curse you, do good to them that hate you, and pray for them which despitefully use you, and persecute you.

How do you let go of unforgiveness and replace it with forgiveness? First and foremost, it is not easy. Forgiveness is a choice. You must desire emotional freedom from the baggage of unforgiveness, the pain, hurt, and the feeling of being disenfranchised. Once you desire that change, seek to identify the areas or the things that caused you hurt and discomfort. Though it may be painful, the process of being free also requires identifying and acknowledging the perpetrator or culprit. Through the eyes and heart of God, begin to see the individuals as victims of satan, see them as someone who was set up, and used to carry out a wicked act against their will. See them as a helpless animal being threatened and led to the slaughter and needing to be delivered from the snare of the enemy. This might be a bit awkward; but, pray for the healing of their heart, the deliverance of their soul from satan, also, pray for their salvation. Your freedom may not be instant; but, if you continue to pray for them, over time, you will have a different and more positive outlook on the situation. You may eventually begin to feel sympathy towards them.

If you feel the need for an outlet and someone to speak to about your struggles, you may also consider speaking to a psychologist or a counselor who may help you to identify the depth of the hurt. They can also help you to acknowledge any other areas in your life that have been affected as a result of the trauma you suffered. Be humble and teachable and prepare to do the work to release unforgiveness.

Please answer the following questions honestly.

> What is your reason for not forgiving?
>
> What does it mean to be a born-again Christian?
>
> What does salvation mean to you?
>
> How is your sin of unforgiveness different from the individual who kills or works witchcraft?
>
> For someone who professes Christianity, is it okay to have hatred, resentment, unforgiveness, bitterness, and a grudge against another sister or brother?
>
> If you should die now, where would you spend eternity? Would you hear "well done" or "depart for me?"
>
> Forgive quickly so that your healing process and freedom can begin.

Prayer

Lord, do not rebuke me in your anger or discipline me in your wrath. Have mercy on me, O God, for I am weak. Lord, heal my heart. Erase every scar, pain, and hurt it has suffered. Lord, you know how long I have been harboring the spirit of unforgiveness. You know how long I have been carrying around this unbearable burden; and, you know how unhappy I have been. Lord, it has been a long time since I have not enjoyed you or my Christian life.

Father God, I am angry. I am bitter. I am hateful; and, I am embarrassed to say that I am a born-again Christian knowing that I am continuously living in sin. Forgive me, O mighty God. My soul

Reason 34 - Unforgiveness

is in deep anguish because I presumptuously disobeyed you and left open doors for the affliction of the enemy. I repent of the sin of unforgiveness right now, in Jesus' name. Hallelujah.

Father God, reveal to me the individual or individuals whom I am holding hostage in my heart. Lord, I am willing and ready to release my burden to you. I am prepared to let go of the hurt and bitterness. I am ready to forgive those who have caused me pain. I am ready to forgive. Lord, I am tired of living in this bondage. Lord God, as I am seeking your forgiveness, grant me the strength and spirit of mercy towards those you hurt me.

Too much of my fasting and prayers have gone unanswered. I have wasted many precious years not being connected to you. Lord, deliver me from this ugly deforming spirit of unforgiveness and uproot every seed and root of bitterness within me, O God. Lord, I release my mind, body, and soul from the spirit of unforgiveness right now.

Spirit of unforgiveness, I rebuke you, I reject you, and I renounce you in the mighty name of Jesus Christ. I cast you into outer darkness and dry places. May the fire of God consume you, in Jesus' name. Thank you, Lord, for setting me free, so I can reign with you throughout eternity and hear "Well done, my good and faithful servant." Thank you, Jesus.

We know that we have passed from death unto life, because we love the brethren. He that loveth not his brother abideth in death. 15 Whosoever hateth his brother is a murderer: and ye know that no murderer hath eternal life abiding in him. (1 John 3:14-15)

"Beloved, how do you cope with lack? Do you have a grateful or an ungrateful heart? Are you the kind of person who forgets what God or others have done for you?"

Reason 35

✱✱✱

Ungratefulness

For although they knew God, they neither glorified him as God nor gave thanks to him, but their thinking became futile and their foolish hearts were darkened. (Romans 1:21, NIV)

Are you familiar with the quote, "ungratefulness is worse than the sin of witchcraft?" Let's think about that. Expressing ingratitude is a form of rebellion, rejection, and despising of the Word of God. Throughout the Bible, it is evident that the human race is the most ungrateful species on the planet. No matter what is done or given to us, it's as if we have never received anything, and no one has ever lifted a finger to assist us in times of need.

It's been said that an ungrateful heart is fertile ground for sin. True indeed. When we rebel or reject the teachings or instructions of God's Word, we are disobedient.

Today is Wednesday, December 25, 2019, what a day to be writing this chapter. First and foremost, I woke up this morning in my right mind, mobility in all my limbs, a roof over my head, and the necessities. In a nutshell, I am most thankful and I am rejoicing for being alive. In spite of not having two dollars to rub against each other–at home, in the bank, or under the mattress–my mind is in such an unexplainable peace. I started out saying all that I have to show you that even though I don't have what I want, God kept His end of the bargain, which is supplying my needs as He promised.

Guess what I did today? At approximately 7:30 am, a young lady came by and joined me in fasting and prayer. We read the Word, prayed, praised, and worshipped. We basked in the presence of God until 11:45 am. I did not allow my circumstances to stop my worship or hinder my spiritual blessing and breakthrough.

I have seen the miraculous hand of God move in my life and in my circumstances too many times to count. Two weeks ago, during my morning worship, while listening to some worship songs on YouTube, my internet and television were disconnected. I started laughing, then I continued with my praise and worship. I began to pray. I said, "God if you never give me another dime or do anything else for me, I will always love you. I will continue to adore and worship you. You are awesome. You are the lover of my soul. You are my provider. Lord, when I look back over my life and see all that you have given me and done for me, I will be forever grateful and indebted to you. Thank you, Lord."

I went on for an hour just praying thanksgiving prayers sincerely from the depth of my soul.

On Monday, 12/23/19, my auto insurance company called and told me that my policy would be canceled on 12/25/19. Sitting in my email, is a disconnection notice from the light and power company, while the telephone is ringing off the hook by other bill collectors. Beloved, I am not saddened, I am not depressed; and, I am not worrying. If I cannot fix my situation, I refuse to do or entertain any of the above. Wallowing in self-pity and worrying would be a lack of faith, trust, and belief in the word and promises of God. Despite my present situation, I do not consider myself poor, struggling, suffering, or facing hardship; and, I certainly don't feel that way.

For me, it would be more than ungrateful to get mad or blame God for the challenges I face, considering that the fingers, the brain, the breath, and the mind that I am using right now are gifts from Him. I don't want to be happy and bubbly only when all is well. I chose to host a worship party instead of a pity party because I know this phase will never last forever; and, even if it does, I will say like Job, "Naked I came in this world and naked I will return." I will continue

Reason 35 - Ungratefulness

to adore God. I chose to activate my faith as I waited patiently. My son has no clue about my current situation. One of my five sisters has a slight idea but doesn't know the in-depth story. I may not have what I WANT but rest assured, I have all I NEED.

Why didn't I tell anyone? I don't want to be pitied. I don't want anyone to feel obligated to run to my rescue; and, most importantly, I am eager to prove God's Words to be true, for myself, so that I could have my own testimony. I prefer to go through the process without anyone interfering with what God is trying to accomplish in me during my wilderness experience.

Even though God can use others as an instrument of blessings in my circumstances, I must acknowledge that the assistance comes from God so that I won't develop a dependency on anyone but Him. It is a possibility that God is taking me through periods of drought to develop my character, integrity, trust, faith, and total dependency on Him. If friends or family keep running to my rescue each time I am faced with challenges, it can interfere with God's plan for my life. Gold has to go through a fiery process of purification before it can be called PURE gold.

Beloved, how do you cope with lack? Do you have a grateful or an ungrateful heart? Are you the kind of person who forgets what God or others have done for you? Are you the one who believes that your spouse should be doing for you continuously, and if he or she fails to meet one need, he or she is the worst thing on the planet? Are you the one who thinks that no matter what you were given, you should have gotten more? When an individual goes beyond the call of duty for you, do you view their act of kindness as insignificant? Are you one who loves and praises God when all is well, but turn on Him when there are bumps and ditches in the road? Are you the one who is quick to criticize and find fault with what's being done before you say thank you?

Perhaps you may have forgotten to say "Thank you, Lord" when everything is in place during the years of receiving a paycheck or a clean bill of health. Perhaps you never once stopped to give thanks to God for His provision. Now that you are forced to stop working, whether, through illness or natural disaster, which results in a loss of your paycheck, you realize how you have been taking God's generous supplies for granted.

My friend, whenever you are going through your drought or wilderness experience, don't withhold your praise and worship, don't resent God, don't get mad at Him, and don't entertain the spirit of suicide, depression, or doubt. It is only a test, and each time you fail it, you have to retake it. You must believe that God did not bring you this far to leave you or forsake you. You must understand that this phase shall pass. God is just showing off with you as He did with Job. You must believe that He is stretching you to refill you with an abundance of blessings. It is a possibility that God is teaching you how to be a better manager and steward over your possessions. Yes, you have been praying relentlessly, and it seems as if God is nowhere to be found. Believing is a crucial component in your survival. You must believe that He will fulfill His promise to you, maybe not when you think you deserve it, but in His time.

When you are tempted to express unthankfulness, remember the many times God provided unexpectedly for you. Remember when He delivered you from your lion's den and your fiery furnace and your Pharaoh. As the song says, "You may not know how or you may not know when, but He will do it again." No one cannot bully God into acting now. His timing is always perfect. My friend, don't give up on Him and don't go back to Egypt for help. Perhaps you have said that you are waiting on God but in reality, He is waiting on you to step out in faith. Stepping out by faith doesn't mean walking out of God's perfect will to please the desire of the flesh. Listen keenly to God's instructions, and be sure you are moving under the unction of the Holy Spirit. Don't take matters into your own hands.

Nine of the ten lepers who were cleansed by Jesus demonstrated ungrateful behavior after they were healed from their leprosy. Only the Samaritan returned to say thanks. *And Jesus answering said,*

Reason 35 - Ungratefulness

"Were there not ten cleansed? But where [are] the nine? There are not found that returned to give glory to God, save this stranger. Luke 17:17-18

As the children of Israel journeyed to a fruitful and better place, away from the 430 years of bondage and slavery in Egypt, I can imagine the enthusiasm they felt, knowing that they are finally free from punishment and hardship. However, when things slightly shifted in a direction that didn't please them, they began to murmur, complain, and curse God and Moses, wishing to die. (Numbers 14:2)

After Jesus raised Lazarus from the dead, many went to see Jesus not to say thank you, but to put Lazarus back to death. (John 12:9-11)

During Jesus' ministry, no matter who was healed, raised from the dead, or delivered from demonic possession, there was always someone who expressed ungratefulness instead of being thankful that someone in their midst had the power to heal and deliver their loved ones should they fall ill. Instead, they criticized and sought to kill Him.

Prayer

Dear God, unto you, I lift my soul. Teach me your ways, O God, and show me your path. You are my glory and the lifter of my head. O God of my righteousness, you comforted me when I was in distress. Have mercy upon me, and hear my prayer.

Please forgive me for expressing ungratefulness towards you and all that you have done for me. Deliver me from the sin of ungratefulness, O God, and help me to not entertain it anymore. Lord, my ungrateful attitude has blinded my eyes to your sincere love and the prompting of the Holy Spirit.

In the name of Jesus, I renounce and reject the spirit of ungratefulness. Spirit of ungratefulness, you shall not dictate my actions anymore. I bind you in the name of Jesus and cast you into outer darkness and dry places. Father, please endow me with the spirit of praise and thankfulness. Remove my ungrateful heart and replace it with a thankful heart. Lord, I would like to be as appreciative as Daniel, grateful as David, and loyal as Shadrach, Meshach, and Abednego. Lord, I apologize for taking your kindness and the kindness of others for granted. Forgive me, O God.

Amen.

[16]*Rejoice always,* [17]*pray without ceasing,* [18]*in everything give thanks; for this is the will of God in Christ Jesus for you. (1 Thessalonians 5:16-18)*

Reason 35 - Ungratefulness

"Learn to appreciate what you HAVE before time makes you appreciate what you HAD."

-Author unknown

"A complaining tongue reveals an ungrateful heart."

-William Arthur Ward

"Wavering is proof that you don't believe God or His abilities to help you through life's journey; and, you don't believe what His Word says about you."

Reason 36

***

Wavering

> *⁶But let him ask in faith, nothing wavering. For he that wavereth is like a wave of the sea driven with the wind and tossed. ⁷For let not that man think that he will receive anything of the Lord.*
> (James 1:6-7)

When we pray, we expect a positive response from our heavenly father, that He'll grant us what we ask for. But instead, we may hear, "no", "wait", or just plain silence. Regardless of what we requested, if we don't receive it right away or within what we think is a reasonable time, we are left with a feeling of disappointment and sometimes try to blame God. Have you ever prayed tirelessly about a situation, but it remains the same or grows worse? Can you recall how long you've been praying for that job, that child, that spouse, or that financial breakthrough? Still, there is no favorable answer and no visible progress or indication of improvement or even guidance in a particular situation. Could it be that we are praying wrongly or growing impatient and weary? Or we are wavering?

Wavering signifies uncertainty, lack of faith, disloyalty, instability, and double-mindedness. A person who wavers tends to be confused and rarely makes conscious decisions. They will take one step forward and ten steps backward because wavering has paved the way for fear, doubt, and unbelief to attack. Do not be mistaken and believe that when you waver, you are being humble. In fact, you are dishonoring and discrediting God.

A wavering person rarely gets anything done or accomplishes their goals because they kept going back and forth with decision making.

They place one hand in God's hand and the other in the world. Wavering is a lack of confidence and trust in God. As children of God, you must put the Word of God to the test. If you continue to express incompetence, like the man who hid his one talent, you risk losing what you already have. At some point in your life, you have to stop drinking milk and start eating solid food so you can enjoy your Christian walk with God.

Wavering is proof that you don't believe God or His abilities to help you through life's journey; and, you don't believe what His Word says about you.

Wavering and double-mindedness show that you fail to believe that you are more than a conqueror. You don't believe that you can speak to the obstacles in your life and they will disappear. You refuse to believe that God surrounds you as the mountain surrounds Jerusalem. You don't believe that you have the power and the anointing to trample snakes, dragons, lions, and adders. You don't believe that no weapon formed against you can never hurt you. You don't believe that you have unlimited power in your hands to break every bow of steel asunder and pull down strongholds. You don't believe that God has actually given you the strength to do anything you set your mind to do.

Who you are and what you can do is unlimited; but, you may never find out if you continue to waver and walk in double-mindedness. It's unlikely you will get the desires of your heart or your prayers answered if you keep taking your problems back after giving them to God before He even starts working on them. As James rightly stated, don't expect to get anything if you are not able to make up your mind. God promises overflow. Don't allow it to miss you.

Overcoming wavering and double-mindedness is possible. Find someone to whom you are accountable–someone, who will make sure you do what needs to be done promptly. Set reachable goals to achieve and complete that which you have started and reward yourself for completing them. If you are eagerly anticipating an

Reason 36 - Wavering

answer, which makes you a bit anxious, create some distractions that will take your mind off that which you await. Have you ever jokingly spoken about a matter, and in record time, it came to pass? Your words are powerful, and things tend to come through faster when we speak it, forget it, and don't interfere. Solomon told us in Proverbs 18:21 that death and life lie in the power of the tongue.

Most importantly, you need to understand that God's ways are higher than ours. His reasons, purpose, approach, and techniques are beyond our comprehension. Trust Him to do His work without interfering.

Prayer

Promise keeping God, you are Alpha and Omega, and I worship you, O God. You are awesome in my life, almighty God. You are a wonder. You are magnificent. You are superb. Hallelujah! O mighty God, I give you all the glory, the honor, and the praise. Lord, despite my wavering, you have stood by me. You provided for me; and, you protected me. Hallelujah! Thank you, Jesus, for never leaving or forsaking me. Thank you, Lord. Hallelujah!

Father God, my mind is bombarded with fear, doubt, and unbelief, which causes me to be unstable in my decisions. Lord, I am reminded in your Word that it is impossible to please you without faith. Lord, I realize that my unnecessary wavering prevented my prayers from being answered. So, Lord Jesus, deliver me from the spirit of double-mindedness. Enable me to anchor radical faith in you that whenever I speak to my mountains, I know they will move instantly. Glory to God!

Thank you, Holy Ghost, for the victory over every challenge that may come my way. Lord, I will no longer depend on my understanding of what my natural eyes can see. I will activate my faith and put all my trust in you, whether I understand or not.

Father God, I thank you for laughing, ridiculing, and mocking the evil kings and wicked rulers of the earth who plotted to cut my connection to you and then laugh at my demise. Thank you, Jesus, for bowing down the heavens and fighting for my freedom. In Jesus' name. Amen.

For verily I say unto you, that whosoever shall say unto this mountain, Be thou removed, and be thou cast into the sea; and shall not doubt in his heart, but shall believe that those things which he saith shall come to pass; he shall have whatsoever he saith. (Mark 11:23)

Reason 36 - Wavering

"Wavering and double-mindedness show that you fail to believe that you are more than a conqueror. You can be an excellent investor; but, don't invest in wavering. You can become anything in life; just don't become double-minded."

"Witchcraft is one of satan's magical powers used by humans. It is a form of idolatry and deception. Unfortunately, many Christians practice witchcraft unaware."

Reason 37

***

Witchcraft

Seers will be put to shame. Those who practice witchcraft will be disgraced. All of them will cover their faces, because God won't answer them. (Micah 3:7)

Witchcraft is the practice of using spells, sorcery, or magic. It is also a form of communication with satan and demons. According to Deuteronomy 18:10-12, witchcraft is malicious, evil, and detestable: *Never sacrifice your son or daughter as a burnt offering. And **do not let your people practice fortune-telling, or use sorcery, or interpret omens, or engage in witchcraft, or cast spells, or function as mediums or psychics, or call forth the spirits of the dead.** Anyone who does these things is detestable to the Lord. It is because the other nations have done these detestable things that the Lord your God will drive them out ahead of you.*

One may argue that witches have done good deeds, and witchcraft varies due to culture and society. Regardless of how they try to view it positively, it is the work of darkness; and, therefore, it is a sin. There is nothing positive about evil actions. Furthermore, there is no such thing as a good witch or good magic, as many are led to believe. A kingdom divided by itself cannot stand.

Necromancers, sorcerers, along with other agents of satan, use WITCHES' CRAFT to cast spells, curses, gain wealth, steal wealth, make evil sacrifices, manipulate other people's destinies and purpose, and much more. These agents use demonic spirits to torment your spirit man to the point where your physical man may get frustrated, confused, and depressed. It is also used to control territories, government, people, marriages, religions. Their sole mission is to control, kill, and destroy you. If witches were good people, why would Exodus 22:18 say, "Suffer not a witch to live." *The kings of the earth set themselves, and the rulers take counsel together, against the Lord, and against his anointed, saying, 3Let us break their bands asunder, and cast away their cords from us.* (Psalm 2:2-3) Ephesians 6:12 says further, *Open our eyes and awareness that these are the evil forces with whom we wrestle. Therefore, they are not to be celebrated.*

Witchcraft is one of satan's magical powers used by humans. It is a form of idolatry and deception. Unfortunately, many Christians practice witchcraft unaware. For example, some believers may find it entertaining to read their horoscope (Horror-scope), and get caught up in astrological and zodiac signs. Some eagerly call psychic hotlines, or burn candles while reading a designated Psalm while chanting. Because they are reading the Word of God, they think it cannot be harmful. Some play with ouija (pronounced weegi) boards, while some visit palm or tarot card readers or astrologers.

Have you ever been asked, "What sign are you?" or "What month were you born?" And, after responding, you were told, "Oh, we share the same sign. I am Scorpio as well," or "You are a Cancer just like my aunt." As born-again believers, we should not participate or embrace astrological or zodiac signs. We are represented by the blood of Jesus Christ, not by a month or any of the twelve zodiac signs. The scientific aspect of studying the heavenly bodies is not a sin. However, when one begins seeing the heavenly bodies as gods and a means to predict the future, define one's character, advise about life issues or solutions to problems, and a way to inform someone of what's being done or said about them, that is considered fortune-telling or divining. That's when it becomes sinful.

Many argue that God embraces astrology because it is in the Bible; furthermore, the wise men followed the stars to find baby Jesus. Yes, it is the Bible, but in what context was it used? What are the other words with which it is associated? Yes, the wise men followed the stars but they were not worshipping them or using them for fortune-telling or divining. Over the years, men have manipulated the celestial bodies to fulfill their curiosity and desires, distorting our minds to believe what they want us to believe to be the truth, which they have done to many things that God created for a specific purpose. I encourage you to research the origin and the true meaning behind astrology; and, compare it with the Word of God. Seeking help through astrology or astrologers is an embracing of idolatry and a slap in the face of God.

Whenever you are asked what your sign is, simply say, "I am sorry, I don't believe in zodiac signs. It is contrary to my faith." Think about the signs "Cancer = crab" and "Scorpio = scorpion." Is Cancer or scorpion a good thing? Why would anyone in their right mind proudly announce that "I am a Cancer" or "I am a scorpion?" Look at all the signs. Most of them represent either animals or insects. Is that biblical or Godly? My people perish because of a lack of knowledge. (Hosea 4:6) Remember, satan tells you half-truth and half lie.

You may have grown up seeing or hearing your parents or friends speak highly of these things. As you watched them glued to the radio, anxiously awaiting the reading of their horoscope, refusing to begin their day without hearing what it is read. I have seen individuals cancel appointments and previously set plans because the horoscope reading was unfavorable. Knowing what I know now, I realize that they did not know any better. They were unaware of the hidden danger and were only following tradition.

Reader, now that your eyes have been opened to the truth about these innocent-looking things, God expects you not to associate yourself with any form of witchcraft, astrologers, zodiac signs, palm reading, divining, or calling psychic hotlines. Neither should you send any personal items to the obeah/voodoo man to inquire about what's in your future or if anyone is trying to harm you. Stay clear. All these things are influenced by demonic spirits. They are demonically inspired. *In the past God overlooked such ignorance, but now he commands all people everywhere to repent. (Acts 17:30, NIV)*

Here is another thing many Christians do ignorantly, participating in Halloween. It's more of a trick than a treat. Satan tricked man into believing that Halloween is pure fun; hence, he got the innocent and naive to help him celebrate his high-day. I once read a booklet titled *The Witch that Switched*. She claimed that she was a witch and one of satan's main brides; but, thank God, she switched and became a bride of Jesus Christ. In her booklet, she mentioned that Halloween is the high time for satanists and witches, during which multiple souls are recruited for satan, especially those of teenagers and young people. It's also a time when more humans go missing and are offered up for sacrifices, she added. Reader, many may not see or know about it, but more lives have been lost, more harm and wickedness are being done during this celebration more than any other holiday.

Halloween is a vast subject to cover and explain. You should take the time to research the origin and the real meaning behind this celebration. While on the subject, I will do my best to share with you a little of the information I have gathered.

First and foremost, as you have read above, Halloween is not as innocent as it appears to be or as many have thought. Even though Halloween means "holy or hallowed evening," There is nothing holy about its activities. No one should participate in such a celebration, let alone born-again followers of Jesus Christ. If you carefully scrutinize the activities, apparel, and the festivities that are associated with this festival, you will see that it is glorifying satan and his demons. There is nothing Godly about dressing as human remains (skeletons), witches, fortunetellers, devils, ghosts, psychics, and vampires? All these images promote the kingdom of darkness. That which we call Halloween is known as "All Hollow's Eve" celebrated on October 31st. This celebration is dedicated to Samhain, "the lord of the dead." Pagans refer to this date as the feast of the dead. *He that sacrificeth unto any god, save unto the Lord only, he shall be utterly destroyed. (Exodus 22: 20)*

The rituals associated with Samhain are: building altars to honor and celebrate the dead, bonfires, feasting, dancing, and setting aside food

Reason 37 - Witchcraft

for the demons and spirit guides. What Christmas Eve is to Christmas Day and New Year's Eve is to New Year's Day Halloween (All Hallows Eve) is to All Saints Day. All Saints Day, also known as All Hallow's Day or Hallowmas, is a feast day celebrated on November 1st. On this day, some churches host services, praying for the saints, who have died and are assumed to be in heaven, eating soul cakes, and visiting cemeteries. November 2nd, is known as "All Souls' Day." In this ceremony, the Church would gather and pray for the cleansing and sanctification of souls for those who have died but did not make it into heaven, but are being held in purgatory, according to the Catholic church.

For the living know that they will die, but the dead know nothing; they have no further reward, and even their name is forgotten. 6Their love, their hate and their jealousy have long since vanished; never again will they have a part in anything that happens under the sun. (Ecclesiastes 9:5-6, NIV)

Whatsoever thy hand findeth to do, do it with thy might; for there is no work, nor device, nor knowledge, nor wisdom, in the grave, whither thou goest. (Ecclesiastes 9:10)

Let no one deceive you with empty words, for because of these things the wrath of God comes upon the sons of disobedience. 7Therefore do not become partners with them; 8for at one time you were darkness, but now you are light in the Lord. Walk as children of light 9(for the fruit of light is found in all that is good and right and true), 10and try to discern what is pleasing to the Lord. 11Take no part in the unfruitful works of darkness, but instead expose them. 12For it is shameful even to speak of the things that they do in secret. (Ephesians 5:6-12, ESV)

Parents, you are in control of your children. Many parents debate that they don't want their children to feel left out or less-than; therefore, they allow them to participate in Halloween. Allowing the kids to engage in such festivities permits satan to invade your home and control your children's lives. It may even lead to possession. *Even satan can disguise himself as an angel of light. (2 Corinthians*

11:14, NLT) Christian parents, don't wait until the night of Halloween to educate your children about the dangers of getting involved in this kind of celebration. You have all year to explain and show them why it is wrong.

When the churches host a holy church-party, as some call it, on Halloween night with candy and costumes, they are participating indirectly. You must be able to say, "Kids, we won't be participating in this celebration of the dead. It contradicts God's teachings and expectations of us. We won't be going outside of the house tonight." It's better if they are mad or sad now than have to deal with demonic possession later. If you fail to control your children, something else will. *Woe unto them that call evil good, and good evil; that put darkness for light, and light for darkness; that put bitter for sweet, and sweet for bitter! (Isaiah 5:20)*

Research the origin and purpose of most festivals, organizations, rituals, ceremonies, and even churches, before you get involved. Take nothing at face value; not all that glitters is gold. Put your trust in God. *The Spirit clearly says that in later times some will abandon the faith and follow deceiving spirits and things taught by demons. (1 Timothy 4:1, NIV)*

The Words of a Church Mother/Deaconess

Mr. Lewis, a prominent police officer, limped across the street heading towards the bank. He met an old friend, an older woman, who happened to be a deaconess and church mother of a Pentecostal church. They had not seen each other for a long time so they stood and chatted for a while. One conversation led to the next.

"I see you were limping. What's wrong with your leg?" the deaconess asked.

Mr. Lewis lifted one pant leg and showed her his swollen ankle.

Reason 37 - Witchcraft

Upon seeing the ankle, she responded, "Oh no! You can't sit around with your foot looking like this. This is not normal. You should go peep (look what is wrong)," implying that Mr. Lewis should go to a reader/obeah man. One of my sisters, May, who was a backslider at the time, but was seriously contemplating rededicating her life to Christ, stood nearby. Upon hearing the words that came out of the mouth of the church mother /deaconess, May was overwhelmed with anger and disappointment. "The most painful part, the woman had no clue that I knew her as the cornerstone of the church. Even though I know that's not the custom of the church, I decided to have nothing to do with church or churchgoers," May stated.

[19]Someone may say to you, "Let's ask the mediums and those who consult the spirits of the dead. With their whisperings and mutterings, they will tell us what to do." But shouldn't people ask God for guidance? Should the living seek guidance from the dead? [20]Look to God's instructions and teachings! People who contradict his word are completely in the dark. [21]They will go from one place to another, weary and hungry. And because they are hungry, they will rage and curse their king and their God. They will look up to heaven [22]and down at the earth, but wherever they look, there will be trouble and anguish and dark despair. They will be thrown out into the darkness. (Isaiah 8:19-22)

So Saul died for his transgression which he committed against the LORD, [even] against the word of the LORD, which he kept not, and also for asking [counsel] of [one that had] a familiar spirit, to enquire [of it]; [14]And enquired not of the LORD: therefore he slew him, and turned the kingdom unto David the son of Jesse. (1Chronicles 10:13-14)

Two Pastors' Words of Wisdom for Me

While living in New York, one of my friends invited me to her church. She wasn't just any friend. She had previously been a member of my home-church before moving to the church she wanted me to visit. She was someone whom I admired, trusted, and grew to love over the years. I accepted her invitation, but, while in the church, something felt off, spiritually. A few days later, I told her what I saw and felt.

From her response, I could tell that she was not happy with what I said. She defended the pastor.

"You know that I don't stand for foolishness, and if I sensed or knew anything as such, I wouldn't be going there," explained my displeased friend.

"Okay, I'm sorry if I offended you, my sister. Let's move on from here," I said.

To give her the benefit of the doubt, I went back to the church again. While engaged in a one-on-one conversation with the pastor, he asked, "Is this your picture on this flyer?"

"Yes," I answered.

He began by saying, "Not knowing who the person on the flyer was, the first time I saw it, I said, 'Wow, they are frustrating her.'"

Then he told me, "I am going to give you some instructions that you need to follow if you want to be free from the frustration of your enemies."

The pastor gave me a list of things that I should do and say, but the ones that left my mouth dropped open were when he told me to fill my bathtub with water and pour a gallon of milk into the water, soak myself for a while, and read a particular Psalm. He also instructed me not to dry my body when I got out of the tub but walk backward into my room, remain naked and start praising and worshipping God. The next insane thing that he told me was to write my name multiple times on a piece of paper, put in under my pillow, and sleep on it for a certain amount of nights. At the end of our conversation, he told me to get a container of olive oil from one of his staff.

"I have no money," I told him.

"It's okay. You can take it; and, bring the money back on your next visit," he said, kindly.

Reason 37 - Witchcraft

No! I did not take the olive oil, nor did I do or say anything that he instructed me to do. I have never seen such information or instruction written in the Bible. Furthermore, my spirit grew even more uncomfortable with him and the things he said. My next and final visit to the church, I tried multiple times to talk to the pastor after his morning service; but, he deliberately ignored me each time I tried. He wouldn't give me the time of day. I went to his sister and told her what I observed and what happened. "Pastor is very angry with you because you did not leave the $50 with me for the one-on-one consultation with him; and, he is taking it out on me," she responded.

I replied, "Ma'am, I was not made aware that I should pay for talking to the pastor. He told me to get a bottle of olive oil for $50. I made it clear to him that I did not have any money, and his response was, 'It's okay, you can take it and bring the money back on your next visit. For your information, I did not take the bottle of oil."

After sharing all that transpired between the pastor and me, with my friend who invited me to the church, I noticed that she was not defensive this time; and, she didn't act surprised but somewhat apologetic. I later found out that she had some weird experience of her own that left her in astonishment, which made her run for her life. That was pastor number one.

Pastor Number Two

Pastor number two told me that demons were lingering in my place of business and consequently, that my business was not flourishing. "You should burn sage or frankincense and myrrh in the building, but don't do it alone. You need someone else with you because when the demons manifest, they can hurt you if you have no knowledge of what you are doing." She continued, "Sis, you cannot go into business uncovered. You have to protect yourself from envious and jealous individuals. You have to use wisdom. The sage is excellent. A lady told me to use it, and I did. Trust me, it works. " Ouch! How unfortunate, she is out of business today.

Working witchcraft indirectly

- Lime
- Nutmeg
- Inch measure
- Rice/Corn/Pea grain
- Ammonia
- Blue
- Salt
- Milk
- Garlic
- Horseshoe
- Padlock
- Frankincense
- Myrrh
- Scallion

All of the above and more are natural things made for our everyday use. Of course, God gave most of these natural things to us for our healing and comfort. Absolutely nothing is wrong with any of the items listed below, when used for their intended purposes and with a clean, clear, and Godly mindset.

- **Lime** mixed with garlic and honey can lower high blood pressure or get rid of sore throat and cold
- **Nutmeg** mixed with salt stops diarrhea
- **Ammonia** is used mainly as a refrigerant gas, for purification of water supplies and as a cleaning solution.
- **Rice, corn** and **pea grains** are a well-known source of food products
- The **blue** primary use is to enhance the brightness of white clothing
- **Inch measure** is used by tailors, seamstress, and individuals working in the textile industry.
- The **horseshoe** was created to protect the horse's hooves.
- The **padlock** is used to secure and protect your property.
- There are so many health benefits attached to **frankincense.** It can be used to stimulate hair growth. It works wonders on the respiratory system, such as clearing nasal passages, making it easier for asthmatics to breathe better. It is great for joint pain & inflammation, helps with gastric pain. It is excellent for the skin when mixed with Shea butter, vitamin E, and peppermint oil. The benefits are endless. It's been said that it is also used to fight some form of cancers, as well as insect repellant or deodorant. Some individuals burn it for the aroma, which helps them to sleep, relieve stress, or improve their memory.
- **Myrrh** is a gum, which comes from a tree; it is used for medicinal purposes and perfume.

When did using these items become the act of witchcraft? It is considered witchcraft when your reason and intention for using them shift from their natural use. It is witchcraft when something is used to chase away or restrain the evil spirits that may be attacking you. Reflect on what you are saying and thinking about while you are using these items. Are you using them because you feel as if demons are invading your house or place of business? Are you using them to prevent your money from disappearing? God's people perish because of what they don't know and refuse to learn. As I have mentioned before, many Christians have worked or are working witchcraft unknowingly. It is all about your mindset.

Beloved, don't be fooled and don't be deceived. God is not mocked; and, He is not ignorant of our journey to Egypt for help. *Woe to those who go down to Egypt for help, who rely on horses, who trust in the multitude of their chariots and in the great strength of their horsemen, but do not look to the Holy One of Israel, or seek help from the LORD. (Isaiah 31:1, NIV)*

Some individuals have been encouraged by friends and family to use these things to protect themselves. Some believe in superstition and old wives' fables. Some are engaged because of their culture or tradition, while others were drawn into it because they've visited seers/psychics, obeah/voodoo men, sorcerers, necromancers, or clairvoyants. *But refuse profane and old wives' fables, and exercise thyself rather unto godliness. (1 Timothy 4:7)*

Sadly, those who have gone to these people for help try to justify their action by misquoting and misinterpreting the word of God. I have heard the following numerous times; and, perhaps, you have heard them as well.

- That God calls fools; but, He doesn't keep them;
- The Bible says if you are sick, you should seek a physician;
- The Bible says there is a balm in Gilead;
- The Bible says the world is wiser than the children of light;
- The Bible says you should be wise as a serpent but harmless as a dove.

Reason 37 - Witchcraft

And the list continues.

Even though misquoted, it is incredible how we are quick to say, "The Bible says" when it's convenient to our flesh. Listen, when we use these items with the mindset that they will combat evil, we are telling God, "Your power is not enough. I have to help you. You are too slow. I can't wait for you any longer. I have been praying, but I don't see any result. But I have gotten an instant result from the sage, lime, and frankincense and myrrh."

Beloved, witchcraft is a form of idolatry as well. You know what the Bible says about witchcraft-workers and idolaters—their prayers will not be answered, and neither will they have a place in the kingdom of God. If dabbling in witchcraft is a part of your life, quit while you are ahead. It is not by coincidence you are reading this book. It is God expressing His never-ending, unconditional for you. He loves you so much that He made way for you to get a copy of this book so you would be made aware of the path on which you are traveling. Through this book, He has given you the opportunity to make a U-Turn and repent before it's too late. Don't allow Jesus' death to be in vain. He is waiting for you to humble yourself under his mighty hand, turn away for your evil and turn to him whole-heartedly.

If you are practicing witchcraft knowing or unknowingly, I do hope that these Bible verses will help you to denounce and break loose from any involvement, rituals, traditions, or act of witchcraft. Don't allow your years of sacrificing for Christ to go for naught. Guard your salvation against old wives' fables. Trust in God and lean only on Him. Jesus loves you, and so do I.

If there be found among you, within any of thy gates which the Lord thy God giveth thee, man or woman, that hath wrought wickedness in the sight of the Lord thy God, in transgressing his covenant: And hath gone and served other gods, and worshipped them, either the sun, or moon, or any of the host of heaven, which I have not commanded. (Deuteronomy 17: 2-3)

Therefore made I a decree to bring in all the wise men of Babylon before me, that they might make known unto me the interpretation of the dream: Then came in the magicians, the astrologers, the Chaldeans, and the soothsayers: and I told the dream before them; but they did not make known unto me the interpretation thereof. (Daniel 4:6-7)

Daniel answered in the presence of the king, and said, The secret which the king hath demanded cannot the wise men, the astrologers, the magicians, the soothsayers, shew unto the king: But there is a God in heaven that revealeth secrets, and maketh known to the king Nebuchadnezzar what shall be in the latter days. Thy dream, and the visions of thy head upon thy bed, are these. (Daniel 2: 27-28)And I will cut off the cities of thy land, and throw down all thy strongholds: And I will cut off witchcrafts out of thy hand; and thou shalt have no more soothsayers.... (Micah 5:11- 12)

Seers will be put to shame. Those who practice witchcraft will be disgraced. All of them will cover their faces, because God won't answer them. (Micah 3:7)

Do not defile yourselves by turning to mediums or to those who consult the spirits of the dead. I am the LORD your God. (Leviticus 19:31, NLT)

Prayer

O God, King of the universe, I bow before you in humility with a repentant heart. Lord, I seek your forgiveness for turning to other gods for help. Father, I have disappointed you with my actions. I have ignored your warnings and got entangled in witchcraft. Help me, O God, to not perish because of my foolish choices. In the name of Jesus, I denounce and renounce any and every involvement with witchcraft, knowingly, and unknowingly. Deliver me, O God, from worshiping and embracing astrological and zodiac signs and symbols.

God, erase any secret oaths I have taken and remove the desire to embrace the horoscope. Deliver me from any incantations,

Reason 37 - Witchcraft

enchantments, rituals, spells, curses, and any sacrifices that I have done knowingly or unknowingly. Lord, your Word says that I can't put fire in my bosom and not get burned. So put out every evil fire that I have kindled, O God.

Father, please forgive me for indulging in witchcraft and participating in satan's schemes, in Jesus' name. Father God, I allowed myself to be carried away in this darkness, not realizing that I was opening more doors for the enemy to come in and frustrate me. God, out of ignorance, I have abused the pure things that you made, turning them into a magnet for demons to attach themselves to my family, home, money, business, and health. Lord, I am sorry for breaking your heart with my rebellious attitude.

May the blood of Jesus Christ of Nazareth, the only begotten son of God, cover and protect me from all retaliating, backlashing spirits right now. May the fire and blood of Jesus Christ of Nazareth destroy every red and white witchcraft in Jesus' name. I command hailstones and coals of fire to fall in every coven, where the witches and agents of satan gather against the innocent and me, in the mighty name of Jesus. Through the power in the blood of Jesus Christ, I command every evil coven and its members to be destroyed by fire. Lord, unless they repent and turn their lives over to you, may they not escape the lake of fire that is prepared for satan and his angels.

Elohim, I thank you for teaching my hands to war so that they will break bows of steel. In the name of Jesus Christ of Nazareth, I break every cage made with steel, iron, or stone that is used as a barrier around my life, my finances, my health, my business, my marriage, my success, and my property. I send the fire of God to unveil every cloud of darkness that hovers over my buildings and properties due to caging, curses, spells, chanting, and any other of satan's evil devices and incantations, in Jesus' mighty name.

Jehovah Naheh, the God that smites, thank you for rendering powerless spiritual wickedness in high places, low places, in the heavens, on the earth, under the earth, and the sea, in Jesus' mighty name. Covenant-keeping God, I break all evil covenants that I have made with satan and his demons, knowingly and unknowingly. You have been a shield for me. You have been my protector, my refuge, my strength, and my savior. Lord, thank you for reaching down your great and mighty hands and drawing me out of the enemy's camp when I was surrounded.

Lord, I thank you for saving me, healing me, delivering me, and setting me free from the bondage and sin of witchcraft. I surrender my whole heart to you right now. In Jesus' name. Amen.

Reason 37 - Witchcraft

You cannot drink the cup of the Lord and the cup of demons. You cannot partake of the table of the Lord and the table of demons. (1 Corinthians 10:21)

Listed below are 25 Bible verses that warn against witchcraft and **express how God feels about the evil works of darkness (witchcraft).** They are taken from various versions of the Bible.

1. *Nothing impure will ever enter it*, nor will anyone who does what is shameful or deceitful, but only those whose names are written in the Lamb's book of life. Nothing unclean, no one who does anything detestable, and no liars will ever enter it. Only those whose names are written in the Lamb's book of life will enter it. (Revelation 21:27, GWT)

2. "But cowards, unbelievers, the corrupt, murderers, the immoral, *those who practice witchcraft, idol worshipers, and all liars–their fate is in the fiery lake of burning sulfur.* This is the second death." (Revelation 21:8, NLT)

3. Now the actions of the flesh are obvious: sexual immorality, impurity, promiscuity, idolatry, *witchcraft*, hatred, rivalry, jealously, outbursts of anger, quarrels, conflicts, factions, envy, murder, drunkenness, wild partying, and things like that. I am telling you now, as *I have told you in the past, that people who practice such things will not inherit the kingdom of God.* (Galatians 5:19-21, NIV)

4. I will tear down your walls and demolish your defenses. I *will put an end to all witchcraft,* and there will be no more fortune-tellers. (Micah 5:11-12, NLT)

5. Seers will be put to shame. *Those who practice witchcraft will be disgraced.* All of them will cover their faces, because God won't answer them. (Micah 3:7, NLT)

6. *Rebellion is as sinful as witchcraft,* and stubbornness as bad as worshiping idols. So because you have rejected the command of the LORD, he has rejected you as king. (1 Samuel 15:23, NLT)

7. Do not eat meat that has not been drained of its blood. *Do not practice fortune-telling or witchcraft.* (Leviticus 19:26, NLT)

8. For example, never sacrifice your son or daughter as a burnt offering. And *do not let your people practice fortune-telling, or use sorcery, or interpret omens, or engage in witchcraft, or cast spells, or function as mediums or psychics, or call forth the spirits of the dead.* Anyone who does these things is detestable to the Lord. It is because the other nations have done these detestable things that the Lord your God will drive them out ahead of you. But you must be blameless before the Lord your God. (Deuteronomy 18:10-13, NLT)

9. *And the light of a candle shall shine no more at all in thee;* and the voice of the bridegroom and of the bride shall be heard no more at all in thee: for thy merchants were the great men of the earth; *for by thy sorceries were all nations deceived.* (Revelation 18:23, KJV)

10. Now use your magical charms! Use the spells you have worked at all these years! Maybe they will do you some good. Maybe they can make someone afraid of you. All the advice you receive has made you tired. Where are all your astrologers, those stargazers who make predictions each month? *Let them stand up and save you from what the future*

holds. But they are like straw burning in a fire; they cannot save themselves from the flame. You will get no help from them at all; their hearth is no place to sit for warmth. (Isaiah 47:12-14, NLT)

11. *Someone may say to you, "Let's ask the mediums and those who consult the spirits of the dead. With their whisperings and mutterings, they will tell us what to do." But shouldn't people ask God for guidance? Should the living seek guidance from the dead?* (Isaiah 8:19, NLT)

12. You must be holy because I, the Lord, am holy. I have set you apart from all other people to be my very own. *Men and women among you who act as mediums or who consult the spirits of the dead must be put to death by stoning. They are guilty of a capital offense.* (Leviticus 20:26-27, NLT)

13. So Saul died because he was unfaithful to the LORD. He failed to obey the Lord's command, and *he even consulted a medium* instead of asking the Lord for guidance. So the Lord killed him and turned the kingdom over to David son of Jesse. (1 Chronicles 10:13-14)

14. We know that whosoever is born of God sinneth not; *but he that is begotten of God keepeth himself, and that wicked one toucheth him not.* And we know that we are of God, and the whole world lieth in wickedness. (1 John 5:18-19)

15. Ye are of God, little children, and have overcome them: *because greater is he that is in you, than he that is in the world.* (1 John 4:4)

16. *Take no part in the worthless deeds of evil and darkness;* instead, expose them. (Ephesians 5:11, NLT)

17. *Dear friend, do not imitate what is evil but what is good.* Anyone who does what is good is from God. Anyone who does what is evil has not seen God. (3 John 1:11, NIV)

18. You cannot drink the cup of the Lord and the cup of demons. You cannot partake of the table of the Lord and the table of demons. (1 Corinthians 10:21, NLT)

19. Do not be deceived: God is not mocked, *for whatever one sows, that will he also reap.* (Galatians 6:7, ESV)

20. The one who does what is sinful is of the devil, because the devil has been sinning from the beginning. The reason the Son of God appeared was to destroy the devil's work. *No one who is born of God will continue to sin, because God's seed remains in them; they cannot go on sinning, because they have been born of God.* This is how we know who the children of God are and who the children of the devil are: Anyone who does not do what is right is not God's child, nor is anyone who does not love their brother and sister. (1 John 3:8-10, NIV)

21. Dear friends, *do not believe every spirit, but test the spirits to see whether they are from God,* because many false prophets have gone out into the world. This is how you can recognize the Spirit of God: Every spirit that acknowledges that Jesus Christ has come in the flesh is from God, but every spirit that does not acknowledge Jesus is not from God. This is the spirit of the antichrist, which you have heard is coming and even now is already in the world. (1 John 4:1-3, NIV)

22. But the people who did not die in these plagues still refused to repent of their evil deeds and turn to God. They continued to worship demons and idols made of gold, silver, bronze, stone, and wood—idols that can neither see nor hear

Reason 37 - Witchcraft

nor walk! And *they did not repent of their murders or their witchcraft or their sexual immorality or their thefts.* (Revelation 9:20-21, NLT)

23. "Quick! Get my chariot ready!" King Joram commanded. Then King Joram of Israel and King Ahaziah of Judah rode out in their chariots to meet Jehu. They met him at the plot of land that had belonged to Naboth of Jezreel. ²²*King Joram demanded, "Do you come in peace, Jehu?" Jehu replied, "How can there be peace as long as the idolatry and witchcraft of your mother, Jezebel, are all around us?"* (2 Kings 9:21-22, NLT)

24. Manasseh also sacrificed his own sons in the fire in the valley of Ben-Hinnom. *He practiced sorcery, divination, and witchcraft, and he consulted with mediums and psychics. He did much that was evil* in the Lord's sight, arousing his anger. (2 Chronicles 33:6, NLT)

25. Behold, I am against thee, saith the LORD of hosts; and I will discover thy skirts upon thy face, and I will shew the nations thy nakedness, and the kingdoms thy shame. *Because of the multitude of the whoredoms of the well-favoured harlot, the mistress of witchcrafts, that selleth nations through her whoredoms, and families through her witchcrafts.* (Nahum 3:4-5)

"Even when our motives are hidden from men, God knows the intent of our hearts. It can be very costly when we do the right thing at the wrong time and the wrong way. It doesn't matter how many good deeds we have done, how many demons we cast out, how many hours we spent in His presence, or how many souls we've led to Christ..."

Reason 38

✷✷✷

Wrong Motive

When you ask, you do not receive, because you ask with wrong motives, that you may spend what you get on your pleasures.
(James 4:3, NIV)

As I sat quietly one afternoon, seeking the anointing of God to write this chapter, I heard the Lord clearly speak. He said, "Some people seek me because of what I can give or do for them. Most of them don't want anything to do with me. They don't like me. They don't believe in me, and they don't trust me. Whenever they seek my advice, they have already tried doing it on their own and failed. They will only listen and do what I say if it will work in their favor, and that's what they want to hear. I am treated like trash by many. I am ignored and rejected by most because of my standard of expectation. If they do what is right or what is required of them to be holy, it will hurt their flesh and cramp their lifestyle."

"Many are defiant as rebellious children who disrespected and disobeyed their parents and despised accountability. They refuse to be corrected when observed going down the wrong path or entertaining the wrong company. They grumble among themselves, asking what kind of God am I who allows terrible or evil things to happen to good people, and they blame me for every evil and bad thing that occurs. Many despise me because I am not compromising with their choice of living. As a result, when they seek my intervention, their motives are wrong."

Marriages

"Disrespectfully, women have asked me to release another woman's husband to them. They fasted, prayed, and prophesied that I am getting ready to release their husband (a man who is already married). Some went as far as to approach the man for whom they are lusting, and say, 'The Lord told me that you are my husband.'

"Some have presumptuously asked me to remove the man's wife to satisfy their evil desire. And when I refused to grant their request, they took matters into their own hands, mocking, jeering, tormenting, and disrespecting the man's wife. Believe it or not, some have worked witchcraft to drive the wife insane, turn the husband's mind against her, and even summon the spirit of death to destroy her. That is a spirit of Jezebel at work.

"Men have prayed silently for the removal of their wives because they are drawn away by the lust they feel towards another female. In their hearts, they wish for their wife to divorce them or make a grave mistake, permitting them to tell her that it is over. Some have already identified who they would marry should their wife pass away. Prayers like those I will not answer—the wrong motive.

Material Things

"Over and over, many have sought my divine intervention to supply their wants. I have read their hearts. I know that which they ask is for their pleasure, to live a lavish lifestyle, and to brag on individuals who said they wouldn't come to anything or be anybody. They justify their request by saying, 'There were days when I didn't have anything, now that the Lord has blessed me, I am going to flaunt it because I deserve this and more.'

"As their heavenly Father, it is my pleasure to see my children prosper and rise above where they have been, but it pains my heart when they are seeking my help to hurt someone's feelings. Wrong motives.

REASON 38 - WRONG MOTIVE

Job Promotion

"Individuals have fasted and prayed relentlessly for days, sometimes weeks, to get a promotion on the job. They have made their case so believable that if I weren't God, I would be deceived. I am He who reads the intent of the heart. Nothing is hidden from my eyes. Even though I know their intentions, I obliged them my permissive will. After the promotion was granted, I observed them enslave their fellow workers, promote their unqualified friends, sow seeds of discord, tell lies, and carry news on those whom they dislike so that they could be fired. I have watched them become hateful, wicked, and ruthless. The job has become their idol. Periods of fasting, praying, and Bible reading are of the past, and I am nowhere on their radar. Despite their past dedication and consistency in prayer and fasting, it was all done with the wrong motive.

Charity

"My heart is extremely pleased to see people extending a helping hand to those who need it most. I am also pleased with the favors that are shown to various individuals. However, I am disappointed and hurt when all this is done to promote self, draw attention to self, and exalt self. I am disappointed when they allow ego and self-glorification to get in the way of their blessings. It is annoying to hear complaints about who is ungrateful and unthankful because the flesh was not praised or acknowledged. I hate when my people go to extreme lengths to announce to the world all that they are doing or have done for others." *Take heed that ye do not your alms before men, to be seen of them: Otherwise, ye have no reward of your Father which is in heaven. But when thou doest alms, let not your left hand know what your right hand doeth. (Matthew 6:1&3)*

Beloved, the Lord has spoken. He has made it clear how He feels about us doing things or petitioning Him with wrong motives. Let us be still under the mighty hand of God and search ourselves to see why we do the things we do–why do we want to buy a house–a specific car–start a business– get that position, or title. My friends, it is evident that if we are doing or requesting these things to brag, or because our friends or neighbors have them. Our motives are wrong; and, the Lord will not answer our prayers.

Have you ever asked God for a particular thing, but deep within, you knew you could not manage it because you were not mature or responsible enough to handle it; and, you didn't have the discipline to see it through. Even when our motives are hidden from men, God knows the intent of our hearts. It can be very costly when we do the right thing at the wrong time and the wrong way. It doesn't matter how many good deeds we have done, how many demons we cast out, how many hours we spent in His presence, or how many souls we've led to Christ. Yes, it is possible to spend all our lives in the church, working for God, and miss heaven. Apostle Paul couldn't have said it better, *"But I keep under my body, and bring it into subjection: lest that by any means when I have preached to others, I myself should be a castaway."* (1 Corinthians 9:27)

My friend, I encourage you to build a sincere relationship with Jesus–not only on Sundays or on the Sabbath or once-a-week prayer meeting at church–but at home, 365 days of the year. Fasting, praying, and reading the Word of God will accelerate your relationship with your Creator. If you stay anchored in Him and allow Him to abide in you, your approach to Him would be different and more sincere. He expects us and indeed wants us to come to Him for the things we want, but not with corrupt motives and deceit, selfish desires, unconfessed sin, pride, doubt, and noncompliance. We are helpless and hopeless without Christ.

[3]Now ye are clean through the word which I have spoken unto you. [4]Abide in me, and I in you. As the branch cannot bear fruit of itself, except it abide in the vine; no more can ye, except ye abide in me. [5]I am the vine, ye are the branches: He that abideth in me, and I in him, the same bringeth forth much fruit: for without me ye can do nothing. (John 5:3-5)

Reason 38 - Wrong Motive

Prayer

I love you, Lord, and I lift my voice to worship you. Oh my soul, rejoice. Take joy my King, in what you hear and let it be a sweet sound in your ears.

Father in heaven, I adore you and I magnify your Holy name. Despite the pain and suffering, you knew what you were going to face, yet, you still left the splendor of heaven on my behalf. Lord, I exalt you. Hallelujah! Thank you, Jesus. Although I didn't deserve it, you did it anyway. Thank you, Lord. O Sovereign God, you reign triumphant in my life.

Lord Jesus, please forgive me for using you for my convenience. Forgive me for disrespecting your sovereignty and your abilities. Lord, I am guilty of not wanting to have anything to do with you. I am guilty of being defiant and not trusting you to do for me what I cannot do. God, I have doubted you because I did not believe in you. Lord, please forgive me for my rebellious attitude as well. O God, I humbly bow before you with a repentant heart. I am sorry for the way I've treated you. Lord, you didn't deserve that. Please forgive me.

Lord, cleanse me from self-centeredness and wrong motives. Forgive me for doing my deeds with the wrong intentions and wanting to be praised and recognized by others. Lord, your words have penetrated my core. I am guilty of drawing attention to myself, promoting myself, and desiring that which is not mine to have. Forgive me for my ungodly, selfish, and wicked behavior.

In the name of Jesus, I renounce and bind every diabolical spirit that is operating through me, causing me to engage in evil thoughts or acts to break up marriages, causing the innocent to lose their job, mistreating others, and wishing death on another human being. Empty me, O God, from all this corruption and place within me the right spirit and attitude. In Jesus' name, I pray. Amen.

If ye abide in me, and my words abide in you, ye shall ask what ye will, and it shall be done unto you. (John 5:7)

"It is my earnest prayer that, as believers, you are more watchful, alert, and aware of the things that cause you to sin. And, if you commit a sin, do not hesitate to repent. The adversary is conscious of the fact that he will not be able to devour everyone; but, he knows that there are those who will consciously leave doors open and unconsciously give him permission and easy access to create a stronghold that will take dominion and authority over your life."

Final Words

Author's Reflection

✱✱✱

From My Heart to Yours

Perhaps you are looking for more explanations on other sins or asking why a particular sin was not mentioned. I did not mention them because you already know what they are. Therefore, be careful not to commit them; and, if you do, repent immediately! Most of the sins in the aforementioned paragraphs are regularly ignored and committed without remorse. They are synonymous to the analogy of the straw that broke the camel's back. By itself, one straw does not seem like a lot, in much the same way a small sin does not seem like sin. But, they are sins nonetheless and, in actuality, can become a very heavy weight if not dealt with from its beginning stages. For example, you readily know that lying and stealing is a sin; but, you were probably not thinking that taking something as small as staplers home from work, without asking, is, in fact, stealing. Since you are not thinking that these are sins, you are probably not asking forgiveness because you believe these are small innocent actions. But, they are not just small and innocent because if they are committed without repentance then there is no reconciliation with God. If there is no reconciliation then there is no salvation and if no salvation then everlasting damnation shall be your portion. This is the everlasting mystery that perplex believers and stagnate their prayers because they have unreconciled sins in their lives that have not been addressed.

It is my earnest prayer that as believers, you are more watchful, alert, and aware of the things that cause you to sin. And, if you commit a sin, do not hesitate to repent. The adversary is conscious of the fact that he will not be able to devour everyone; but, he knows that there are those, who will consciously leave doors open and unconsciously give him permission and easy access to create a stronghold that will take dominion and authority over your life. This is why the devil prowls back and forth seeking. If, at first, he is not successful, he will come back again and again to see which door you have, neglectfully, left open. Do not leave any door or window open! Do not be his victim. PRAY!!!!

***

Words of Encouragement

Each reason I wrote, I could see myself somewhere in a sentence, a paragraph, or a chapter. This simply means I am not exempt from the message in this book; and, neither am I exempt from the reprimands or the consequences. Would you reward your child for bad behavior? Do you still love your child despite his disrespectfulness? How eager are you to see a change in that rebellious child or that ungodly spouse? Assuming your answers are correct, how do you think our heavenly parent feels about our bad behaviors? In Jeremiah 29:11, He made it clear that His thoughts towards us are excellent; and, it's His desire for us to live in peace, be successful, and accomplish all of our heart's desires.

It has been seven years since I began writing this book. The closer I got to its completion, the more I got distracted and steered off course. Most times, I was distracted by good things, Godly things. For those of you who have my first book, "Fear Not! There is Still Power In Prayer," which was published in 2013, you will see that synopsis of this book was a part of that book. I make mention of the time I began writing because I would like to encourage you to not quit what you started, whether it's a book, a business, a house, a ministry, or anything that is worth fighting for, even if it seems extremely long, don't give up on your dream. Whenever you are about to give birth to your triplets—purpose, promise, and potential—expect delays, especially when the delivery will be life-changing.

Beloved, Christianity is not a religion. It is a relationship with Jesus Christ. I admonish you to stop playing and start praying. You are loved beyond comparison. On the flip side of that equation, there is an adversary at work. Whether or not you believe it, receive it or acknowledge it, the devil and his demons are real. What we are seeing and hearing on the news, globally, is just one of the many strategies satan is implementing to rage war against the body of Christ.

May I have your undivided attention? As we speak, satan and his agents are scheming how to get God's chosen, on his side so we will denounce Christ. We know about the closing of churches and the order to stay away from each other. Satan knows the power of unity and corporate prayer; therefore, if he can weaken us in that area, we may be more vulnerable to his attack.

Look what the Bible says about the benefits of being together. In Mark 6:7, Jesus sent His disciples out in twos; why? So that if one fell ill, the other would be able to assist. And in Hebrews 10:25 (AMP): ...not forsaking our meeting together [as believers for worship and instruction], as is the habit of some, but encouraging one another; and all the more [faithfully] as you see the day [of Christ's return] approaching.

As iron sharpens iron, so one man sharpens [and influences] another [through discussion]. (Proverbs 27:17)

Five of you will chase a hundred, and a hundred of you will chase ten thousand, and your enemies will fall before you by the sword. (Leviticus 26:8)

As long as God does not give up on us, by yourself, you will chase one thousand, but you and I together will chase ten thousand demons. (Deuteronomy 32:30)

Two are better than one; because they have a good reward for their labour. 10For if they fall, the one will lift up his fellow: but woe to him that is alone when he falleth; for he hath not another to help him up. 11Again, if two lie together, then they have heat: but how can one be warm alone? 12And if one prevail against him, two shall withstand him; and a threefold cord is not quickly broken. (Ecclesiastes 4:9-12)

So you see, satan is always trying to oppose the instructions of God. Coming together as the body of Christ, satan and his demons will be terrified.

People of God, persecution of the church is right around the corner; and, war, famine, terror, and death is at our doorstep. Some of us will be beaten, burned alive, beheaded, or tortured! Will you exercise your faith and stand up for Jesus Christ, as Stephen did when he was being stoned to death? Despite the pain and suffering that Stephen felt, He took it, gracefully, to the point where he asked God to forgive his murderers.

Brethren, shortly after this pandemic is over, we shouldn't be surprised if we see the collapse of the economy and a significant food shortage. Saints, we are heading towards a cashless system (as it was in Ezekiel 7:19, so it will be in time to come. History does repeat itself). The mark of the beast will be forced upon us. The new world order will be introduced; and, the beast will be revealed. (Revelation 13:13-18) What are your plans? Which side will you choose, God or satan? Will you deny Jesus, as Peter did? Will you take the mark/chip to save your life, feed your physical man, and by so doing, miss any chance of entering the kingdom of heaven? Or, will you refuse it and risk being starved, tortured, and killed for Jesus' sake? Satan is not your friend, no matter what you do for him or how much you allow him to use you.

Matthew 24:37 states that, As it was in the days of Noah, so it will be at the coming of the son of man. (NIV) What does this mean? It means that while God is patiently pleading, warning, and showing us signs of mercy, we still take no heed. Our hearts are hardened, leaving us unprepared. We mock God and fail to believe that there will be a second coming, followed by the judgment. Presumptuously, we insist on doing things our way–craving earthly possessions, seeking fame, building platforms to establish our names, organizing parties, and partaking in all sorts of ungodly entertainment.

Finally, in the last days, we will see atrocities escalating like never before. True love and commitment will deteriorate. Our genuine affection towards each other will be watered down; and, we are no longer committed to the unity of love through the institution of marriage. As it was in the days of Noah, so we rebelliously reject the call of God unto safety and salvation. Therefore, destruction shall be our portion if we do not adhere to the commands of God.

My friend, I can't stress this story enough. Take heed of the story of the five foolish virgins referenced in Matthew 25. You are running out of time. If you are not ready, it is time to prepare your heart and get ready. Now is the time for you to build a relationship with Jesus Christ. Get your house in order so you can grow and allow the anointing to flow. Be watchful. Step out of your comfort zone and get rid of your complacent attitude.

From January to December, we know which holidays are coming, so, we prepare and celebrate. Sadly though, after hearing and seeing all the signs pointing to the return of Christ, we still refuse to make ourselves completely available for Him. We have gotten a glimpse of the chaos that is on the horizon; but, we believe it is business as usual. One thing I know is that the return of Jesus Christ is sure; and, it is closer than we can imagine. In Deuteronomy 30:15, God said, "I set before you life and death ... choose life." Not making a choice is, in fact, a conscious choice.

My sister, my brother, this is not the time for malice, unforgiveness, resentment, and strife. Go, find those whom you have wronged, and those who may have wronged you and apologize--ask forgiveness. In turn, you must also forgive.

I pray that you will not see this book as just another book, but as a road map and a manual on how to maneuver your day-to-day life, how to love each other, how to live, talk and walk, holy. May your eyes be opened to the things you take for granted, as you prepare yourself to be a better born-again child of God.

May you take extensive note of the little things of which you had no idea could stop your prayers from being answered and cause you to live in continuous sin. As you rededicate your life to the Holy Ghost, seek to find out your purpose here on earth. It is not enough to be saved and sit in the church, growing complacent and comfortable. Sooner or later, we all will be leaving this life as we know it; so, I implore you to go in search of those who need to hear about Christ and His saving grace. Tell someone about God's salvation plan for humanity. Sound the alarm so no one's blood will be on your shoulders.

There are many individuals whom God has marked and called, but they have not yet answered. They are still out there in the rum bars, the prostitute houses, covens, in the beds of fornication, and drug dens committing various kinds of sin. Hence the scripture, "And other sheep I have, which are not of this fold: them also I must bring, and they shall hear my voice; and there shall be one fold, and one shepherd." (John 16:20) The Lord has called us to be fishers of men. Let us stop witnessing to those who are already saved and throw out the life-line to those who are drowning in sin.

***

Call To Salvation

Dear reader, if you have not yet accepted Jesus Christ as your personal Lord and savior, it is not too late. If you are reading this book, you still have the opportunity to say yes to Jesus. There is still hope.

Take a look around you. As I am writing these final words for this book on April 5, 2020, the whole world is in uproar caused by what men consider to be a virus (COVID19). Panic and fear blanketed the atmosphere while faces are veiled with uncertainty. People are dying by the thousands, and many are wondering, "Will I be next? Will I be a part of that number?"

Many have passed on without getting the chance to say, "Lord, have mercy." Many did not get to repent of their sins and accept Jesus Christ as their Lord and Savior. Many will not experience eternal life with Christ. Did they know that they were going to die so young and so soon? No! But death respects one. It does not work with a schedule, and no appointment necessary.

Beloved, what is your relationship with Jesus Christ? If you should die today, where would you spend eternity? If you are not already born again, give Him your whole heart today. Seek Him while He may be found and call upon Him while he is near. He laid down His life for us, His sheep. Don't allow His selfless sacrifice to go in vain.

You've likely been hearing for a long time that He is coming, but you haven't seen Him as yet. Well, my friend, look closer. He is at your doorstep. Whatever or whoever is holding you back is not worth losing your life for. Let it or them go. Your soul is more valuable. I beseech you, say yes to Jesus now. Neither tomorrow nor next week is promised to you. By then, it may be too late. Don't tell yourself that you are waiting until you get married, or buy a house or get rich. Make God your priority; and, everything else will fall in place.

As many as I love, I rebuke and chasten: be zealous therefore, and repent. [20]Behold, I stand at the door, and knock: if any man hear my voice, and open the door, I will come in to him, and will sup with him, and he with me. [22]He that hath an ear, let him hear what the Spirit saith unto the churches. (Revelation 3:19-20 & 22)

***

Repentance Prayer

Dear God, I am a sinner.

I have strayed far from the fold. Be my shepherd, and lead me in the path of righteousness.

Father God, I am willing and ready to say yes to You. I accept your invitation to salvation, O God. I know you have sent your Son Jesus Christ to die for my sins so we could have a closer relationship and spend eternity together.

Thank you, Jesus. Lord, please forgive me for every sin that I have ever committed. Cleanse my mind from every evil thought, O God. Lord, give me a spiritual blood transfusion and a spiritual heart transplant.

I acknowledge that Jesus Christ is Lord. I believe in the death, burial, and resurrection of Jesus Christ. I believe in the Father, the Son, and the Holy Spirit. I believe in the baptism of the Holy Ghost. I believe that Jesus Christ is the only way to God and salvation. In John 14:6, Jesus says, *"I am the way, the truth, and the life: no man cometh to the father, but by me."*

Thank you for saving my soul.

In Jesus' name. Amen.

***

Note of Thanks

Indeed, it is a pleasure to be a part of your circle. I am most grateful to you for purchasing this book and helping me spread God's words of encouragement to our brothers and sisters. Thank you for allowing me to minister to your spirit man, your mind, your flesh, and your emotions. Your support, over the years, has meant so much to me. Those who would not let up on me until the book has come to its completion, thank you. I am encouraged by the many calls asking when I was going to finish writing "38 Reasons" and get it out to the public. Thanks for believing in me and the assignments given to me by God. Your words of encouragement and prayers have uplifted me and taken me to a whole new level.

God bless you all.

References

Millicent Alexander-Spencer. Chapter 28 -Pride.

Miriam-Webster; https://www.merriam-webster.com/

https://www.biblegateway.com/

About the Author

***

Jasmine was born Nichole Gordon on the island of Jamaica. She is the seventh of nine children. Her talents span many fields. She is the founder of Ministries Without Boundaries International, a non-profit organization that ministers to the material needs of others. Since 2011, she has hosted an annual banquet and concert on both Mother's Day and Father's Day, bringing smiles to the families in her community. As an evangelist and chaplain, Jasmine strongly believes that once someone's earthly needs are met, they will be more inclined to hear God's message of love and hope.

Despite maintaining such a busy schedule, Jasmine still finds time to engage in her "secular ministries," which include professional nursing, coaching, consulting, and developing online courses. She is also a radio personality, the CEO and owner of a very successful assisted living facility, and the author of three published books: *Fear Not! There is Still Power in Prayer*, *38 Reasons For Unanswered prayers*, and *Daily Restorational–52 weeks of Devotion*.

In a nutshell, Jasmine is an entrepreneur who empowers and coaches individuals in the health field, as well as ordinary men and women who are hungry for change, to reach and maximize their full potential. Through her online courses, workshops, conferences, seminars, and retreats, she is able to guide and support clients across the world.

Jasmine is also a proud mother of her 32-year-old son and grandmother of a 4-year-old grandson. She presently resides in Palm Bay, Florida, where you will most likely find her engaged in planning or coordinating uplifting events for the community. Jasmine is always seeking to guide, encourage, and empower others. She strives to see the potential for greatness in other people and works toward bringing it to the forefront. Jasmine is most fulfilled when those around her transform and begin living their best life.

Those who know Jasmine and have been touched by her presence or her ministries know that she may indeed be the next philanthropist in her community. Jasmine–a trailblazer and woman of profound strength and resilience. What will she do next?

Contact the Author

You are welcome to email or write the author with comments about this book. You are also welcome to contact her for bookings. Jasmine is available for book club presentations, book signings, or speaking engagements for your group or organization (conferences, workshops, retreats, seminars, women's groups, women's ministries and women's clubs).

Contact her at:

www.mwbint.org

Email:
mwb8870@gmail.com

718.781.0671
804.720.6080

Connect with her on social media:

Facebook:
https://www.facebook.com/jasmine.gordon.75

Instagram:
jasminegordon88

Twitter:
jasmine gordon
@jasminegordon

YouTube:
http://bit.ly/jasminegordonyoutube

www.ingramcontent.com/pod-product-compliance
Lightning Source LLC
Chambersburg PA
CBHW071220080526
44587CB00013BA/1439